PRAISE FOR *WINNING WITH AI*

"What got you here won't get you there—and that's never been more true than with AI. Li and Walsh deliver what leaders actually need: not more AI hype, but a disciplined blueprint for creating real value in ninety days. This is the playbook for leaders who are done experimenting and ready to win."

—**Dr. Marshall Goldsmith,** Thinkers50 #1 Executive Coach and *New York Times* bestselling author of *The Earned Life, Triggers,* and *What Got You Here Won't Get You There*

"AI transformation is ultimately about people, and Li and Walsh understand this truth deeply. Their ninety-day blueprint goes beyond implementation to create the conditions for human magic to flourish alongside AI. *Winning with AI* offers a practical and human-centered way for purposeful leaders to approach the AI era."

—**Hubert Joly,** Harvard Business School professor, former Best Buy CEO, and bestselling author of *The Heart of Business*

"I have seldom read a book in which I agree with so many of its ideas. The focus on value, speed, limiting pilots, leadership—every ingredient is there for helping enterprises make effective and strategic use of AI in a relatively short time."

—**Thomas H. Davenport,** Babson College distinguished professor, MIT Initiative on the Digital Economy fellow, and author of *The AI Advantage, All-in On AI, Working with AI,* and *Agentic Artificial Intelligence*

"*Winning with AI* is refreshingly practical. It gives leaders clear guidance on what to do, what to avoid, and how to deliver value fast without losing sight of people, ethics, or strategy."

—**Tsedal Neeley,** Harvard Business School professor and coauthor of *The Digital Mindset: What It Really Takes to Thrive in the Age of Data, Algorithms, and AI*

Charlene Li   Dr. Katia Walsh

WINNING *with* AI

The 90-Day Blueprint for Success

amplify
an imprint of Amplify Publishing Group

amplify
an imprint of Amplify Publishing Group

www.amplifypublishinggroup.com

Winning with AI: The 90-Day Blueprint for Success

For more information, please contact:
Amplify Publishing, an imprint of Amplify Publishing Group
620 Herndon Parkway, Suite 220
Herndon, VA 20170
info@amplifypublishing.com

ISBN-13: 979-8-90026-329-8

To Ben and Katie, thanks for your unending and
unconditional love and support.
–Charlene

To Tom, Emily, and Tommy, with love and thanks
for all your encouragement.
–Katia

CONTENTS

THE THINGS THIS BOOK TELLS YOU THAT OTHERS DON'T

YOU KNOW AI IS IMPORTANT but aren't sure what to do with it. You need a practical, no-fluff blueprint on how to win with it—right now. This book is that blueprint. And it will tell you what nobody else will:

1. **You don't need an AI strategy.** AI is a technology, and a strategy shouldn't be defined by technology. Instead, use AI to serve your business strategy.
2. **You are asking the wrong question.** Stop asking: What can I do with AI? Start asking: What can AI do for me?
3. **Use cases are not a strategy.** Important equation: many use cases = procrastination. Focus on driving value, not on a laundry list of AI uses.
4. **You need an AI value owner.** To drive focus and scale, appoint one leader who lives, breathes, and dreams AI outcomes.
5. **RIP AI pilots.** Pilot purgatory kills momentum. Build for scale or don't build at all.
6. **Speed is the new moat.**[1] With AI today, first-mover advantage is back. Fast followers end up slow losers.
7. **Learn fast; don't fail fast.** Forget what they tell you. No one rewards failure. Instead, learn fast.
8. **Don't let feasibility hold you back.** If AI can really help matters—even if data and tech are not ready—find a way to make it work.
9. **You don't need perfect data.** Waiting for clean data means

waiting forever. AI works with good enough.

10. **Don't fixate on the foundation**. You're *not* building a house. You're combining the data, tech, talent, and process at the same time to show value fast.
11. **Have a plan and change it all the time**. Rigid plans fail. Write strategy in ink, tactics in pencil, and evolve as you learn.
12. **It's not just tech you need; it's people**. People are the most important part of getting value from AI. Win their hearts before their clicks.
13. **There is no one right way to win with AI, but there are wrong ones**. No magic formula exists; fatal mistakes do. Watch out while not losing speed.
14. **Legacy companies can leapfrog**. Legacy isn't a liability–it's the opportunity to skip the middle steps and jump to the future.
15. **Focus on value . . . but don't lose imagination**. Deliver with AI today and shoot for the moon.

INTRODUCTION

WHY SHOULD I CARE ABOUT AI? Is there any real value AI can bring to my organization? How do we get started with AI? What should we do and not do? How do we show value? And how do we make sure it lasts?

These questions have befuddled most leaders since November 2022, when the release of ChatGPT marked the mainstreaming of AI in the world. As veterans in helping companies create value with emerging tech, especially AI, we wrote this book for you. This is the blueprint for leaders who ask these and other valid questions. You are right to ask them. And you've come to the right place for answers.

Consider two companies that started using AI at the same time, with similar ambitions to create value. Eighteen months later, Company A had launched fifteen pilots, all unrelated to company strategy, and exercised a great deal of caution, which they saw as necessary due to AI's novelty. When their board asked what impact AI was having in the organization, they had nothing to show.

By contrast, Company B recognized that AI could help them accelerate their market-leading business strategy. They understood that waiting for the technology to stabilize would mean missing out on immense opportunities. So, Company B focused on a business priority–the call center. They added voice AI agents and embedded customer data into the scripts of human agents for fast, personalized call handling. They used generative AI to introduce new product features in support of the business strategy. They moved in agile sprints and saw results in weeks. Within a few months, they achieved a 15 percent margin increase and a 20 percent rise in customer satisfaction. Soon after, their new AI-powered offerings contributed to increased market share across their most strategic business segments.

The difference between the two companies isn't about the technology. It's about driving measurable business value that leads to wins. Company B had embraced the three principles that separate AI winners from losers:

First, they connected AI directly to business strategy. They anchored every AI effort to their most significant business priorities rather than treating AI as a technology initiative. When the CEO said, "Increase market share by 10 percent," the team immediately asked, "How can AI help us get there faster?"

Second, they understood that speed wins. Speed has never mattered as much as it does today in helping a company be a winner in emerging tech. "Speed is the new moat," says Vikram Mahidhar, an AI thought leader and investor. It's a nod to the idea that every company needs something to keep competitors at bay. In this case, it's not patents or products–it's how fast you can move. In today's business world, with AI's dynamic pace, speed is the edge–Company B moved from idea to value in weeks, not quarters, much less years.

Third, they stayed focused. Instead of multiple pilots and proofs of concept, Company B set priorities and went after them with unwavering commitment.

This book will help you become like Company B–a winner. It's your 90-day blueprint for setting your organization up to create value with AI.

YOUR GUIDES

We're **Charlene Li** and **Katia Walsh**, two veterans in helping businesses thrive with technology change. We bring two distinct, but complementary, perspectives to this blueprint.

Charlene is a *New York Times* bestselling author of six books and has spent over two decades guiding organizations through disruptive tech transformations. She provides the proven framework for leading change in uncertain times and was named one of the most creative people in business by *Fast Company*.

Katia is a pioneer in driving business value with AI. She was one of the world's first chief AI officers, with a track record that includes leading digital, data, and AI at Prudential Financial, Vodafone, Levi Strauss & Co., and Harvard Business School. She brings the battle-tested, in-the-trenches wisdom of building and scaling AI inside some of the world's largest and most iconic brands.

Together, we offer both the *what* and the *how* of winning with AI. We interviewed over fifty executives and analyzed dozens of real-world AI implementations to understand what separates the winners from the losers in creating value with AI. We share a conviction that leaders deserve a practical blueprint for driving value with AI. This book is it.

THE PROBLEM: YOU'RE STUCK IN PILOT PURGATORY

If you feel more like Company A, you're not alone. You've probably launched AI pilots, attended AI conferences, and led a team that has experimented with ChatGPT. But you're waiting for the promised transformative impact.

Meanwhile, you're surrounded by headlines about AI, your employees are wondering about the implications of AI for their jobs, and your board wants a plan. Maybe it feels pointless to create a plan that you know will have to change in three months. We are convinced, however, that in times of great uncertainty, organizations must have a strategy—a clear direction of travel.

But you need to move fast—so plan for speed.

THINK BIG, START SMALL, SCALE FAST

In the face of change, it's natural to feel a mix of FOMO (fear of missing out) and FOGI (fear of getting in). You feel the urgency to jump in but worry about the risks.

This conundrum is what we refer to as the "knowing-doing gap." Leaders *know* AI is important, but they struggle with *doing* what's necessary to actually lead the transformation. This is where progress stalls, leaving potential value locked behind a wall of uncertainty.

To close the gap, think big, start small, and scale quickly:

- **Think big**. Craft a bold vision that serves your organization's strategy. Look beyond the immediate use of AI and envision your organization in a new light, able to achieve what was never possible before. Think about how AI can help transform your business and accelerate your strategy.
- **Start small**. Begin with applications that are focused and manageable, yet valuable, delivering quick wins, demonstrating tangible benefits, and building momentum. They are not isolated pilots but committed AI applications that work together, compounding for a transformative impact—your big vision.

- **Scale fast**. As you gain traction, ensure that you have in place the building blocks for sustainable AI value–the mindset, skills, data, technology, and decision structures to deliver and grow as an AI-powered organization.

If you're feeling like you're running as fast as you can with AI–planning, piloting, learning–yet somehow not getting anywhere, you're not alone. You're experiencing what Lewis Carroll captured in *Through the Looking-Glass*. Alice and the Red Queen race through the forest at breakneck speed, yet the scenery never changes. When Alice points out that such running should take her somewhere, the Queen delivers an uncomfortable truth: "Now, here, you see, it takes all the running you can do, to keep in the same place. If you want to get somewhere else, you must run at least twice as fast as that!"

Welcome to AI's "Red Queen Race." Keeping pace with your competitors means you are standing still. **This blueprint is your coach, helping you run twice as fast.**

YOUR 90-DAY BLUEPRINT FOR GETTING STARTED WITH AI VALUE

AI is evolving at unprecedented speed. Anyone with a digital device can use it. Business success goes to organizations that move from idea to value faster than their competitors. This book provides a practical 90-day blueprint to help your organization drive value with AI. It's a step-by-step plan that works in our current reality and prepares you for sustained success and to scale in the future. Each week offers specific, actionable guidance you can implement immediately. You'll get concrete tools, like the Double-S Matrix for prioritizing AI applications, Goldilocks governance for making decisions, and detailed action plans that tell you precisely what to accomplish each week.

We've structured this book into four parts:

PART 1: GETTING STARTED (WEEKS 1 TO 3)

The first three weeks are about laying the groundwork. Before you can develop an AI roadmap, you need to gather the right people, develop guiding principles, and find effective leadership to mobilize the organization.

- **Week 1: Your AI starter kit**. You can't lead what you don't understand. This week is about demystifying AI through hands-on experience. You'll assemble your core leadership team, secure the right tools for safe experimentation, and develop the confidence to move from uncertainty to action.
- **Week 2: The responsible AI advantage**. To move fast, you need good brakes. Here, you'll establish the ethical principles and responsible AI policies that both ensure safety and enable rapid progress. Trust us: This isn't about slowing down; it's about moving fast because you have the confidence to tackle emerging tech safely and at speed.
- **Week 3: Who owns AI?** AI value cannot build without a clear leader. This week, you'll make the most critical decision for success: defining who will lead your AI efforts and how you will organize to break down silos and drive enterprise-wide value.

PART 2: CREATING YOUR AI ROADMAP (WEEKS 4 TO 7)

Now you'll shift your focus to the strategic work of building your AI roadmap. But this isn't a traditional, static planning exercise. It's about creating a dynamic plan that directly connects AI's potential to your most critical business priorities, ensuring you focus your efforts where they will have the most impact.

- **Week 4: Creating value with AI**. Before you can prioritize, you must understand where AI creates value. You'll move beyond the random use case trap of ideating what you can do with AI to exploring the full spectrum of where you can put AI to work in service of your strategy. You'll examine the three broad areas of AI value: customer engagement, internal efficiencies, and business reinvention.
- **Week 5: Grounding AI in your strategy**. You don't need a separate AI strategy. Rather, you need to deploy AI in support of your existing business strategy. This week, you'll map AI applications directly to your business strategy, focusing on clearing the main obstacles and seizing the biggest opportunities that define the company's top goals.

- **Week 6: Crafting a dynamic AI roadmap.** A plan that's obsolete in three months is useless. This week, you'll create your Six-Quarter Walk–a rolling eighteen-month roadmap that provides clear direction while maintaining the flexibility to adapt to a fast-changing environment.
- **Week 7: Focusing on AI's building blocks.** A vision with no way to execute it is a dream. This week presents a crucial reality check of your organization's mindset, skill set, toolset, and decision-making process to identify what you have and what you will need to put in place to build sustainable AI value.

PART 3: BUILDING BLOCKS FOR AI VALUE AT SCALE (WEEKS 8 TO 11)

Once you have a clear and realistic roadmap in hand, this phase focuses on delivery and ensuring that AI value creation sticks. This is where you put in place the deep organizational infrastructure–the building blocks–required to deliver on your plan and ensure the value you create is scalable and sustainable.

- **Week 8: Establishing the AI Mindset.** If your culture resists change, your well-laid plans will fail. This week, you'll focus on shifting your organization's culture by establishing a mandate to integrate AI into everyday work, broadening the organization's exposure to AI, and clearly and consistently communicating its impact.
- **Week 9: Developing an AI-fluent workforce.** Your people are your greatest asset. Here, you'll learn how to prepare your people for human-AI collaboration, turning fear into trust and building a team of "superhumans" who can use AI to amplify their own expertise.
- **Week 10: Assembling the AI toolset.** Don't get locked into yesterday's technology. This week, you'll learn to implement technology in a way more like building a LEGO house than building a cathedral. This modular approach creates a flexible and adaptable toolset that can evolve as quickly as AI itself.
- **Week 11: Designing AI's decision system.** Bureaucracy kills speed. But lack of structure impedes progress. Here, you'll establish the lean decision-making structures that balance speed with safety, creating a governance framework that empowers your teams to innovate with confidence.

PART 4: LEADERSHIP AND THE FUTURE (WEEK 12 AND EPILOGUE)

You've completed your roadmap and put in place the organizational capabilities for sustainable AI value. But strategy, culture, skills, technology, and governance—no matter how strong—can remain isolated without one other critical element: leadership. The final week addresses what determines whether your 90-day effort produces lasting transformation or scattered initiatives that fade.

- **Week 12: Leadership as accelerant of AI value.** This week brings everything together, focusing on how to lead with AI and reach unprecedented scope, speed, and scale. You'll see how AI amplifies the core leadership responsibilities, how to lead AI-fluent people, and how to prepare for the next wave of value creation through integrated intelligence, combining the best of human and artificial intelligence.
- **Epilogue: Imagine.** Beyond the ninety days lies a question: What will you do with what you've built? We'll leave you with a vision of what's possible when organizations truly master AI value creation—and a challenge to help shape the future that's emerging.

By the end of these twelve weeks, you'll have moved from scattered AI experiments to a systematic approach that will help you create measurable value as you assemble the building blocks to scale over time.

HOW TO USE THIS BOOK

Now that you've seen the roadmap, here's how to make it work for your company:

- **Follow the complete 90-day sequence** if you're starting from scratch. The plan unfolds systematically, from preparation to creating strategic value.
- **Jump to where you need help** if your AI efforts are already underway. Do you have your AI leader and policies in place? Start with part 2's AI roadmap. Already have a solid AI roadmap? Fine-tune your delivery with the building blocks in part 3.

- **Select the option that best suits your organization**, considering its unique situation. Scan the chapter summaries and see which ones resonate most deeply, then dive deeply into that chapter.

The goal isn't rigid adherence to our plan—it's using our framework to create your path to AI value. Think about what works for your organization and adapt accordingly.

IT'S GOING TO BE MESSY . . . BUT IT'S WORTH IT

Let's be clear about two things: First, this is a messy endeavor—change always is. Second, and more importantly, the stakes are higher than you might think.

This isn't really about implementing technology. It's about deciding what kind of organization—and what kind of future—you want to create. If your ambition stops at making your current operations more efficient, you'll get exactly that: a more efficient version of what you already have. However, if you're willing to use AI as a catalyst to reimagine your business model, redefine customer relationships, and rethink the value you can create, then you can build something unprecedented.

The organizations that win won't be those that executed the most pilots or achieved the best ROI on automation. They'll be the ones that dared to ask bigger questions: What is possible now? What customer problems can we solve that we couldn't before? What can we create that our industry said was impossible?

It will be uncomfortable and, at times, nerve-racking. AI represents an unprecedented shift; navigating it requires a willingness to embrace discomfort. In our experience, every transformation includes a "messy middle"—a liminal space between what was and what will be. It feels uncomfortable because it's unclear, uncertain, and unknown. But it's also an opportunity to be curious, explore new possibilities, and challenge your limits.

Winning with AI means sustainably creating tangible value, built with ethical and socially responsible practices that underpin the AI systems we deploy. Winning with AI means introducing, nurturing, and expanding new skill sets that future-proof organizations and their people. Winning with AI means driving a cultural transformation that delivers value at speed, supports focus, and challenges the status quo. It means letting go of individual ego in service of the organization, and accepting that we don't know everything and must continually learn.

With this blueprint as your guide, you'll have the tools and clarity to get started, embrace the messy middle, and emerge not just stronger but with the ability to pull ahead. The organizations that master the connection between AI and business strategy, that build speed as their new competitive moat, will define the next decade of business.

The journey of a thousand miles begins with a single step.

–Lao Tzu

One

YOUR AI STARTER KIT

THE FIRST WEEK in your 90-day blueprint for AI success is all about getting ready. This phase addresses the uncertainty that many leaders face when considering how to use AI effectively. You'll start by safely experimenting and learning, which will turn the uncertainty into fuel for value creation.

This chapter is your AI Starter Kit—everything you need to launch into being an informed leader of AI value creation, without becoming overwhelmed.

In the following pages, we'll help you do the following:

- **Understand AI** and its current potential.
- **Grasp the importance** of mobilizing an organization's senior leadership.
- **Set up a secure AI environment** for exploration.
- **Assemble and prepare your minimum viable team (MVT)** to drive AI value.
- **Use AI firsthand** through pragmatic exercises.
- **Capture learnings** and successes to build organizational momentum.

By the end of this week, you'll understand and have the hands-on experience to begin building your roadmap for value creation with AI.

UNDERSTANDING AI'S POTENTIAL

AI today is the result of decades of accumulated research and business applications. At the time of this writing, three types of AI feature in the business landscape: predictive AI, generative AI, and agentic AI. Understanding how they work—individually and in combination—is the starting point for creating value with AI (see figure 1-1).

Figure 1-1: Three types of AI explained

AI TYPE	Predictive	Generative	Agentic
ROLE	The Oracle	The Creator	The Agent
WHAT IT DOES	Analyzes patterns, creates classifications, predicts outcomes, and optimizes toward multiple goals	Creates new content based on patterns	Takes actions autonomously toward specific goals, while continuing to learn
BUSINESS EXAMPLE	Sales forecasting, fraud detection, recommendation and personalization engines (e.g., Uber arrival time, streaming video recommendations)	Writing, image and video design, code generation, and content personalization	Automated tasks based on probabilistic input (not rules-based), autonomous workflows, process reinvention
WHEN TO USE	When you need to understand current data and behaviors and drive desired outcomes	When you need to produce content (text, images, video) at scale	When you need sustained, autonomous execution of tasks over time

PREDICTIVE AI: THE ORACLE

Predictive AI is your organization's data-driven crystal ball. It analyzes historical data patterns to project future trends, transforming raw data into recommendations for driving desired outcomes. Many people still believe predictive AI is only about providing actionable insights. It is much more. In this case, AI models identify patterns and use them to make predictions that help achieve concrete goals, such as personalizing customer experiences, accurately planning inventory, or increasing consumers' likelihood of responding to specific messaging.

Examples of predictive AI applications in business are abundant, and your organization likely already uses them extensively. It's part of CRM systems for sales forecasting, email platforms for spam detection, financial software for fraud prevention, and marketing tools for customer communication, personalization, and lead conversion. Predictive AI provides you with predictions and recommendations that you can act upon to gain business value. However, predictive AI cannot generate anything new or take actions independently; this is the domain of other, more recent types of AI.

Here are some examples of predictive AI transforming businesses today:

- **Retailers** forecasting demand with greater precision. This reduces excess inventory, improves margins, and boosts customer satisfaction by providing better product availability.
- **Financial institutions** detecting and preventing fraud in real time. By identifying anomalous patterns, predictive AI helps prevent financial crime and reduce risk exposure.
- **Streaming and e-commerce platforms** relying on predictive AI for customer engagement. This includes personalized content or product recommendations.
- **Healthcare systems** improving patient outcomes. Predictive models assess risk and suggest preventative interventions, such as identifying patients likely to be readmitted.

These examples illustrate how predictive AI uses existing data to provide foresight and inform targeted action. It enables organizations to anticipate, optimize, and personalize their strategies. However, this type of AI does not generate new content and does not operate independently.

GENERATIVE AI: THE CREATOR

Like predictive AI, generative AI relies on and analyzes vast amounts of data. Generative AI, however, uses that information to create something new, such as text, images, audio, code, and videos. The technology is also predictive–it works by predicting the most likely next word, phrase, or element based on context. However, it goes a step further than predictive AI by using these predictions to generate new content.

The generation of new content is crucial because it explains both the remarkable strengths and the limitations of generative AI. It can create content because it can predict what good writing or effective communication looks like based on millions of examples. But it can also produce so-called *hallucinations*–plausible-sounding information that is incorrect. While future models and technical advances may address this limitation, business leaders should consider generative AI as a helpful thought partner that's not always accurate and requires information verification.

Here are some examples of generative AI transforming businesses today:

- **Marketers** generating personalized email campaigns in minutes rather than hours.
- **Legal professionals** drafting contract templates that are tailored to meet the specific needs of each client.
- **Product managers** creating detailed specifications from basic requirements.
- **Customer care representatives** providing consistent responses across customer needs.

While predictive AI deployment requires engineers and data scientists with specialized skills, the basic use of generative AI can be universal. All that is required to start using generative AI is conversation, a skill that most people master at a young age. We will later cover how to master the ability to create specific prompts for interacting with generative AI. However, the fact is that there are no barriers to getting started; all you need is a computer or phone with a browser or an app that serves as the user interface for generative AI models.

Although generative AI surpasses predictive AI by generating actions based on user input, it remains dependent on user input and continuous engagement and therefore cannot act independently. This is where agentic AI comes in.

AGENTIC AI: THE AGENT

Agentic AI marks a significant evolution, moving beyond content creation to a system that uses AI models to perform tasks autonomously. An AI agent is goal-oriented and can plan, act, learn, and adapt independently, without step-by-step human instructions. Think of it as an independent system, capable of managing complex multistep processes that unfold over time.

To understand how agentic AI works, it's helpful to contrast it with the traditional rules-based automation most businesses use today. Many of these automated systems are *deterministic*—in other words, they follow a rigid script of "if this, then that." For example, a traditional analytics script follows a fixed programming rule, for example, "Pull sales data from the last thirty days and create a bar chart showing sales by region." It does precisely what the instructions specify and cannot deviate from them.

Agentic AI, however, is *probabilistic*; in other words, it operates without a rule, but instead uses a range of probable outcomes, taking an action based on the highest probabilities of success in a specific context. Rather than following a script, an agentic system serves a goal. Imagine an AI agent working toward a goal such as "Find our most promising new customer segment." To achieve this, the agent autonomously explores multiple datasets, for example, sales histories, customer profiles, or social media trends. It predicts which analytical paths are most likely to yield valuable insights. It then tests various hypotheses and presents a final recommendation, accompanied by supporting evidence. It's strategizing the best route to achieve a business objective.

Agentic AI becomes even more powerful in a multiagent system, in which multiple agents collaborate, share information, and check each other's work to achieve the overarching business goal. As you'll explore in chapter 10, this involves an ensemble of specialized AI agents working together, with an "orchestration layer" acting as the project manager.

Agentic AI's breakthrough lies in its ability to autonomously pursue objectives over time, moving beyond the prompt-and-response interactions of generative AI.

Because of AI's autonomy in this case, it is crucial to ensure that human judgment and oversight are at the core of any agentic AI deployment. Your role as a leader is to set goals, define ethical guardrails, ensure there are appropriate controls in place, and allow agents to execute their tasks effectively.

Examples of agentic AI that are transforming businesses today include the following:

- **Customer service centers** using autonomous AI agents to resolve inquiries. These agents handle entire conversations–from answering a call to understanding the issue to offering solutions and even following up. They can do this without human intervention; however, human monitoring is always advisable for continuous relevance and to ensure the AI agents remain consistent with their intended tasks.
- **Operations teams** deploying AI agents to automate workflows. For instance, AI agents in supply chain organizations autonomously track orders, update timelines, and reroute deliveries as conditions change. Again, they can do so independently, although human monitoring remains essential.
- **Sales organizations** automating outbound sales calls and follow-ups. Although this use is not yet prevalent at the time of this writing, sales organizations are starting to see success with AI agents. Based on sales lead data, pipeline status, and sales goals, AI agents initiate and manage outreach campaigns, adjusting follow-ups and strategies in real time.
- **Entrepreneurs** building AI agents that act on their behalf. In tech startups, it's not uncommon for AI agents to manage email inflows, summarize email content, assign tasks, issue reminders, schedule meetings, and even respond to customer queries using the founder's voice and style.

We cannot overstate the importance of these advances. Generative and agentic AI aren't just helpful–they're transformative. Their use frees up people to focus on strategic and meaningful work, while machines handle repetitive and reactive tasks. As agentic systems become more capable, they'll reengineer processes and workflows, reshape entire functions–from customer service and marketing to operations and IT–and revolutionize business, industries, and society.

CONTINUOUSLY ADVANCING: ROBOTICS

As AI continues to mature, expect to see it move beyond digital systems and into the physical world. The convergence of agentic AI with robotics is already benefiting industries such as distribution, logistics, and manufacturing. For example, autonomous mobile robots in warehouses independently navigate aisles, pick products, and optimize inventory placement based on real-time demand signals. In logistics, companies are piloting AI-driven delivery drones and autonomous trucks to streamline last-mile delivery. On factory floors, agentic AI, combined with robotics, monitors production lines, detects quality issues, and automatically reconfigures workflows to minimize downtime. This shift doesn't just improve efficiency–it enables businesses to translate digital scripts directly into physical actions.

Don't let the term *robotic* confuse you. In the case of combining agentic AI with robotics, we're referring to intelligent machines that operate in the physical world. By contrast, robotic process automation (RPA), which we explain below, focuses on automating repetitive digital tasks on a computer screen, with no learning or adaptation required.

RELATED TECHNOLOGIES TO KNOW

The three main types of AI–predictive, generative, and agentic–often incorporate other specialized AI technologies to perform specific tasks. Consider these related technologies as essential components that enhance the overall power of the AI system or solution your organization is building. Here are some of the specialized AIs you'll likely encounter:

- **Robotic process automation (RPA):** This technology handles highly structured, repetitive, and rules-based tasks by mimicking human actions on a computer, such as copying and pasting data or filling out forms. Unlike AI, RPA follows a deterministic script and doesn't learn or adapt. It is best thought of as a tool that a more advanced agentic AI can use to understand the context and execute a specific part of a larger workflow.
- **Natural language processing:** This technology enables computers to understand, interpret, and generate human language, bridging the gap between how people communicate and how computers process

information. Natural language processing forms the foundation for modern chatbots, document analysis, and translation services.

- **Speech recognition:** This technology converts spoken language into text. It functions by analyzing sound waves, breaking them down into fundamental sounds (phonemes), and predicting the most likely sequence of words. Speech recognition powers voice assistants and the transcription of meetings and calls.
- **Computer vision:** This technology enables machines to "see" by interpreting and understanding visual information from images and videos. It uses models to identify patterns, objects, and activities, powering everything from quality inspection on a manufacturing line to medical imaging analysis.

Each type of AI builds on the others, creating compound value when they work in concert. Understanding the current range of AI helps you see the technology's full potential while focusing on what's actionable today.

Your 90-day blueprint centers on generative AI as the starting point because the technology offers these features:

- **Immediate accessibility.** Generative AI works through natural language conversations. No coding is required, and no complex integrations are needed. If you can ask questions and specify instructions, you can use generative AI productively today.
- **Rapid value demonstration.** Unlike predictive AI, which requires extensive data preparation, or agentic AI, which demands a sophisticated setup, generative AI creates measurable value in minutes. Draft a strategic memo, analyze a competitive landscape, and brainstorm ideas–the results are immediate and tangible.
- **Universal applicability.** Just about every role in an organization involves communication, analysis, or problem-solving. Generative AI enhances all three, making it relevant across departments and skill levels.
- **Foundation for AI orchestration.** The prompting skills and AI collaboration techniques you develop with generative AI are essential for

working with other types of AI (we'll get into prompting later in this chapter). Understanding how to direct and evaluate generative AI prepares you to combine multiple AI technologies.

- **Learning ground.** Generative AI's conversational nature makes it an ideal training ground. You can experiment, make mistakes, and iterate quickly, without technical training or knowledge.

Some organizations have used generative AI to transform their entire business model, for example, moving from traditional call centers into high-value financial risk management. However, generative AI is forgiving enough to allow you to learn while creating value.

The companies creating transformational value aren't choosing among types of AI; they use all of them strategically. A customer care transformation might use predictive AI to route inquiries, generative AI to draft personalized responses, and agentic AI to handle routine issues autonomously while escalating complex cases to human intervention.

Now that you understand the types of AI, let's start setting up your organization to create value with it.

TRANSFORMATION REQUIRES TOP LEADERSHIP

Several research reports show that most CEOs believe AI will be transformational, with one survey in early 2025 finding that 89 percent of global CEOs ranked AI as the most critical technology for ensuring future profitability and competitiveness.[1] Yet, when it comes to leading that transformation, CEOs do not always walk the talk. They delegate AI deployment to research and development departments that are disconnected from business priorities, or they hand it off to IT. As a result, only 22 percent of organizations have a visible, defined AI roadmap.[2] And here's the kicker: Those with a roadmap are twice as likely to see AI-driven revenue growth.[3]

The reluctance is understandable. Many CEOs feel out of their depth with AI technology, preferring to let technical experts lead.

"I don't understand the algorithms," one Fortune 500 CEO told us. "Why shouldn't IT handle this?" The answer is simple: AI isn't a technology transformation–it's a business transformation that happens to use technology.

CEO leadership fundamentally changes what is possible with AI, as only the chief executive has both the authority and the overall organizational perspective that true transformation requires. The CEO controls resource allocation across all functions, can break down organizational silos, and possesses a cross-functional view to identify AI opportunities spanning departments. Critically, a CEO's engagement with AI in service of the company's strategy signals a shift in how the business will compete.

Without CEO involvement, individual departments inevitably filter AI applications through their siloed functional perspectives. The CIO focuses on technical feasibility, the CFO optimizes for cost reduction, and the COO prioritizes efficiencies and process automation. Meanwhile, transformational opportunities that require cross-functional coordination and resource reallocation often fail to receive executive consideration, let alone materialize.

The companies that win with AI share a characteristic: Their CEOs have invested time in understanding the strategic implications of AI. They used AI tools themselves, participated in strategic planning sessions, and integrated AI into regular executive team discussions.

Paul Hudson, CEO of Sanofi, is clear that "winning the AI revolution" requires active, personal engagement from top leadership.[4] As he puts it, "If you're planning to delegate the AI revolution, then good luck to you. You must be prepared to bring the energy." Hudson personally chairs annual reviews of AI initiatives, selects attendees, asks key questions, and actively removes barriers for his team, underscoring his philosophy that breakthrough technologies demand direct involvement from the CEO, not delegation to technologists or functional leaders.

OVERCOMING CEO RESISTANCE TO LEADING AI

Many CEOs feel uncertain about leading AI due to a lack of technical understanding or concerns that focusing on AI will divert attention from their perceived "other" business priorities. In our work with various companies, we encounter many responses from senior leaders that indicate, at best, a lack of understanding and, at worst, resistance to change. Let's address some of the most common concerns we hear from senior leaders:

"I don't understand the technology well enough to lead this."

Our response: You don't need to understand the full intricacies of internal combustion engines to develop an automotive strategy. The same applies to AI–your role in creating value with AI is strategic, not technical. Connect AI directly to your current priorities. For instance, focusing on growth allows you to mobilize AI to accelerate customer acquisition. To create efficiencies, deploy AI in core processes. If you are rethinking your value proposition and competitive advantage, consider using AI to generate ideas and envision how your business could evolve by integrating AI throughout its operations.

"We have more pressing priorities right now."

Our reply: AI isn't separate from your business priorities–it's the way to achieve them. Growth strategy? AI personalizes customer experiences at scale. Competitive positioning? AI creates differentiation through superior service at lower costs. Acquisition decisions? AI accelerates due diligence through richer and faster research. Operational excellence? AI eliminates bottlenecks and reduces completion times. Customer engagement? AI delivers proactive solutions. The companies winning with AI deploy AI in direct service of their top business objectives.

"The CEO can't lead AI; they have too many other responsibilities/direct reports, stakeholders, etc."

We say: The CEO must always be personally involved and visibly champion AI to create value for strategic purposes. If AI is truly to deliver value, the CEO must lead with conviction, making time for personal engagement, upskilling themselves, and leading by example. In addition to helping their organization advance with AI, CEOs who personally lead AI's deployment solidify their careers, open future growth opportunities, and expand their influence and impact.

In the very rare exceptions–and let's be clear, we do not recommend it–that the CEO cannot personally spearhead AI deployment, they must appoint another senior-most leader. That leader's role, like the CEO's, needs to be inherently cross-functional and strategic. At this early stage of AI adoption, when the organization is still exploring use cases and building foundations, the best alternative is often a chief strategy officer or chief transformation officer, as their mandate for enterprise-wide strategy naturally connects with the transformational potential of AI.

Avoid at all costs delegating strategic AI leadership to purely functional roles and traditional leaders. Doing so will severely limit the scope of AI deployment, the ability to create value at scale, and the change needed to influence a holistic organizational transformation. Instead of business transformation, you will end up with incremental improvements, at best. Common pitfalls to steer clear of include giving the role to these leaders:

- **CFO**. Generally, their remit requires them to prioritize cost reduction over growth.
- **COO**. This role typically requires a focus on operational efficiency rather than transformational opportunities.
- **Traditional IT leaders, such as a CIO**. Executives in this group may seem a natural fit; however, they more often fill roles as "service providers" than as transformational leaders who can drive cross-functional change.

To be clear, the CEO's leadership is paramount, and that's what we recommend. However, even in rare instances when the CEO cannot personally lead strategic AI value creation, their visible involvement remains essential and nonnegotiable. Without it, we've seen numerous organizations struggle to achieve the cross-functional coordination and resource allocation necessary for genuine business transformation and value creation with AI. We do not want you to face the same.

Now that you understand the critical nature of CEO leadership for AI success, it's time to mobilize the initial team to drive that success.

ASSEMBLE YOUR MINIMUM VIABLE TEAM

To get started with AI, you need a small committed group that can move fast, make decisions, and learn quickly. This group is your minimum viable team–a lean group that leads the way, connecting immediate AI deployment with value. This is a small cross-functional team of strategic leaders tasked with serving as the initial engine for getting your organization set up to create value with AI. The MVT's purpose is to learn and iterate quickly, make informed decisions, and build momentum through actions that benefit the entire organization.

BUILDING YOUR MVT

The MVT is a temporary yet necessary strategic catalyst that enables your organization to create value with AI. It should move with the speed and agility required to develop your initial AI roadmap and build momentum. As you'll see in later chapters, this team and its work provide the foundation for the organizational model of AI value creation and governance, enabling the scaling and sustaining of value and the integration of AI across the organization. In that sense, the MVT's goal is to work itself out of a job by creating a plan so effective that the rest of the organization can carry it forward.

Your success with AI depends more on the people driving it than the technology powering it. The main limitation to AI success is the ability to envision a different future and take steps toward it. Traditional, siloed departments often move too slowly and lack a cross-functional perspective. To overcome this inertia, you need a dedicated team.

Roles to include in your MVT

Your MVT requires diverse strategic perspectives to ensure that AI applications support business strategy. In addition to the CEO, consider these critical roles:

- **Digital or emerging tech lead.** Someone who understands how technology and data strategy support business success. Avoid traditional IT administrators; instead, choose someone who can translate business needs into technology requirements.
- **Commercial and customer lead.** A customer-obsessed leader who understands current customers, pays attention to new customers, and can foresee evolving needs. This person might be a business unit, product, or marketing leader.
- **Human resources.** HR leadership is crucial for AI success. Choose someone who can anticipate how tasks, jobs, and careers will evolve and adapt the culture, hiring, training, and development processes accordingly.

Consider additional roles based on your business priorities but resist the temptation to include everyone. The goal is to maximize the team's ability to move quickly and make decisions effectively. Start small and agile–follow the "two pizza rule": If two pizzas can't feed your team, it's too large to move quickly and make decisions effectively.[5]

We recognize the importance of inspiring people, capturing their hearts and minds, and sparking their enthusiasm. But that is different from what we see in many organizations that waste valuable time to bring everybody along. The reality is that there will be people who resist, and we cannot plan for a pace that waits for the slowest to catch up. Instead, we must accelerate the pace while working diligently to communicate effectively, manage change, and prepare the workforce for the incredible transformation that AI represents. We will cover the importance of speed when discussing the roadmap for AI in chapter 6.

KEY CHARACTERISTICS OF MVT MEMBERS

Given the importance of speed, the MVT members will deliver the most value when balancing the following:

- **Strategic vision with pace.** People who can connect AI with long-term organizational strategy and, at the same time, serve top business objectives quickly.
- **Collaborative spirit with decision-making ability.** Look for individuals who work effectively across departments and can also make decisions quickly. AI moves too fast to be building consensus on every choice, deliberating at length, and spending time to convince everyone.
- **Handling uncertainty with action orientation.** MVT members must be able to make decisions with incomplete information and adjust the course as necessary. They should feel energized by uncertainty, not paralyzed.
- **Ethical considerations with business pragmatism.** Team members should possess a strong moral compass, coupled with a clear understanding of business realities.
- **Planning and open-mindedness.** The MVT must work toward a concrete roadmap for value creation with AI, while remaining flexible and embracing new possibilities.

The best MVT members often feel that the role is a stretch because it requires them to operate at the edge of their comfort zones, engage in continuous learning, and master adaptability.

HOW YOUR MVT OPERATES: FAST, FOCUSED, AND VALUE DRIVEN

Your MVT is the ignition switch for your organization's AI value engine. Think of it like a SWAT team or COVID-era war room—lean, decisive, and laser focused on progress. This team doesn't carry out every AI initiative itself. Instead, they're the orchestrators—driving coordination, clearing bottlenecks, and ensuring that learning turns into momentum.

The MVT holds ten-to-fifteen-minute, daily stand-up meetings. These are fast-paced check-ins to make decisions, assign follow-up actions, and escalate obstacles. It's how the organization stays focused on value creation and avoids getting bogged down.

To function effectively, the MVT must follow a few core practices:

- **Assign work outward, not inward.** The MVT isn't responsible for doing all the work. Their job is to delegate, connect, and follow up—ensuring that the right teams handle the right work and that someone remains accountable for follow-through.
- **Make decisions across silos.** Ensure MVT members represent different functions or domains. This diversity enables the team to act on behalf of the whole organization, surfacing blind spots and creating solutions that work across silos.
- **Embrace uncertainty while creating clarity.** AI moves fast—perfect information is a luxury. The MVT pushes forward, making calls, testing ideas, and learning quickly.
- **Provide transparency and traceability.** As a central coordination team, the MVT becomes a source of truth. Use shared documents or dashboards to track decisions and their underlying reasons. This clarity builds trust and keeps momentum from stalling.

- **Work in short feedback loops.** Whether it's reviewing a prototype, a policy draft, or an initial roadmap, the MVT must provide quick feedback and act on it. The goal is to move and improve rapidly.

When the MVT operates this way, it sets the tempo for the next 90 days.

TROUBLESHOOTING—THE "DEPARTMENTS OF NO"

As soon as you assemble your MVT, you can expect a knock on your door. Leaders from legal, security, and compliance will want a seat at the table, viewing a fast-moving strategic AI team as a potential source of risks.

This situation presents a challenge. The MVT moves with speed, while these vital functions may operate with deliberate caution. We recommend that legal, security, and compliance leaders serve as advisors to the MVT—but not as members. As you'll see in the next chapter, their expertise will soon be essential when you formally build the responsible AI policies that enable your organization to move quickly and safely.

There is, however, a path for these leaders to influence the MVT. The critical question is whether they can operate as enablers rather than as gatekeepers. An enabler asks, "How can we help the team move forward quickly and safely?" A gatekeeper asks, "How can we slow or stop this initiative to prevent risk?" If they can adopt the enabler mindset, their presence will serve as an accelerator.

SET UP YOUR GENERATIVE AI ENVIRONMENT

When selecting your initial AI tools, your highest priority must be the secure and private handling of your company's information. This is why using the free consumer versions of these tools for company work isn't an option. The key difference comes down to data protection. Consumer-focused AI tools often use your conversations and inputs to train their models, and the information from your interactions becomes accessible to the open internet, potentially including Google searches. This situation creates an unacceptable risk: If an employee pastes a draft of a confidential strategy memo, sensitive customer data, or unannounced financial figures into a consumer AI tool, they expose proprietary information and compromise security.

This issue is the most critical reason to subscribe to enterprise versions of these tools, such as ChatGPT Team or Enterprise, Claude for Work, or Google Gemini for Business.[6] Their core value proposition is data privacy. These tools contractually guarantee that your organization's conversations remain private and inaccessible for training AI models or internet searches. It is imperative that you immediately start using enterprise versions of these tools, providing a secure technical environment for yourself and your MVT.

The goal this week is to get started quickly with one of these tools. There is no wrong choice among reputable enterprise providers. The best way to understand AI's potential is through hands-on use; the cost of delay far exceeds any potential future costs from switching tools.

FIVE ESSENTIAL HABITS FOR RESPONSIBLE AI USE

As you start using AI tools, keep these fundamental practices in mind:

- **Pause and reflect**. When AI generates an answer, take a moment to consider it critically. Is this consistent with your expectations and professional assessment? This simple pause activates your critical thinking and prevents you from automatically accepting AI output.
- **Fact-check diligently**. Never assume AI-generated information is accurate. AI can confidently present incorrect information in convincing formats. Verify facts through independent sources, particularly for data, statistics, or specific claims.
- **Explore multiple options**. Ask AI tools for alternatives rather than accepting the first suggestions. Try phrases such as, "Give me three different approaches to this problem" or, "What are alternative ways to think about this challenge?" Use your expertise to select the most appropriate option.
- **Maintain data privacy**. Be extremely cautious about inputting sensitive or confidential information. Consider the potential consequences if such data were to become public. When in doubt, use hypothetical examples or anonymized data to get AI assistance while protecting sensitive information.

- **Respect intellectual property.** Be aware of copyright issues when using AI-generated content, especially in public-facing materials. AI training data includes copyrighted material, and generated content might inadvertently reflect existing work. Continually review and modify AI outputs to ensure originality.

These habits create muscle memory for responsible AI use. When you encounter ethical uncertainties, err on the side of caution and document these instances–they'll inform the comprehensive policies we'll develop next week.

HANDS-ON LEARNING: YOUR FIRST AI EXPERIENCES

In this section, we provide concrete exercises for you and your MVT to gain and expand your hands-on AI experience. Experiential learning is crucial for AI adoption, and it's essential that your MVT starts from the same baseline. Even if some team members have been using AI regularly, these structured exercises can still be helpful as they include best practices for maximizing the benefits of AI interactions. These exercises will also ensure that everyone has comparable foundational experience and develops shared vocabulary around AI use.

PREPARING FOR YOUR FIRST AI EXPERIENCES

By now, your MVT should have access to one of the secure, enterprise-grade AI tools discussed earlier, allowing you to begin using it in a structured way to understand its strategic potential. The following exercises will move your team beyond casual experimentation, reveal deeper business applications, and build a shared vocabulary around what's possible. We recommend that all MVT members complete these exercises, even those who are already advanced AI users.

For these exercises, a broad conversational AI tool, like the ones mentioned prior, is ideal, as they provide an open-ended environment for the strategic thinking and analysis required. This differs from workflow-integrated tools like Microsoft Copilot, which are powerful for executing specific productivity tasks within existing applications. For the creative and strategic exploration ahead, a dedicated conversational tool provides the best starting point.

THE FOUNDATION: WELL-CRAFTED PROMPTS

Crafting detailed prompts is the key to unlocking AI's potential. Clear, specific, and detailed prompts significantly increase output accuracy and minimize hallucinations. Think of prompting as a form of delegation, where the more precise your instructions are, the better the results.

Effective prompts include five elements:

1. **Role**. The persona or perspective you'd like the AI tool to adopt
2. **Instructions**. A set of directions for specific tasks you want the AI tool to perform
3. **Context**. Background information for the AI tool to guide understanding and aid its prediction
4. **Output**. Guidelines for the desired format, such as a text document, a spreadsheet, or a style of writing or presentation
5. **Refinement**. Iterative feedback that you provide with every tool output to improve the AI generation to meet your needs and goals

Example prompt: "As a business strategy consultant with expertise in retail (*role*), analyze the attached quarterly report and identify the top three growth opportunities for our expansion into European markets (*instructions*). Focus on markets where we have existing supply chain strengths (*context*). Present your analysis as an executive summary with specific recommendations and supporting rationale for each opportunity (*output*)."

This prompt provides a clear role definition, specific instructions, relevant context, and desired output format, setting up the AI for follow-up *(refinement)*.

THREE PRACTICAL EXERCISES

These exercises reflect everyday leadership tasks to build confidence and demonstrate AI's value across business scenarios. Ask every MVT member to complete each exercise to ensure a shared baseline experience, then discuss the learnings together. In addition to gaining comfort with the tools, you'll have a new leadership practice that can guide how you collectively think through deploying AI to create value in the organization.

EXERCISE ONE: CREATE CONTENT USING AI

Challenge: Overcome the tyranny of the blank page

AI's role: Your ghostwriter and thought partner

Steps:

1. **Define your content need and audience.** Choose a specific content type you need–a presentation for the board, an email to customers, a report for your team. Avoid confidential information.
2. **Craft a detailed prompt.** This should include all five elements. For example: "As a chief marketing officer with deep expertise in B2B software, draft a presentation for our quarterly business review explaining why our customer retention rates have improved 15 percent this quarter. The audience is the executive team, which wants to understand both the contributing factors and how we can sustain this improvement. Include specific data points, strategic implications, and recommendations. Format as a 10-slide presentation outline."
3. **Generate and critically review.** Send your prompt and carefully evaluate the output. Does it contain insights you hadn't considered? What's missing from your industry knowledge? How would your audience react?
4. **Refine and iterate.** Based on your review, adjust prompts or ask for modifications, such as, "Expand on slide 7 with more specific metrics" or, "Adjust the tone to be more data driven."
5. **Test with colleagues.** Share drafts with team members for feedback. Use their insights to refine for clarity and impact.

The goal is to understand how AI can accelerate your thinking and writing process, while your expertise guides and refines the output.

EXERCISE TWO: RESEARCH A PROSPECTIVE CUSTOMER MEETING

Challenge: Prepare a comprehensive research report for a sales meeting

AI's role: Your research assistant and strategy analyst

Steps:

1. **Define research objectives**. Choose a customer or prospect–either someone you're meeting soon or a top account you'd like to understand better.
2. **Gather company intelligence**. Use detailed prompts requesting specific information. For example: "As an experienced business development analyst researching prospects for enterprise software sales, conduct background research on [Company Name]. I need to understand their business model, recent financial performance, current technology initiatives, major competitive challenges, and any recent leadership changes or strategic announcements."
3. **Analyze and synthesize**. After reviewing initial results, refine your queries. Ask for deeper analysis, such as, "Based on this research, what are the three biggest operational challenges this company likely faces?"
4. **Connect to your offerings**. Provide information about your products or services and ask AI to identify opportunities for improvement. "Based on your analysis of [Company Name] and our platform features, what are the most compelling value propositions we could present?"
5. **Develop talking points**. Instruct the AI to generate discussion points that demonstrate an understanding of the business while positioning your solutions as relevant and valuable.

This exercise demonstrates AI's research potential while highlighting the importance of your business judgment in interpreting and applying the insights.

EXERCISE THREE: AI AS THOUGHT PARTNER

Challenge: Refine, expand, and challenge your ideas
AI's role: Executive coach and advisor
Steps:

1. **Present a strategic challenge**. Choose a business challenge you're facing–entering a new market, improving operational efficiency, responding to competitive threats, or developing a new product strategy.

2. **Engage AI as an advisor.** Craft prompts that use AI as a thinking partner. For example: "As a seasoned strategy consultant with expertise in [your industry], review my analysis of [strategic challenge]. What are the strengths and weaknesses of my current approach? What important factors might I be overlooking?"
3. **Challenge your assumptions.** Use AI to stress-test your thinking. For example, ask, "What would a skeptic say about this strategy?" or, "How might this approach fail, and how could we mitigate those risks?"
4. **Explore scenarios.** Ask the AI tool to help you think through possibilities and scenarios. For example, "If our main competitor responded by [specific action], how should we adapt our strategy?"
5. **Integrate and refine.** Take the AI tool's output and incorporate valuable elements into your strategic thinking. Continue the dialogue to refine ideas, but remember that the final judgment remains yours.

This exercise reveals AI's capability as a thought partner, while reinforcing that decision-making requires human judgment, industry knowledge, and organizational context that AI cannot provide.

THE KEY: ASK AI FOR CLARIFICATION

Here's a technique that transforms AI from an answer machine into a collaborative partner: At the end of your prompts, add, "Before you start working on this task, ask me any clarifying questions you may have."

This simple addition changes the entire dynamic. Instead of generating responses based on potentially incomplete understanding, an AI tool will often ask questions that help you provide fuller context and get results that are more relevant and comprehensive.

For example, when asked to draft a customer email, an AI tool might ask, "What specific action do you want customers to take after reading this email?" or, "What tone would be most appropriate for your customer relationship?"

These questions often reveal gaps in your original prompt and lead to more relevant outputs.

CAPTURING AND SHARING BEST PROMPT PRACTICES

Develop a systematic approach to capture both findings and value from your AI experiments. These discoveries will transform AI from individual tools into organizational assets.

Treat prompts as valuable intellectual property. Document, share, and protect them accordingly. A well-crafted prompt that saves two hours of work every week is worth thousands of dollars annually in productivity gains.

Leading organizations quickly recognize that AI discoveries shouldn't remain isolated achievements. When employees discover new ways to use AI effectively, those insights need to be systematized and shared across teams. Companies that create repositories of successful prompts and techniques—documenting what works and why—see AI adoption accelerate naturally as teams build on each other's discoveries rather than starting from scratch.

This approach involves treating AI lessons like any other business asset—capturing them, refining them, and scaling them across the organization.

DOCUMENT TAKEAWAYS AND VALUE

To transform individual discoveries into organizational assets, you need a simple way to document and share what the team is learning. Create two complementary repositories for your AI experiments:

1. **Prompt and technique library.** A centralized collection of effective prompts and successful approaches. This collection should provide context on why each prompt is effective and how to adapt it for various situations.
2. **Value tracking system.** The goal is to capture tangible evidence of impact without the burden of formal ROI calculations. Ask team members to log a simple one-sentence value statement when they have a significant win. For example: *Used AI to draft the quarterly board presentation outline, which saved about three hours and helped surface a new stakeholder analysis we hadn't considered.* Focus on this lightweight tracking for the first few weeks to build a collection of success stories that will demonstrate momentum.

Creating your AI knowledge hub

The best place to house these repositories is wherever your team already works. The key is to make sharing low-friction. Consider a two-part approach:

- **For active discussion and sharing,** create a dedicated channel in a tool like Slack or Microsoft Teams. These tools enable team members to share interesting prompts, ask questions, and post their value statements in real time.
- **For the permanent library,** use a more structured tool. A designated page on an internal wiki (like Confluence or SharePoint) or a shared document can serve as the curated, searchable home for the most effective prompts and techniques that emerge from the discussion channel. A shared spreadsheet can be a simple and effective log for tracking value statements.

Initially, these repositories should be accessible to the entire MVT to expand access as AI use grows throughout the organization.

YOUR WEEK 1 ACTION PLAN

This first week is about turning uncertainty into action and building a foundation for the next 83 days. Before moving on to Week 2, complete these four critical steps to launch your AI efforts:

- **Assemble your minimum viable team.** Identify and assemble a small, agile team comprising your most strategic and open-minded individuals. Ensure your team can make decisions and move quickly.
- **Provide access to a secure AI tool.** Select a reputable, enterprise-grade generative AI tool and give access to every member of your MVT. The goal is to start learning and experimenting immediately.
- **Complete the foundational AI exercises.** Ensure every MVT member completes the three hands-on exercises: creating content, researching a customer, and using AI as a thought partner.

- **Start your prompt and value library.** Treat your team's discoveries as valuable intellectual property by establishing a system to document and track them. Establish a prompt library to share effective techniques and a simple value tracking system to capture the impact of your AI use.

SUMMARY

You've now completed Week 1 of your 90-day preparation to create value with AI. In this chapter, you accomplished the following:

- **Learned about the types of AI** that dominate business today, with a focus on generative AI.
- **Established CEO leadership** as the driver of transformational AI for value creation.
- **Set up secure AI tool access**, understanding that speed to learning beats analysis paralysis.
- **Assembled your MVT** with diverse perspectives and an eye to moving quickly.
- **Discovered the power of well-crafted prompts**, using a five-element structure and clarifying questions.
- **Gained hands-on experience** through three practical exercises: content creation, customer research, and thought partnership.
- **Learned to treat AI discoveries** as intellectual property, documenting both learning and measurable value.

With the essentials in place–anchored by CEO leadership–you're ready for Week 2. In it, we'll cover the ethical and responsible AI frameworks that enable rapid deployment while maintaining trust and safety.

You can't go fast without good brakes.

–Charlene Li

Two

THE RESPONSIBLE AI ADVANTAGE

WELCOME TO WEEK 2 of your 90-day blueprint for winning with AI. Last week, you tackled your AI starter kit, learned about the current types of AI, assembled a core team, secured access to tools that protect your data, and gained hands-on experience. This week, you will learn how to put in place a full safety system that enables you to derive value from AI. You cannot create value without safe, ethical, and responsible practices. Yes, you want to move fast, but without breaking things.

Think about Formula 1 racing. The drivers who win championships have immense confidence in their safety systems—brakes, crash barriers, and fire suppression—which allows them to focus entirely on speed and strategy. The same principle applies to the use of AI. The organizations that will win with AI will be those that adopt robust, responsible AI practices, enabling them to innovate safely.

In this chapter, you'll embrace AI safety as the springboard that makes speed possible. You'll develop a responsible and ethical AI policy, grounded in your values; learn to navigate ethical trade-offs; and establish the system to make ethical decision-making as natural as any other business process.

This week, we'll help you do the following:

- **Draft your AI policy** using the template and prompts provided.
- **Identify a point person** for your initial AI Ethics Office.
- **Run one ethical scenario** with your team to practice values-based decision-making.

By the end of this week, you'll have what every winning Formula 1 team has: confidence in your safety systems, letting you focus on creating value.

THE SAFETY-FIRST MINDSET: WHY TRUST ENABLES SPEED

Companies that are moving the fastest in AI adoption are those with the highest ethical standards.

Why? Because ethics brings trust, which eliminates friction. When your team knows where the guardrails are, when your customers trust your intentions, when your board has confidence in your approach—that's when you can move safely at the speed AI demands.

According to the 2024 Edelman Trust Barometer, there is a significant "trust gap" in AI innovation.[1] While 50 percent of people globally trust the technology sector to do what is right, only 39 percent trust AI to do so. This gap ties directly to management. A full 43 percent of respondents said they would reject AI in products and services if they believe the innovation does not undergo extensive scrutiny. That's both a public relations problem and a business problem, directly impacting adoption, revenue, and competitive position.

AI presents challenges that don't have clear-cut answers. How do you ensure your new AI-powered marketing system doesn't inadvertently exclude certain customer groups? How do you balance the immense value of data personalization with individuals' fundamental right to privacy? When does an automated process cross the line from helpful to manipulative? These questions don't have one-size-fits-all solutions; they touch on everything from AI model design and data to your organization's core values.

The AI winners deliberately build in the ability to navigate ethical challenges. When ethical questions arise, they have systems, processes, and people in place to handle them. When opportunities arise, they possess the decision-making skills to navigate the accompanying ethical challenges.

To help get you on the same path, let's make sure you understand the difference between two often-confused terms: responsible AI and ethical AI.

- **Responsible AI** means designing, building, and operating AI systems with a structured set of best practices. It means you have the discipline to ensure AI use is safe, secure, fair, accurate, and accountable. Responsible AI provides the brakes that give you the confidence to move fast.

- **Ethical AI** involves navigating complex moral dilemmas where there is no single "right" approach. It comes into play when principles conflict, such as balancing personalization with privacy or weighing the efficiency of automation against its impact on jobs. It's a decision-making discipline rooted in your organization's core values, guiding you when choices are unclear.

Value from AI requires balancing tensions: safety and speed, values and innovation, principles and pragmatism. Mastering this balance will bring a competitive advantage in areas such as attracting talent, earning customer loyalty, and tackling regulatory changes. However, the right balance depends heavily on the specific industry context and the potential impact of AI failures.

The appropriate level of risk tolerance varies significantly by industry. In sectors managing critical infrastructure, the stakes are inherently higher, demanding a more conservative approach. Iskra Nikolova, a former executive in the telecom industry, explained in an interview with us that unlike consumer applications like Facebook, which deploy software changes multiple times daily, telecommunications networks require a slower, more deliberate pace.

"We cannot afford to have outages . . . this is critical infrastructure, national infrastructure," she said. "Changes are typically made weekly or monthly, not daily, because failure is not an option." Nikolova compares this stringent approach to industries like the military or space exploration (NASA), where processes are necessarily conservative because "things should not and cannot go wrong." This context shapes telecom's AI adoption. As Nikolova noted, AI needs to become "more like humans" in its ability to judge risk before it can be trusted in high-stakes operational situations. This highlights how industry context and risk profile are crucial inputs when defining responsible AI practices and the speed of deployment.

THE AI TRUST PYRAMID: YOUR SAFETY SYSTEM

The AI Trust Pyramid is a practical framework for implementing responsible AI. Its structure works much like Abraham Maslow's hierarchy of needs, where people

Figure 2-1: The AI Trust Pyramid

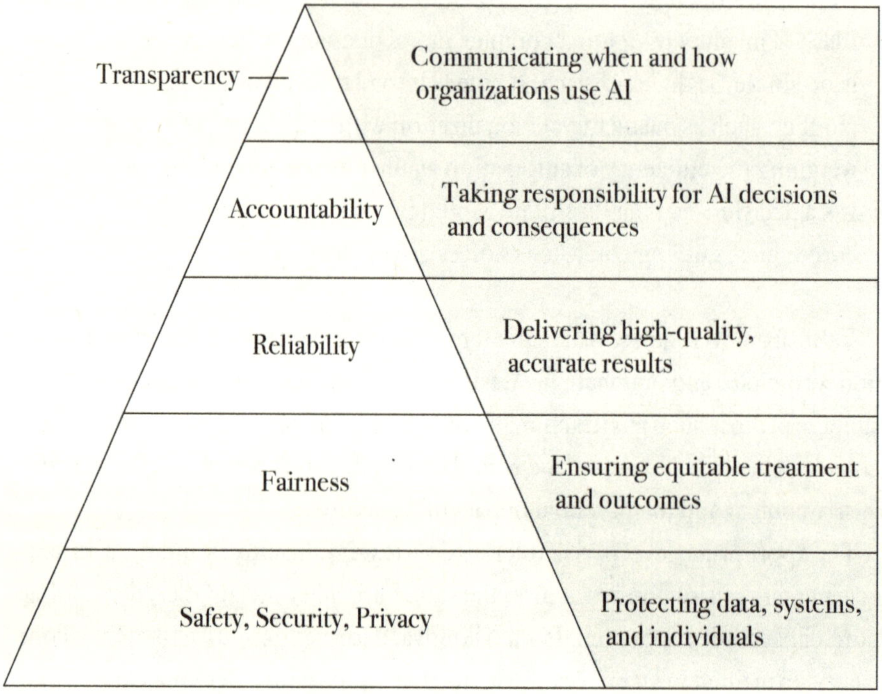

must satisfy foundational elements before they can reach higher-level elements.[2] This hierarchical structure provides stability and confidence. Each of the five elements builds upon the one below it; if a lower-level element, such as safety, fails, the entire structure risks collapse (see figure 2-1).

Companies that master all five elements differentiate themselves, build stronger customer relationships, and create resilience against AI-related risks. Let's walk through each element.

ELEMENT 1: SAFETY, SECURITY, AND PRIVACY

Safety, security, and privacy are the nonnegotiable baseline on which everything depends. You cannot build trust in AI without rock-solid safety, security, and privacy practices. You can't have fairness, reliability, or transparency without ensuring safety, security, and privacy.

This foundational element requires you to focus on three integrated areas:

safety, which involves ensuring AI systems don't cause unintended harm; **security**, which entails protecting systems and data from misuse; and **privacy**, which involves safeguarding personal information throughout its lifecycle.

This element requires that your core actions always do the following:

- **Protect confidential information** with user access controls, data encryption, and cybersecurity measures.
- **Safeguard customer and employee data** in compliance with regulations like the EU General Data Protection Regulation (GDPR) and the California Consumer Privacy Act (CCPA).[3] Even if you are outside these jurisdictions, it's a good idea to comply with their regulations as they represent the highest privacy standards–you can't go wrong by doing so.
- **Continuously test for adversarial attacks** by actively probing your AI systems for vulnerabilities. As you guide AI deployment, work closely with cybersecurity experts to implement and evolve safety, security, and privacy protections. For example, just as in cybersecurity, you can proactively work with "benevolent hackers" who deliberately push and test a system's limits.

Global information technology company HP exemplifies this approach. "We had a robust process in the company on data privacy training," said Prashant Jain, HP's former regional head of marketing, who implemented AI-led transformation programs for marketing at HP, told us. "It's refreshed religiously every 6 to 12 months. HP also ensures that any AI tool that is used by any HP employee first has to be cybersecurity approved."

Similarly, Unilever, which has been scaling its global AI assurance program since 2019, evolved its Responsible AI Principles to meet the demands of evolving regulation, such as the European Union AI Act. Unilever now manages over five hundred AI systems worldwide and conducts systematic privacy impact assessments for new technologies and maintains an incident response plan, all of which strengthen consumer trust. These reviews are undertaken by cross-functional teams to identify, manage, and mitigate risks before and after AI deployment.

We will cover technology safety and security in more detail in chapter 10.

ELEMENT 2: FAIRNESS

AI systems can perpetuate or amplify existing biases, unintentionally leading to potentially discriminatory outcomes.

The business case for fairness goes beyond upholding a principle of nondiscrimination. Companies that minimize AI bias can tap into broader markets, reach previously underserved customer segments, and avoid costly legal and reputational damage. Conversely, companies that fail to reduce bias do not accurately reflect the reality of the markets they serve; expose themselves to missed opportunities, at best; and, at worst, face consumer turmoil and limited ability to attract talent, among other risks.

Step one in achieving this element is to define what fairness means in your context. There is no universal definition of fairness, and the technical and academic debates are complex. However, the choices for a leader generally boil down to two approaches: Do you focus on the fairness of your *process* or the fairness of your *outcomes*? Your organization's values should guide your decision.

Process-based fairness applies the same impartial rules and processes to every person, focusing on removing subjective bias from the decision-making process itself. For instance, a marketing team could program its AI system to offer a discount to customers who have spent over $500 in the past year. The rule applies equally to everyone, regardless of their background or demographics.

Outcome-based fairness ensures the results from the AI system are equitable across different groups of people. This lens acknowledges that applying the same rules to everyone could lead to unbalanced results. For instance, a company might find its AI customer care voice agent has a lower success rate for nonnative English speakers. To achieve a fairer outcome, they could invest in specialized data sources to train the voice agent for different dialects, ensuring all customer groups have a comparable experience.

Regardless of which approach you choose, minimizing bias requires vigilance. You can't eliminate bias–it's ever present in data, systems, and human judgment. However, by defining fairness and committing to a specific approach, you can create systems that actively promote fairness. The essential strategies to do this include the following:

- **Using diverse datasets** that span demographics, geographies, cultures, and contexts.
- **Involving diverse teams** in development and testing to identify blind spots and challenge assumptions.
- **Employing multiple models and tools** with different architectures and training methods. This situation is where open-source tools are particularly powerful. They represent the voices and talents of many developers around the world, with their diverse backgrounds, knowledge, and perspectives.

Creating AI systems that promote fairness requires investing in prevention measures and constantly assessing and improving business and technical approaches.

ELEMENT 3: RELIABILITY

At its core, reliability means an AI system that behaves consistently and predictably every time you use it. This layer involves building the confidence that an AI system will perform as expected, whether it's drafting a marketing email or analyzing financial data. Reliability doesn't mean perfection; it means consistently meeting a *defined* standard of quality and accuracy for a specific task. For example, a creative AI assistant is reliable if it consistently produces high-quality first drafts. In contrast, a medical diagnostic AI is only reliable if it consistently meets its promised 99.9 percent accuracy rate, as the stakes are significantly higher.

The business stakes of unreliability are immense. When an AI system is erratic, it erodes the most critical asset for adoption: your team's trust. If employees cannot rely on a tool, they will develop workarounds, disregard its outputs, or abandon it, ultimately negating the investment. In customer-facing applications, the consequences are even more direct. An unreliable AI tool can lead to inconsistent customer experiences and flawed product recommendations and can ultimately damage your brand's reputation.

Achieving reliability is the result of deliberate practice. It requires rigorous testing before deployment and, just as importantly, continuous monitoring once an AI system is live. Achieving reliability also demands clear communication about the AI system's intended purpose and limitations. This clarity prevents people from using a tool for tasks it wasn't designed to handle, a common source of perceived failure and mistrust.

This dependable and predictable performance is what enables your team to trust and integrate AI into their daily work. Reliability entails both the engine delivering predictable power and the brakes engaging consistently, allowing the driver to move at speed.

ELEMENT 4: ACCOUNTABILITY

Accountability needs to extend throughout the organization, with clear roles and decision-making processes that empower people.

Every function in your organization needs to understand its role and responsibilities. Frontline employees—the operational users who interact daily with AI tools—should be able to spot issues and know who to contact when things go wrong. Departmental leaders are accountable for ensuring the AI tools their team uses uphold company standards. Technical and compliance leaders must ensure the tools operate within their organization's defined risk tolerance.

Accountability becomes more complex when an AI system works across functions. For example, imagine the marketing team uses a powerful AI tool for a lead-generation campaign, resulting in a 50 percent increase in customer inquiries. However, the surge in call volumes overwhelms the customer care department, causing long wait times and an eventual decline in customer satisfaction. If the company starts losing potential deals due to this poor service experience, who is accountable? Is it the head of marketing, whose campaign was a huge success by traditional metrics? Or the head of customer care, for not having enough staff to handle the higher call volume? Or the technology leader, who deployed the AI tool for the marketing team? Answering this question *before* the AI tool's release is a critical step in establishing ownership.

What's clear is that accountability is even more critical with the rise of agentic AI, which acts autonomously on behalf of an organization. An AI agent is not a legal entity (yet)—the business or organization cannot hold an AI agent accountable. For every AI agent your organization deploys, you must designate a responsible individual to oversee its actions and ensure it delivers reliable results within the intended task and context. This ownership answers the crucial question: When the AI agent does something unexpected, who do you call? Without a clear line of human accountability, you are granting autonomy to a black box—a risk no leader should take.

ELEMENT 5: TRANSPARENCY

Transparency in AI involves three dimensions: disclosing *that* you are using AI, observing *what* the AI model is doing, and interpreting *why* it is doing it.[4]

1. **Disclosure:** Announcing the use of AI is the most basic form of transparency. It means informing people when they are interacting with an AI system versus a human. This process sets expectations and builds trust. For routine internal tasks, disclosure may become less critical over time, much like no one feels the need to announce they used a calculator or an internet search engine. But for customer-facing applications or systems that impact people, disclosure is a nonnegotiable starting point.
2. **Observability:** Tracing AI actions goes deeper than disclosure by providing an audit trail of *what* an AI system did and *how* it performed those actions. Many AI models have features, sometimes referred to as a scratchpad, that display their chain-of-thought reasoning—the sequence of steps, decisions, and data points used to arrive at an outcome. This feature is not the same as explaining the *why*—that's interpretability—but it allows you to trace a model's logic. For example, when an AI agent independently reallocates marketing funds, observability provides a clear log of the actions it took, which is essential for accountability and transparency.
3. **Interpretability:** Understanding *why* an AI model arrived at a specific output or recommendation is the difference between knowing the molecular science of baking a cake versus simply having the recipe. You don't need to delve into the science, but you do need to understand the process to trust the outcome. This focus on interpretability enables stakeholders to act effectively on insights generated by AI.

Deciding where transparency is required versus optional will change over time. As more people adopt AI, routine tasks such as drafting email responses are likely to require less human intervention. However, for high-stakes applications, such as healthcare treatment plans or loan approvals, disclosure is necessary, but not sufficient. In these scenarios, trust demands observability and interpretability. Similarly, if an AI model denies a loan application, you should be able to see the key factors–like credit score, debt-to-income ratio, or loan amount–that drove that decision.

The need for observability and interpretability becomes even more critical with the rise of agentic AI, where AI moves from suggesting a course of action to independently executing it.

As your organization and stakeholders become more comfortable with AI, the requirements for trust will mature. As mass adoption approaches, we assume AI is helping manage our calendars and don't care whether we're engaging with a person or an AI agent. But for high-stakes and autonomous AI systems, there will always be an imperative to provide transparency, observability, and interpretability.

NAVIGATING ETHICAL TRADE-OFFS

The AI Trust Pyramid is your guide for responsible AI. But it doesn't eliminate difficult choices. Making tough trade-offs is where ethical AI comes in. Ethical AI is the ability to navigate complex dilemmas when values collide.

As every leader discovers, with AI ethics, the most complex decisions arise in situations where legitimate principles conflict, or where the right choice depends entirely on your values and context. The organizations that win with AI are those that anticipate challenges and enable decision-making to handle them before the need arises. Let's look at three scenarios that illustrate the trade-offs you'll encounter.

SCENARIO 1: TRANSPARENCY VERSUS CLIENTS' BEST INTEREST

A financial services firm deploys a powerful AI tool to help its advisors create retirement plans for clients. During testing, the company discovers something remarkable: The AI model's recommendations consistently outperform those of human advisors. The data suggests that investments made by clients following the AI-recommended plan will surpass those of human advisors.

This ability creates a sharp ethical dilemma. The company holds transparency as a core value, suggesting they should always disclose when they use AI. However, they have a fiduciary duty to act in their clients' best interests. They have learned from focus groups that many clients are wary of AI and would likely reject an AI-generated plan.

Should they uphold the value of transparency and disclose AI use, knowing it will likely lead some clients to choose a plan that is not in their best interest? Or should they prioritize their clients' best interests and refrain from fully disclosing the origin of the plan that will benefit them the most, thereby compromising their commitment to transparency? This dilemma presents a direct conflict between two deeply held principles.

SCENARIO 2: TWO PATHS TO A FUTURE-READY WORKFORCE

Imagine your company has the opportunity to deploy an AI system that automates much of the work of a two-hundred-person department, promising to cut operational costs by 60 percent. This dilemma is often the most emotionally charged trade-off a leader will face. The alternative is an AI tool that would make people more productive but requires a significant training investment and delivers only half the cost savings.

The first path presents a strategy for acquiring next-generation talent. You could reinvest the immediate cost savings to hire *new* people. Those new hires would possess the critical and creative skills to work alongside AI. This option provides a fast and direct path to building the workforce you need to stay competitive.

The second path is a long-term investment in your current employees. It buys you time to upskill them for higher-value roles that require human discernment and creativity–work AI can't do. This approach can foster employee loyalty and avoid potential labor issues. The risk, however, is significant: What if training employees isn't as successful as you hope? Or what if it fails to keep pace with the evolving skills your business will continue to need? You could end up with lower savings *and* a workforce not equipped for the future.

The displacement of a large, loyal portion of your current workforce is a profound ethical and strategic dilemma. Do you bet on transforming your current employees? Or do you choose to replace them, accepting the human cost of that decision? Both paths have significant implications for your culture, brand, and bottom line.

SCENARIO 3: THE SYNTHETIC CUSTOMER DILEMMA

A regional US home improvement retailer has collected detailed customer data over eight years, including purchase histories, service calls, satisfaction surveys, and personal stories shared during major purchases, such as kitchen renovations or deck installations. Their privacy policy states this data is used for "improving products and services and enhancing the shopping experience."

With new product launches, the marketing team needs to quickly test new advertising campaign concepts. The team suggests saving the time and costs required to conduct new studies of the concepts and instead tap into AI to create "synthetic" customer personas using existing data collected over the years. These artificially created archetypes would follow the patterns of what people have said in the past and predict what similar people will say in the future, thus enabling marketers to test the new campaigns with their customer audiences. Moreover, this allows for the testing of unlimited permutations of product positioning and messaging, which excites the marketing team. The legal department is also supportive, finding no legal stipulation that says it can't be done, and, further, sees the use of synthetic data as a new means for protecting real customers' privacy.

However, the fact is that the original customer data use permissions did not extend to feeding that data into AI models for designing artificial customer segments. Is creating synthetic customers for marketing optimization a legitimate extension of improving customer experience? Or does it cross an ethical line by repurposing personal insights without explicit permissions to create artificial customers? What if customers found out that retailers were using their personal stories to create AI versions of themselves, essentially testing psychological sales tactics? What would you do as a business leader? What would you want companies to do when they serve you as a customer?

SOLVING AI ETHICAL DILEMMAS

How do you respond to ethical dilemmas? Perfect solutions don't exist. As you encounter ethical trade-offs during your AI deployment, remember that the right decision often depends on your specific context, values, and strategy. What matters is that you are deliberate about your choices, systematically consider different stakeholder perspectives, and remain adaptable as technology and circumstances evolve.

The consideration of stakeholders is critical. Each group–your employees, customers, partners, and investors–views ethical challenges through a different lens. Their perspectives will expose blind spots and reveal potential unintended consequences that might otherwise go unnoticed. Actively seeking out diverse viewpoints leads to a robust decision and builds the trust on which AI adoption depends.

YOUR RESPONSIBLE AND ETHICAL AI POLICY: START WITH VALUES

Most companies approach AI policy backward. They begin by considering regulatory requirements, industry best practices, or competitor analysis. However, effective AI policies begin with your organization's values–the beliefs that it holds as an entity and exemplifies in its decisions and actions.

An effective policy must address both the *what* and *how* of approaching AI. The *what* is your ethical AI stance. It's grounded in your values and answers the question "What do we believe is the right way to use this technology?" This approach provides the moral compass for your decisions.

The *how* is your responsible AI practice: the concrete rules, systems, and day-to-day processes that bring your ethics to life. It answers the question "How do we ensure AI use is safe and consistent?" A policy addressing only the *what* is a noble statement that lacks teeth. A policy with only the *how* is a brittle set of rules that will fail to guide people through unexpected challenges. By combining the two, you create a policy that is both practical and a reflection of your organization's character.

Your values should also guide your AI choices. For example, if your organization prioritizes employee development over operational efficiency, this will inform your approach to AI deployment. Since customer privacy is paramount to your brand, it should inform every AI application you consider. If risk management is paramount in your industry and company, it will also determine how you handle ethical dilemmas in AI deployment.

VALUES FIRST, NOT REGULATION

A values-driven AI policy creates three categories of AI use:

- **Beneficial and encouraged:** AI use that supports your mission and accelerates your business goals. These are the AI applications you want to see flourish across your organization.

- **Questionable and requiring caution:** This is a murky territory where the benefits are unclear and pose risks. Decisions in this category require you to implement additional oversight, approval processes, and other safety measures.
- **Prohibited:** AI use in this case violates your organizational values or could harm your stakeholders. These applications either don't serve your interests or could create unacceptable risks, making them a hard no.

For example, a healthcare organization might use AI to expedite patient treatment. However, the same organization would prohibit applications that could compromise accurate diagnoses. A financial services company that values personal connection may be cautious about using AI applications that could compromise this personal touch.

This values-first approach creates a policy that's uniquely yours, not a generic template. It also makes the AI policy more meaningful to employees by connecting it to the organizational purpose they understand and support.

SOUTHWEST AIRLINES: MOVING FAST WITH GUARDRAILS

When generative AI emerged, Southwest Airlines CIO Lauren Woods knew her team needed to move quickly and use the right lens. Before establishing policies, they grounded their approach in Southwest's core values: servant's heart, warrior spirit, and fun-loving attitude. "We wanted to look at generative AI and large language models through that lens of 'this is what we are, this is how we do business,'" Woods explained in an interview with us.

With values as their foundation, she assembled a small cross-functional team with dedicated resources from technology, artificial intelligence, operations, legal, and cybersecurity. "We made it small so we could go really fast," she said. This lean structure bypassed typical bureaucratic processes, allowing them to establish clear policies within weeks, under guidance such as not allowing the use of confidential company, customer, or personal information in public AI tools.

The team also became a critical funnel for vendor relationships, preventing departments from inadvertently signing contracts where, Woods said, "Those small little terms and conditions say, now all that information is owned by somebody else." This values-driven, CEO-backed approach accelerated Southwest's deployment of AI solutions for customer service, customer experience, and software development.

YOUR AI POLICY

Creating your responsible and ethical AI policy should be an iterative process. This is where your minimum viable team (MVT) from Week 1 should keep the lead but is also where other leaders should be involved.

Appendix A includes a sample Responsible and Ethical AI Use Policy template that you can use as a starting point.

Here is a three-step process to follow:

Step 1: Involve other functions. Include both senior leadership and high-potential employees from legal, compliance, information security, privacy, and risk functions. They can provide expert advice on policy development, ensure it serves both organizational values and compliance requirements, and provide ongoing feedback as the policy evolves. But the MVT will continue to lead and own policy implementation.

Step 2: Use AI to create an initial outline. What better way to gain hands-on experience than using AI to kickstart the process? Upload your existing information security policies, code of conduct, and employee handbook to an enterprise-grade, secure AI tool (as we covered in chapter 1). Then provide a clear prompt, like this:

"Please draft a responsible AI use policy outline that incorporates our existing data and information handling and security policy, code of conduct, and employee handbook. The policy should cover:

- Uses of AI that we would support and encourage
- Uses of AI that we would find questionable and urge caution regarding
- Uses of AI that would violate our existing policies and code of conduct
- The importance of considering content appropriateness and

respecting copyright and intellectual property rights

- The specific responsibility of employees and related accountability measures
- Ways and examples of implementing, monitoring, and updating the policy

Before drafting the policy outline, please ask any questions to ensure you have all the necessary information."

Step 3: Human review and refinement. Remember that your AI-generated outline is a starting point. Review it carefully for accuracy, completeness, and consistency against your existing policies. Seek feedback from functional experts and employees across the organization who work in operations, customer care, product development, and human resources. This review will help you determine whether the policy is directionally correct and assess whether it's too restrictive at the expense of genuinely empowering employees. Your next step would be to incorporate significant elements of the feedback.

Some stakeholders may challenge the very idea of yet another policy or object to the technology's use in the organization. Regardless of the reasons, address their concerns by emphasizing that an AI policy ensures appropriate governance. The reality is that people are already using AI in their work. Without a policy to guide its use, the organization exposes itself to risk.

LEARNING TO PRACTICE RESPONSIBLE AND ETHICAL AI

Your AI policy should be a living document that you refresh as technology and regulations evolve. This adaptation occurs through practice, involving a combination of regularly scheduled reviews, clear channels for employees to provide feedback, and ad hoc updates in response to major technological or regulatory shifts.

For Week 2, your goal is to develop a draft policy that can guide the immediate adoption of AI, preparing you to implement it thoroughly over the coming weeks. The AI policy will provide clear direction that your team can follow as they begin working with AI tools.

The real test of your AI policy is how effectively it guides decision-making in real situations. Make it practical, accessible, and valuable.

THE AI ETHICS OFFICE: THE GUARDIAN OF RESPONSIBLE AND ETHICAL AI

Responsible AI principles are essential, but they won't on their own prevent ethical problems. When ethical questions inevitably arise, your organization needs systematic processes, clear escalation paths, and expert guidance to navigate complex trade-offs.

This is why you need to establish an AI Ethics Office. It oversees the practical implementation of the responsible AI practices we outlined in the AI Trust Pyramid. It ensures systems are safe, fair, and reliable. The AI Ethics Office will naturally be the central point for navigating ethical dilemmas as they arise. By providing clear guidance and practical tools, it ensures that AI development reflects your core values and accelerates responsible innovation. Its role is to help teams move beyond asking "Is this permitted?" to wrestling with the more complex and crucial question "Is this right?"

Many organizations stumble here. They establish ethical principles but fail to apply them consistently. They slip when business pressure mounts, deadlines loom, or complex circumstances demand quick decisions. The solution is to build ethical decision-making directly into your organization's daily operations, making it as natural and integral as any other business consideration.

Let's be clear about timing: You won't create an entire system for ethical AI deployment this week. Creating the AI Ethics Office is long-term work that will evolve over the coming months as you expand AI deployment across the organization.

THE AI ETHICS OFFICE IN ACTION

Effective ethical oversight comes from embedding ethical considerations directly into the natural flow of AI development and deployment. The AI Ethics Office's primary role is to guide the organization in implementing its principles and values. This means embedding two key sources of guidance into daily operations: the organization's core values and the five elements of the AI Trust Pyramid. The office accomplishes this through three core work streams:

1. Develop practical tools and frameworks

To make abstract principles concrete, the AI Ethics Office creates and maintains practical frameworks and processes that integrate directly into existing workflows.

These frameworks and processes encourage teams to consider ethical implications at key stages of a project's life cycle and include these elements:

- **Consequence-scanning exercises,** like using a "red team" to brainstorm how a new AI tool could fall into misuse or cause harm to customers.[5]
- **Ethical AI design checklists** that put the AI Trust Pyramid into practice. They provide a simple way for organizations to review projects against each of the AI Trust Pyramid's five elements.
- **Stakeholder impact assessments** involving systematic reviews that require organizations to identify all audiences reached by an AI tool and evaluate its potential impact. This involves mapping out everyone the system might interact with–from end users and employees to community members and supply chain partners–and analyzing how the AI tool could affect each group.
- **Bias detection protocols**, which are the technical standards for testing AI systems during development, deployment, maintenance, and scaling. For example, this could involve running tests to determine if a loan-approval model exhibits a different false rejection rate for applicants across racial or gender groups. Mitigating this will ensure the model performs equitably.

2. Manage escalations and critical concerns

As the hub for addressing complex ethical issues, the AI Ethics Office creates and manages clear, confidential channels for employees to escalate concerns when they identify a potential problem that exceeds existing guidelines. This ensures that challenging questions don't remain unresolved. The office is also responsible for fielding inbound concerns from outside the organization, such as those from customers or the public. In this way, the AI Ethics Office serves as the single point of contact for all matters related to AI ethics.

3. Build organizational conscience

Finally, the AI Ethics Office is responsible for building the organization's conscience through expert guidance and training. Retailer H&M Group provides an excellent example of building AI ethics at scale. Facing the challenge of integrating ethical AI practices across its 171,000 employees, the company's AI leadership team developed an Ethical AI Debate Club.[6] In its sessions, facilitated by the AI Ethics Office, employees debated realistic AI dilemmas, often taking on positions with which they disagreed to force a critical examination of all perspectives. The program was instrumental in creating champions of ethics across the workforce. The work did not end after initial deployment. Continuous focus on AI ethics evolved to include "exploration guides." These guides included specific probing questions to help employees navigate ethical dilemmas. H&M established a culture of ethical decision-making, fostering an organization that can apply AI ethics and continue to advance.

EMBEDDING RESPONSIBLE AI IN THE ORGANIZATION

The AI Ethics Office collaborates with frontline teams across the organization. These teams will use the tools and frameworks provided by the central office to embed the principles of responsible and ethical AI into their daily workflows. This means systematically pausing at key checkpoints to ask the right questions:

- **When prioritizing** where and how an organization deploys AI for value creation, assess both potential risks and opportunities.
- **In data collection and preparation**, assess risks of bias, privacy implications, and fairness considerations.
- **Throughout model development**, implement bias detection protocols and build in the technical hooks required to enable future transparency and interpretability.
- **During testing and validation**, confirm that systematic testing for fairness has been conducted across demographic groups and that the model performs reliably across its intended applications.
- **In deployment and monitoring**, establish ongoing surveillance for unintended consequences and clear escalation paths.

The goal is to equip employees with the awareness to spot potential issues and the knowledge of when to use the provided tools or escalate a concern to the AI Ethics Office.

SUSTAINING RESPONSIBLE AND ETHICAL AI

The goal is to develop an organizational capacity for ethical reasoning, moving beyond isolated decision-making. Here are some ways employees can practice ethical reasoning:

- **Scenario-based learning** that helps individuals recognize ethical challenges before they escalate into crises. For example, facilitating regular AI Dilemma of the Month discussions based on real-world or hypothetical situations, similar to the H&M Ethical AI Debate Club model.
- **Decision support systems** that provide clear escalation paths for navigating complex trade-offs. For example, embed an ethical AI-by-design checklist in your product management software, making the ethical review a required step before advancing to the next stage.
- **Communities of practice** that create networks of ethics champions who share experiences and support each other. For instance, consider creating a dedicated Slack or Microsoft Teams channel for AI champions to ask questions, share experiences with challenging situations, and receive advice from the AI Ethics Office.
- **Continuous learning systems** that capture lessons from both successful and problematic decisions to improve future decision-making. For example, such systems might involve conducting exercises on major AI applications that simulate potential failures in advance, and building a searchable library of case studies and lessons learned from past AI deployments.

Committing to ethical AI decision-making can strengthen stakeholder trust, avoid costly mistakes, and position an organization as a leader in conscientious innovation.

STAYING AHEAD OF REGULATIONS

The rapid evolution of the AI regulatory landscape can feel overwhelming. You face the complexity of international regulations—such as the EU AI Act—alongside a patchwork of laws in the US. The good news is that most emerging regulations reflect the responsible and ethical AI principles we've been discussing.

THE REGULATORY REALITY

The regulatory environment is fragmented, uncertain, evolving, and varies widely across geographies. This creates complexity, but it shouldn't paralyze progress.

The silver lining? Most regulations focus on the same core areas: safety, security, and privacy; fairness; reliability; accountability; and transparency. Sound familiar? These mirror the five elements of the AI Trust Pyramid.

One area that deserves special attention is intellectual property. AI-generated content does not easily fit into existing copyright laws; many popular AI tools emerged from publicly available content that likely included copyrighted materials without explicit permission. Creators and rights holders have mobilized and launched lawsuits against AI companies.

The legal landscape is complex, and legal uncertainty creates a significant question for companies as they tackle AI and content. Some organizations are choosing to address intellectual property proactively, potentially turning a responsible practice into a business advantage.

Adobe, for example, decided to train its Firefly generative AI model on its own Adobe Stock library, openly licensed content, and public domain images with expired copyrights.[7] This way, Adobe proactively ensured it had permission for the content it used to develop AI models. By avoiding the legal and ethical gray area of using publicly available–and possibly copyright-protected–data, Adobe built what they call a "commercially safe" model. They are so confident in this approach that they offer full legal indemnification to enterprise customers. This indemnity serves as a differentiator, easing enterprise concerns about AI and establishing the trust necessary for wide-scale adoption.

This is a clear example of how a values-driven decision–in this case, respecting creator rights–can directly translate into a competitive advantage.

YOUR PREPARATION STRATEGY

Grounding your work in the practices of responsible AI and guiding it with the principles of ethical AI can help you prepare for emerging regulation. This enables you to move faster, avoid penalties, and establish a reputation as an industry leader in trustworthy AI.

Key steps to position your organization for compliance include the following:

- **Assign clear responsibility for AI regulation monitoring**. Task your legal team or AI Ethics Office with active monitoring. They need to stay informed about regulatory developments in their industry and operating jurisdictions and provide regular briefings to ensure leadership reacts to credible signals, not just news headlines.
- **Establish clear documentation to ensure transparency and prepare for future regulatory inquiries**. Partner with your legal and compliance teams to purposefully record the evidence of your due diligence–such as key decisions, their rationale, data sources, and model testing results–to create a defensible record without introducing legal risk.[8]
- **Help shape future AI policy by contributing to public discourse where it matters**. This involves shaping future AI policy through responses to public comment requests from federal regulatory bodies, participation in industry groups, and engagement with state-level lawmakers, where much of the initial regulatory activity is occurring. This proactive engagement helps inform future regulations and gives you a voice in them.
- **Anchor compliance in your values**. Regulations will always lag behind technology. Following the principles of ethical and responsible AI prepares your organization for future regulations, not just where they are today. Regulatory uncertainty shouldn't slow AI deployment; it should motivate you to proceed in accordance with ethical principles.

YOUR WEEK 2 ACTION PLAN

Here are three specific actions you can take to put the principles from this chapter into practice.

- **Draft your AI policy**. Use the prompt from this chapter for an AI tool to generate the first draft of your AI Use Policy. Send this initial draft to your legal and compliance functions to begin the feedback process.
- **Identify a point person for your initial AI Ethics Office**. Identify one person in your organization who can serve as the initial point of contact for a future

AI Ethics Office. This could be a part-time responsibility for now, but establishing an owner is the first step in building accountability.

- **Run one ethical scenario with your minimum viable team**. Choose one of the three ethical dilemmas from this chapter—customer guidance, workforce transformation, or content generation—and lead a discussion. Focus on understanding how your team approaches ethical trade-offs in AI deployment.

SUMMARY

You've explored something crucial this week: the systems that will enable you to move quickly and safely. Like those Formula 1 drivers who push to the limit because they trust their brakes, you now have the safety to innovate with speed. You have grasped the basics of responsible AI:

- **The AI Trust Pyramid**, a five-element system covering safety, security, and privacy; fairness; reliability; accountability; and transparency.
- **Ethical decision-making scenarios** to navigate complex trade-offs when competing values collide.
- **AI policy**, a values-driven approach to governing AI use.
- **The AI Ethics Office**, which provides systematic support for integrating ethical decision-making into daily work.
- **Regulatory readiness**, preparation for emerging compliance requirements through responsible and ethical AI principles and practices.

With your safety systems in place, you're ready for Week 3, getting a head start on making AI a driver of value in your organization.

Leadership is the capacity to translate vision into reality.

—Warren Bennis

Three WHO OWNS AI?

CONSIDER TWO MANUFACTURING companies that started deploying AI with similar investments and ambitions. Company A launched various AI proofs of concept across marketing, operations, and HR. Eighteen months later, they had a dozen disconnected initiatives with no enterprise-wide impact. Result: When their board asked for an AI value overview, no one could provide it.

Company B, on the other hand, appointed a chief AI officer six months after it began its AI efforts. This leader developed a holistic approach to support the company's strategy; coordinated AI applications across customer service, supply chain, and product development; and launched a focused effort with plans for scale. Result: A 15 percent increase in margin from optimized customer experience and two new AI-powered services that captured market share.

The difference? Company A treated AI as a technology rollout that IT serviced on an ad hoc basis in siloed departments. Company B treated AI as a value driver that required dedicated strategic leadership and a coordinated, business-focused approach.

This is the choice every organization faces: scattered AI projects that never scale, or strategic AI leadership that drives transformation and measurable value. The companies winning with AI organize differently and mobilize a new structure that enables them to create value with AI across the enterprise.

You're now in Week 3 of your 90-day blueprint for winning with AI. You've learned the essentials of the technology and established responsible and ethical AI frameworks. Now it's time to address the most critical decision for AI success: Who will be 100 percent accountable for driving AI value across your organization?

This week, you will accomplish the following:

- **Understand why AI value creation** requires dedicated leadership that goes beyond traditional IT or other functional roles.
- **Learn the organizational options** for establishing AI leadership and when each approach works best.
- **Define the profile of your AI leader,** who will drive organizational transformation and business value.
- **Make the leadership decision** that will determine your AI success.
- **Begin building the organizational structure** that enables AI execution at scale.

The stakes couldn't be higher. Organizations with dedicated AI leadership achieve a 10 percent higher ROI on AI investments and are 24 percent more likely to outperform their peers in innovation.[1] But only 26 percent of organizations have established a dedicated AI leadership role.[2]

Don't become a cautionary tale. The window for establishing an AI advantage is closing rapidly.

THE LEADERSHIP GAP THAT KILLS AI SUCCESS

Every week, we hear the same story from frustrated executives: "We have AI pilots everywhere, but nothing is scaling." The symptoms are universal, marked by scattered initiatives, siloed approaches, and disappointing results. But the root cause isn't a technology failure. It's a leadership failure.

Most organizations view AI in the same way they handled cloud computing or mobile apps—as a technology deployment managed by IT or individual business units. This approach guarantees mediocrity because AI isn't a technology project. It's a business initiative for value creation that happens to use technology.

THE ACCOUNTABILITY GAP

The fundamental problem is a lack of accountability. When multiple leaders share responsibility for AI, nobody takes ownership of the outcome. The chief information officer optimizes for technical feasibility, the chief financial officer focuses on cost reduction, and the chief marketing officer pursues conversion and customer engagement. Meanwhile, transformational opportunities that require cross-functional coordination fail to materialize.

Organizations need someone who wakes up every morning with one job: ensuring the company creates value with AI. This person must have the authority to break down silos, allocate resources, and drive decisions that individual department heads cannot make alone.

AI transformation requires dedicated leadership with enterprise-wide authority, working directly with the CEO.

DETERMINING YOUR AI LEADER

Establishing effective AI leadership requires two critical decisions: defining the type of leader needed and determining how to organize that leadership within your existing structure. Most companies skip the first step and jump straight to organizational charts, which explains why so many AI initiatives underperform.

First, let's define what it takes to lead AI transformation. Then we'll examine the approaches legacy organizations typically take, including why the most popular approach almost always fails.

ESSENTIAL CHARACTERISTICS: THE CHANGE AGENT PROFILE

The role of leading AI requires someone who can bridge AI's technological potential with business value and organizational transformation. This isn't the most brilliant technologist or the most seasoned business executive–it's someone with a specific combination of characteristics that drive value creation through the use of AI. Your AI leader must fit this description:

- **A proven change agent**. They've driven transformation and value creation with emerging technology. They understand how to inspire a bold vision, start in a focused way, mobilize resources, and maintain momentum–despite likely organizational resistance. They relentlessly challenge the status quo, envisioning new opportunities, solutions, and even business models made possible by AI. This isn't someone who thinks like a traditional service provider responding to business requests.
- **Technically credible**. They possess AI knowledge to evaluate opportunities,

pose probing questions to vendors, guide engineering teams, and assess the technical feasibility of implementation. They understand how to transform data into live-streaming repositories for AI models to mine and use, and ensure that data flows support AI applications. They can match business value with technical possibilities. They don't have to be the most sophisticated AI engineer or architect—they need to guide and inspire them.

- **A value creation driver**. The winning AI leader wakes up every morning focused on creating measurable value through AI. They connect AI applications to revenue growth, cost reduction, expanded reach, and competitive positioning—any of the business goals an organization has—with clear metrics and accountability. They also think strategically about where AI creates growth, not just efficiency.
- **A problem solver and solution builder**. They drive the creation of AI applications that solve business problems. They understand how to turn technical possibilities into AI products that deliver results. They know how to scale and don't get stuck on prototypes. They focus on execution and business outcomes, not innovation theater.
- **A business leader with entrepreneurial pragmatism**. They understand business dynamics, the regulatory environment, and customer expectations. They possess intellectual curiosity and persistence in working through obstacles, combined with pragmatism that delivers quick, practical solutions. They succeed through partnership and influence rather than hierarchy, with an entrepreneurial willingness to tackle any challenge, big or small.

These characteristics require someone who can operate simultaneously as a change agent, strategist, and business value integrator. The scope is intentionally broad because AI transformation affects every aspect of an enterprise, requiring coordination across organizational boundaries that traditional functional leaders often struggle to cross.

WHAT THIS LEADER IS *NOT*

Just as important as knowing your AI leader's profile is recognizing what that leader is not. Many organizations make the wrong choice by appointing or elevating people with the wrong profiles, expanding legacy executives' scopes, or expecting them to fill multiple incompatible roles.

Your AI leader is not any of the following:

- **A traditional IT executive**. This choice is the most common mistake organizations make—expecting their legacy IT leader to also lead AI deployment. Traditional IT leaders focus on running enterprise systems, managing risk, and serving as internal service providers—what one senior consultant at Bain described in an interview with us as "procurement officers" rather than builders. "The moment you mention the word 'build,' they worry because they've never built anything," he observed. This creates a credibility gap that undermines the ability to attract the technical talent AI transformation demands. "They cannot find anyone to get things done because they don't have the knowledge and credibility to attract others who have the knowledge and credibility."
- **A business leader without a technical foundation**. Some organizations swing too far in the other direction, appointing someone with a business track record and credentials but zero technical understanding. Without AI knowledge and technical chops, this person can't evaluate opportunities, assess vendor offerings, or guide engineering teams effectively. They'll be swayed by every AI sales pitch, which will undermine their credibility with engineers.
- **A technical guru without influence**. Don't assume that sheer technical brilliance is enough to drive transformation. Pure engineering experts often lack the crucial soft skills to translate their work into tangible business value. Unable to influence peers or communicate a strategic vision to nontechnical leaders, their groundbreaking projects often fail to gain traction and get stuck in the lab.
- **A pure data governance expert**. Some organizations may promote their data management executive into an AI leadership role, thinking it's a natural fit. However, someone who has spent years perfecting data quality processes often lacks the pragmatic mindset necessary to deploy data for value creation through AI applications. They get stuck on ensuring data is perfect rather than making it good enough to create a business impact.

- **An innovation facilitator.** If you have someone running design workshops and innovation labs, don't assume they can drive AI transformation. Facilitation and ideation are valuable, but they differ significantly from executing technology initiatives that deliver measurable business results at scale.

These defaults may seem logical at first, but they fundamentally mismatch what AI value creation requires with what these leaders can deliver. The stakes are too high for organizational convenience.

THREE APPROACHES ORGANIZATIONS TYPICALLY TAKE FOR AI LEADERSHIP

For the most part, every organization with which we've worked follows one of the three approaches outlined below. Each has benefits and challenges, but the success rates vary dramatically.

APPROACH 1: PUTTING AI WITH THE EXISTING CIO

What it looks like: By default, the current IT leader incorporates AI into their existing responsibilities.

Why organizations choose this approach: This approach feels logical and low-risk. The rationale is that the CIO leads technology and already manages enterprise systems.

Why it almost always fails: The vast majority of current technology leaders in legacy organizations are traditional CIOs. They focus on keeping enterprise systems running, managing risk, and operating as internal service providers. They focus on system deployment, integration, and maintenance rather than organizational transformation or business value. Most view themselves as cost centers whose primary role is to minimize disruption rather than create value through emerging technology.

When AI falls under traditional IT leadership, it risks becoming part of the typical IT machine, where technology infrastructure is rolled out cautiously, implemented over years or even decades, and not measured by business outcomes. The scope limitations of traditional IT leaders and organizations will prevent AI from delivering value across the organization.

ARE YOU INCREDIBLY LUCKY?

There is a chance your organization may already have an executive who fits the profile of the AI leader we outlined above. They would likely be a chief digital officer, chief transformation officer, or in still rarer instances, a next-generation technology leader (see Approach 3).

Suppose you have recently brought in or currently have someone who fits the AI leader profile and reports directly to the CEO—congratulations. In that case, you're ahead of 99 percent of organizations around the world.

But be brutally honest in your assessment. Don't shortchange your AI efforts for the sake of convenience and expediency. The stakes are too high to settle for someone who's "close enough." Many organizations may believe they have the right person, but often they don't, which is why AI initiatives underperform.

APPROACH 2: BRINGING IN A PARALLEL AI LEADER

What it looks like: Recognizing the constraints of traditional IT, organizations hire a chief AI officer (or similar role) who reports directly to the CEO and operates alongside the existing technology organization. This implies the establishment of a separate new AI department or function within the organization.

The logic: This preserves operational stability in core IT functions, while establishing dedicated AI leadership with strategic authority and cross-functional scope.

Why it could work: This approach provides a dedicated AI focus without disrupting existing technology operations. The AI leader can recruit specialized expertise, coordinate across business functions, and drive transformation, while the CIO maintains enterprise systems.

The challenges: This approach creates inherent tension between the two owners of technology. Organizations are often reluctant to give the new AI leader control over various aspects, including digital products, data platforms, data management, data engineering, analytics, and machine learning. This approach leads to territorial friction, increased coordination overhead, and organizational confusion about which leader to consult for what is seemingly all technology. Additionally, as AI permeates enterprise hardware and software, it's becoming increasingly challenging to separate AI from IT.

Reality check for Approach 2: This approach requires clear scope boundaries to minimize territorial friction and organizational confusion. But even with clear scope and boundaries, everyday conflicts such as these emerge:

- The AI leader requires clear authority over data management and engineering to enable AI applications, while the CIO seeks to maintain control over information security and enterprise systems.
- Budget decisions become complex when AI initiatives require infrastructure and engineering resources controlled by different leaders.
- Vendor management becomes fragmented when AI solutions must integrate with existing enterprise systems.
- The AI leader aims to move quickly on cross-departmental data aggregation, new tools, and new tech vendors, but the CIO wants to work through security and governance issues at their own pace.

Here's how organizations might divide responsibilities (see figure 3-1):

Making Approach 2 work: We don't recommend this approach because it forces the CAIO–often hired from outside the organization–to navigate extreme politics, manage structural conflicts, build a new organization from scratch, and prove value quickly, all at once. While it can work, it comes at a significant cost for the new, fledgling AI organization, which frequently encounters issues with the traditional IT teams and vice versa.

If you were to take this approach, be clear about the risks of organizational confusion, diminished scope, and a particularly uphill battle for the new leader, on top of the usual resistance an organization might harbor against AI. You might be choosing this path as one of least resistance and with the noble goal of not alienating or disrupting traditional IT. However, this approach incurs costs for the new CAIO organization you are introducing, and you are not setting them up to succeed.

If you remain committed to this approach, define and consistently enforce clear boundaries regarding ownership. As a CEO or MVT, ensure visible support for the AI leader's authority, scope, championship, and credibility. Establish shared success metrics and regular coordination protocols. Accept that this approach requires more management overhead than unified technology leadership. This

Figure 3-1: CAIO versus CIO responsibilities

CAIO TYPICALLY OWNS	CIO TYPICALLY OWNS
• AI strategy and roadmap • Data management and governance • Data engineering • Analytics and business intelligence • Data and AI product management • Data science and machine learning • AI vendor management	• Information/cybersecurity • Network and infrastructure • Hardware and device management • Enterprise applications (ERP, CRM, finance systems) • End user computing and tech support • IT vendor relationships

approach also limits the full impact of your efforts due to organizational and structural issues.

APPROACH 3: BRINGING IN A NEXT-GENERATION TECHNOLOGY LEADER

What it looks like: The organization replaces a traditional IT leader with someone who can drive both technology infrastructure and AI transformation.

Why this approach is most effective: It eliminates the structural, organizational, and coordination challenges of Approach 2, while ensuring AI receives strategic leadership. All technology functions–IT, information security, digital products, data, analytics, and AI–operate under unified leadership with clear accountability for business transformation and value creation.

The implementation path: This requires the most organizational change and CEO conviction. Many CEOs shy away from making major technology leadership changes because they fear the potential disruption to the organization. It takes confidence, courage, and conviction that this move is unavoidable. Ironically, this approach is also the least disruptive for an organization, as it unifies technology work, connects it to organizational strategy and value creation, and ensures the most effective and efficient management of resources.

Here are two implementation options:

- **Replace a traditional CIO** with a next-generation technology leader who can drive value creation through all things technology and AI.

- **Add a new technology and AI leader** above the current IT executive, effectively layering them. This would enable the technology organization to take responsibility for AI with a leader who fits the profile, while maintaining IT systems management within the same function in the enterprise. Consider this in the same light as other major technological shifts. Organizations that undertook early digital transformation often concluded that their traditional IT executives were too focused on maintaining legacy systems, prompting them to add new digital leaders or significantly redefine technology leadership roles to drive the shift from analog to digital. Companies whose leaders acted decisively to implement digital transformation–including making necessary leadership changes–achieved stronger financial performance and competitive advantage.[3]

MAKING THE DECISION

This decision cannot wait while you analyze every angle. Every week without dedicated and competent AI leadership has a cost to your organization. With the pace of AI advancement, waiting is a greater downside risk than moving too fast.

Take a hard look:

- Does your current technology leadership fit the profile needed for AI transformation? Do they possess the change agent ability, business value focus, and technical knowledge to lead AI teams, as well as the strategic acumen to drive the AI value roadmap?
- Can your organization support the structural and coordination complexity, as well as the overhead, of parallel technology leadership?
- Can you afford to maintain the status quo in the interest of what you see as avoiding internal disruption, while existing competitors and new challengers are disrupting your business?

Choose quickly: Companies that win with AI establish dedicated leadership accountability early and iterate based on results. Analysis paralysis costs more than imperfect choices.

If you take a hard look at your current technology talent and are realistic about organizational constraints, the right approach becomes clear. Approach 1 is not an option unless you've already brought in a chief digital officer or another flavor of a next-generation technology leader. Approach 2 causes significant organizational friction, frustrates both the new AI organization and traditional IT function, and can limit the full potential of AI value creation.

Approach 3 is the only viable option because it eliminates cross-technology friction, organizational confusion, and unnecessary overhead and coordination, and provides unified technology leadership. But this option demands the CEO's courage to make tough leadership decisions. In our experience, organizations that follow Approach 3 are best positioned to achieve the greatest success with AI transformation and value.

The leadership decision you make this week sets the foundation for everything that follows in your AI transformation.

SETTING YOUR AI LEADER UP FOR SUCCESS

Once the leadership decision is made, the MVT's role shifts to that of a champion. Even with the right approach and the right person in place, AI leadership requires active support from the CEO to succeed. The AI leader will face organizational resistance, resource constraints, and the pressure to deliver results quickly while building entirely new AI competencies.

The most capable AI leader cannot overcome organizational inertia without the CEO's unique authority and influence. Success depends on three areas where only the CEO can provide the necessary support:

- **Executive air cover remains essential throughout the transformation.** AI leaders often need to make decisions that create short-term friction for long-term value, such as consolidating redundant systems, changing established processes, or redirecting resources from familiar initiatives to emerging opportunities. The CEO's visible support during these moments determines whether the AI leader drives necessary changes or gets trapped in organizational politics. When resistance emerges—and it will—the CEO's authority breaks through departmental boundaries and competing priorities that would otherwise paralyze progress.

- **Stakeholder expectation management requires ongoing attention from the CEO.** Board members, key customers, and investor relations need realistic timelines and clear success metrics that only the CEO can credibly communicate. AI transformations follow different patterns than traditional technology rollouts, often showing minimal visible progress for months before achieving breakthrough results. Set realistic expectations about the timeline–even the best AI leaders need six to twelve months to fully understand your business context, build the right team, and establish effective processes. The governance dashboard should provide the data you need to maintain stakeholder confidence during inevitable periods of uncertainty.
- **Resource commitment testing occurs throughout the AI adoption process.** Successful AI initiatives often require additional investment to scale beyond the pilot stage, while unsuccessful initiatives need clear sunset criteria. Final resource decisions often require the CEO's authority to break organizational deadlocks that individual department heads cannot resolve on their own. The buck stops with the CEO when competing priorities demand tough choices between proven initiatives and emerging opportunities.

During any transition period, continue leveraging your MVT from chapter 1. This team fills the AI leadership role during your transition, ensuring AI momentum doesn't stall as you establish the organizational structure. The CEO must continue to drive the connection between business objectives and AI value creation, as well as to clear roadblocks, until the dedicated AI leader is fully operational.

Most importantly, commit to clearing roadblocks for your AI leader. The primary reason AI transformations fail is not a lack of technology or strategy–it's organizational resistance and executive ambivalence when tough decisions arise. Your leadership decision this week sets the foundation for everything that follows in your AI transformation.

BUILDING THE ORGANIZATIONAL STRUCTURE: THE HUB-AND-SPOKES MODEL

Once you establish AI leadership, you need an organizational structure that enables AI value creation at scale. Even the most capable AI leader cannot drive transformation alone—they need a team that provides specific technical expertise, does hands-on work, and delivers the AI roadmap, which you will soon know how to develop as part of this 90-day blueprint. The most effective organizational structure is known as the "hub-and-spokes" model (see figure 3-2). It combines the AI leader's centralized direction and cross-functional resources with embedded resources in business domains for optimal ability to deliver business value in specific areas and scale across them.

Figure 3-2: Organizational model options

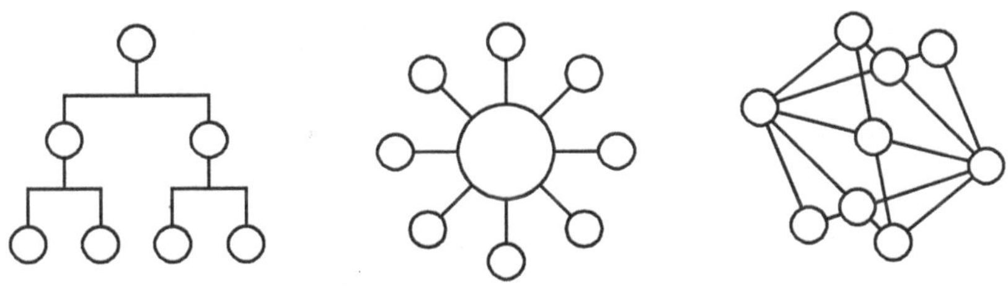

Centralized | Hub-and-spokes | Decentralized

This model succeeds where purely centralized or fully decentralized approaches fail. Pure centralization creates bottlenecks and disconnects AI from business realities. Complete decentralization leads to fragmented efforts and inconsistent approaches. The hub-and-spokes model combines the strategic coordination of centralization with the business expertise and agility of people embedded in specific organizational functions and units.

HOW THE HUB-AND-SPOKES MODEL WORKS

The hub is a lean center that includes the AI leader along with functional experts across strategy, data management, data sourcing, data engineering, data science and machine learning, product management, AI architecture, engineering, and user experience. The people who work in the hub provide strategic direction, technical expertise, standards, and processes to create value with AI.

The point is to lead with a big vision, starting in a focused way within an individual business unit and scaling fast across other business units. That is the magic of the hub-and-spokes model. It is particularly effective in attracting talent, fostering diversity that enables movement across functions and roles, and providing the scale to penetrate the entire organization. This is achieved by working in individual units and having the remit to drive enterprise-wide AI applications and their associated value. The hub-and-spokes model also drives the overall organization's development of the skill set, mindset, toolset, and decision set required to transform with AI.

The spokes represent AI resources from the AI leader's organization embedded within each business function and/or geographic unit. These individuals are fully integrated into their departments, working alongside coworkers in specific business areas to practice bilingual work that combines technical data and AI expertise with in-depth knowledge of the business domain. The people in the spokes have dual reporting responsibilities, back to the hub and also to the function, business unit, or geography. These individuals speak the domain language, possess the relationships and proximity to drive local adoption, and continually sharpen their business acumen while staying connected to the hub for expertise, strategic guidance, technical direction, and resources.

This structure creates a powerful dynamic between the AI leader's hub-and-spokes resources. People can rotate between domains while advancing their technical skills. The scale of the hub, combined with the domain-specificity of the spokes, drives focused AI applications, while building overall scale and strategic value across the enterprise.

In addition to driving value through focused AI applications and scale, this model is more effective at attracting top talent and is also more cost-efficient, as it avoids duplications in headcount, effort, and vendor use.

MAKING THE HUB-AND-SPOKES MODEL SUCCESSFUL

Many organizations implement this structure in name only, creating organizational charts that look collaborative but in practice maintain functional silos. Success requires intentional design of the relationships, processes, and incentives that make coordination natural rather than forced. Success factors include the following:

- **Clear role definition**. Document who makes which decisions and owns which outcomes. Avoid overlap and gaps that create friction or confusion.
- **Regular coordination**. Establish a rhythm of communication between the AI hub and spokes, such as weekly check-ins to maintain momentum and consistency and monthly reviews to facilitate adjustments.
- **Shared success metrics**. Ensure that people in both the hub and the spokes work toward the same goals, as one team. Domain experts in individual functions collaborate with their hub partners to scale innovations in one area and apply them to another, then scale them fully across functions to achieve enterprise-wide AI value.
- **Career development paths**. Create opportunities for rotation and talent mobility between hub and spokes placements and roles. This approach builds and grows talent while breaking down silos.

The hub-and-spokes model becomes self-reinforcing, creating a virtuous cycle where the overall AI roadmap comes to life with practical local execution and focused, domain-specific AI applications scaled across the organization, delivering on that roadmap. This is the only organizational model that can launch delivery of value from AI, accelerate AI adoption throughout the organization, and scale business benefits at speed across the enterprise.

YOUR WEEK 3 ACTION PLAN

Here are five specific actions you can take to put the principles from this chapter into practice.

- **Articulate why AI transformation requires dedicated leadership**. AI requires a different approach than traditional IT or other individual business functions and calls for a new kind of cross-functional leadership.
- **Define your AI leader profile**. Identify the traits and experience that characterize your AI leader—regardless of whether they come from inside or outside your company.

- **Evaluate your options for establishing AI leadership.** Take a hard look at existing leaders in the organization and determine if they fit the AI leader profile—chances are they do not.
- **Make the tough leadership decision.** Replace a legacy IT leader or place above them a new, next-generation tech executive fluent in digital, data, and AI.
- **Begin shaping the structure to support execution.** Lay the groundwork for the AI leader's success and start working with HR to shape what the hub-and-spokes model would look like in your organization. Begin adjusting incentives, resources, and reporting lines to ensure effective collaboration.

SUMMARY

You've now completed Week 3 of your 90-day blueprint to set yourself up for value creation with AI. You've made the most pivotal decision yet: choosing who will lead AI for business value. This chapter helped you understand why AI success depends on leadership that drives transformation, not just technology adoption.

Here are six key takeaways from this week:

- **AI leadership is the tipping point for success.** Without dedicated leadership, AI remains scattered and underdelivers.
- **The right leader drives transformation.** AI isn't an IT project—it's a business transformation that requires leadership with a focus on value creation.
- **You have one leadership option.** Bring in a next-generation tech leader who will upgrade your entire tech organization and lead AI value creation.
- **Your AI leader must own cross-functional impact.** Their role spans strategy, coordination, value creation, cultural change, and responsible AI practices.
- **A hub-and-spokes organizational model enables acceleration and scale.** The spokes create value locally with a focus that accelerates business units' AI adoption, while the hub's strategic guidance and enterprise scope deliver scale.
- **Speed matters.** The faster you make your leadership decision, the sooner you'll generate business value—and avoid falling behind.

With these essentials now in place–AI starter kit, responsible AI practices, and strategic AI leadership–you're ready to move into the next phase. In Week 4, you'll shift focus to identifying where AI can support your business goals and priorities, creating value where it matters most.

Ask not what I can do with AI—ask what AI can do for me.

–Katia Walsh

Four

CREATING VALUE WITH AI

ONE OF US was sitting across from a CFO who had been watching his company's series of AI experiments with growing skepticism. "Look," he said, leaning back in his chair, "I've seen the demos. AI can automate some processes, potentially improving their efficiency. But honestly? I'm not seeing the transformational value everyone keeps talking about."

In response, we asked simply, "What are your top three strategic goals for this year?"

He rattled them off without hesitation: "Accelerate revenue growth in our underperforming markets. Reduce customer churn by improving retention. Streamline our capital allocation process to improve ROI."

"Now," we said, "let's talk about how AI could help you achieve each of those goals."

For the next twenty minutes, we explored possibilities he'd never considered: AI-powered market analysis to identify the highest-potential customers in underperforming regions; predictive models to flag at-risk customers weeks before they churn; and intelligent systems to simulate and analyze thousands of investment scenarios to optimize capital deployment.

His entire perspective shifted. "I was thinking about AI all wrong," he admitted. "I should have been asking how it could help us achieve our biggest goals."

That CFO's experience is universal. Too many leaders view AI solely through an efficiency lens, seeing it only as a means to automate existing processes or squeeze out marginal improvements. However, AI's power lies in how it can help you achieve your business objectives in ways that were previously impossible.

You're now in Week 4 of your 90-day program to set your organization up to win with AI. To date, you've assembled a core team to drive AI adoption, established responsible AI guidelines, and started work on an AI leadership and organizational model. Now, it's time to shift to strategy–not just asking what you can do with AI but how AI can drive sustained value for your organization.

Many companies stumble at this stage, falling into the "use case trap" and focusing on individual AI applications in isolation. While it's natural to begin with specific use cases, treating AI as a collection of disconnected tools can limit its impact. AI doesn't create value in a vacuum; its sustainable potential occurs when different AI applications interact with and reinforce one another, compound their effects, and collectively contribute to an organization's overall strategy and top priorities.

This week marks an important transition. You're moving from the early preparation phase into the work of creating your AI roadmap.

This week, you will take these steps:

- **Move beyond isolated and narrow use cases** to understand AI's full value potential.
- **Explore how AI creates value** through engagement, efficiency, and reinvention.
- **Learn the AI Value Portfolio Framework** to assess and diversify AI investments.
- **Build a shared understanding** of AI's transformative potential across your organization.

By the end of this chapter, you'll have a comprehensive view of where AI can create value in your organization–the foundation for connecting AI to strategy and building your roadmap.

WHAT IS AN AI APPLICATION?

Before exploring how AI creates value, it's essential to understand what we mean by "AI application." This isn't just semantic clarity–it will shape how you think about AI's potential and avoid limiting yourself to narrow technical implementations.

An AI application is any process, product, or solution that organizations develop using AI to deliver concrete business value. It goes beyond just an AI tool, such as an interface to a generative AI model. It includes the people using that tool and the processes it may streamline—even revolutionize—to create value. It's more than an individual use case because it also includes the cultural transformation that may result from applying AI to a business problem.

What makes something an AI application isn't the sophistication of the technology, but whether it harnesses AI—predictive, generative, or agentic—to create measurable business value. There are many examples of AI applications, which we will cover in this chapter. This broad definition is crucial because it prevents you from prematurely limiting your thinking to only obvious automation opportunities. When you view AI applications as business solutions that happen to rely on AI—rather than trying to find a problem that fits an AI tool—you will start unlocking greater value and the possibility for organizational and business transformation.

Throughout the rest of the book, we'll be using the term *AI applications* to refer to the broad use of AI on business problems that result in value creation.

THE THREE AREAS OF VALUE FROM AI

AI generates business value in three areas (see figure 4-1). Understanding each area, its focus, and typical applications is essential to creating your AI roadmap in the following chapters.

Each value area represents a distinct way AI can generate value. However, these areas are not isolated—they interact and build upon one another. Companies may start with engagement and expand into efficiency and reinvention, or they may pursue multiple areas simultaneously.

- **Engagement** enhances how companies interact with customers and employees, creating deeper relationships through personalization and predictive insights. This drives revenue growth and loyalty by focusing on your most important stakeholders—your customers—and primarily involves your go-to-market teams: marketing, sales, and customer care.
- **Efficiencies** focus on doing what you already do, but faster, cheaper, and with fewer errors. AI automates repetitive tasks, optimizes workflows, and reduces costs. This is often where companies see the fastest returns,

Figure 4-1: The three AI value areas

VALUE AREA	FOCUS	TYPICAL APPLICATIONS
Engagement	External: Enhancing customer, employee, and stakeholder relationships and interactions	• Personalization, at scale • Proactive customer care outreach and problem-solving • Customer retention and turnaround system to reverse negative sentiment • Dynamic, customized retail assortment • Employee training with AI-powered simulations
Efficiencies	Internal: Automating operational processes and workflows, optimizing internal systems, and transforming existing ways of working within the same business model	• Process optimization and automation • Document processing at unprecedented velocity • Customer service automation • Dynamic cost and pricing optimizations • Predictive maintenance of equipment and infrastructure • Transformed demand planning and inventory management–moving from unconnected Excel spreadsheets to automated systems of prediction
Reinvention	External and internal: Discovering new business models and revenue streams that were not possible before this stage of AI	• New products or service offerings • New customer segments • New markets • Business model innovation • Industry disruption, for example, replacing human agents with AI

freeing up resources for higher-value work. This area focuses your attention inward to examine internal operations and processes for improvements.

- **Reinvention** enables entirely new business models, unlocks new revenue streams, and allows you to serve new customer segments. This is the most transformational–and often the riskiest–area of AI value, where you start doing something completely different from what you have done in the past. It takes imagination, problem-solving, and courage to pursue what nobody else has tried. But the rewards can be enormous. Examples of reinvention from past emerging technologies include Amazon's early customer-centricity bets with digital commerce, Uber's power shift from taxis to riders, and new ways of storing data from physical data centers to the cloud.

Understanding the value AI creates in engagement, efficiencies, and reinvention forms the foundation for strategic AI thinking, moving beyond the narrow automation mindset that limits so many organizations.

THE EFFICIENCY TRAP

Most organizations start by trying to deploy AI to increase efficiency. The problem is that many organizations never progress beyond this point. They become comfortable automating existing processes and capturing time savings but often overlook AI's broader strategic potential. While efficiency gains are valuable, they're not differentiating as competitors easily replicate them.

Competitive advantage typically comes from engagement and reinvention. Companies that limit themselves to efficiencies are using a strategic weapon as a cost-cutting tool. Don't let purely operational thinking constrain your strategic vision and potential.

Now, let's explore how each of these value areas plays out in practice, starting with engagement.

ENGAGEMENT: ENHANCING CUSTOMER EXPERIENCE THROUGH AI

To stay competitive, your business must go beyond traditional, broad market segmentation and generic marketing tactics. You need a new model for customer engagement—one that enables your company to anticipate customers' needs, act before they even realize they have a need, tailor customer interactions, and deliver value with unmatched accuracy. AI can help you build a better customer experience by being predictive, proactive, personalized, and precise. We call these the new Four Ps of AI-powered business today.[1]

PREDICTIVE VALUE: ANTICIPATING FUTURE NEEDS WITH AI

AI's predictive power can reshape how businesses forecast and prepare for customer behaviors. Its continuous learning ensures that predictions adapt to shifting customer needs and actions, while real-time data updates sharpen its ability to adjust to location and minute-by-minute events. By transitioning from passive data collection to real-time data-driven predictions, companies can achieve desired outcomes, such as enhanced customer engagement.

Predictive analytics could identify patterns and make forecasts based on past behaviors; however, AI takes this further. It doesn't just predict what might happen—it can simulate detailed infinite combinations of what-if scenarios and outcomes, giving businesses a dynamic tool to explore possibilities and determine optimal action plans. For example, video streaming subscription services incorporate AI to analyze user engagement patterns and predict the risk of churn. This allows them to intervene strategically, offering viewers incentives to stay and locking them in. This all happens in concert, with proactive outreach and personalized offers timed for the precise moment customers are most likely to consider them.

PROACTIVE VALUE: TAKING ACTION BEFORE CUSTOMERS CAN REACT

Predictive AI enables proactive customer engagement, allowing you to act before a customer reacts, as seen in the previous example of churning.

When one of us led data and AI at a major global telecommunications company, we designed machine learning models that predicted when a customer's mobile phone would stop working. This was important because the moment when a mobile phone stops working provides a window for customers to shop for new phones—and new mobile service providers. Armed with the predictive machine learning models, we then designed an end-to-end system that proactively contacted customers and, with their permission, performed a "device health check" on their phones. Upon confirmation of the models' prediction that the device was indeed at the end of its life, the company offered new devices specifically targeting the individual users' needs and preferences.

In another example, utility companies use AI to identify potential service disruptions and proactively notify customers likely to experience an outage, providing them with solutions and time frames to set expectations. This not only averts customers' frustration but also strengthens trust through timely, customer-centric service.

And in a hypothetical third example, a B2B software provider might use AI to analyze how a client's team interacts with its platform, proactively surfacing underused features that could improve efficiency. If AI detects frequently missed deadlines, it may suggest automation tools or even generate a brief, personalized tutorial to help users work more efficiently.

PERSONALIZED VALUE: THE SEGMENT-OF-ONE IN ACTION

Today's customer expects a highly personalized experience. AI enables you to deliver tailored interactions to them, thanks to data ranging from past purchases to browsing habits. For example, AI drives online clothing retailers' ability to offer product recommendations tailored to a shopper's style, preferences, size, and budget.

Beyond marketing, AI-powered chatbots and virtual assistants recall user history and provide more relevant support than ever. Such interactions not only resolve issues more efficiently but also create a sense of familiarity and care, reinforcing brand loyalty and customer satisfaction. Personalization has become so prevalent that the traditional marketing concept of customer segmentation is no longer applicable. We live in the era of "a segment of one," where every consumer receives bespoke messaging and targeted promotions based on near-infinite permutations for outreach. This approach identifies the most relevant messages not only for a specific person but for that person in a specific place at a specific time.

PRECISE VALUE: ACCURACY IN EVERY INTERACTION

AI's ability to process massive volumes of data at high velocity enables marketers to tailor, refine, and continuously update their approach. They may send more relevant messaging, customize promotions, or maintain precise inventory management that adapts to the market conditions, in some industries, by the minute. For example, e-commerce platforms use AI to dynamically adjust prices, balancing customer demand with the need to remain competitive and optimize profitability.

AI also enhances the power of promotional messaging by tailoring its mechanics to match the mood, cultural sensitivities, and attitudes of specific target segments. For instance, when one of us worked in a global retail company, our AI efforts revealed that different messages around the same kind of promotion elicited different reactions in some countries compared to others. A promotion offering "30% off" attracted customers in one country, but in another, a similar incentive marketed as "1+1 = 3" better grabbed shoppers' attention and led to higher sales. The ability to precisely target the messaging came from using AI, which predicted the optimal message in each country, despite the discount itself being of a similar size. AI's accuracy–sometimes delivered at record speed–reduces errors and helps leaders confidently make timely, data-driven decisions, ultimately improving both customer experiences and business outcomes.

BEYOND CUSTOMERS: EMPLOYEE ENGAGEMENT

Engagement isn't just about customers–it extends to employees. When people working in an organization feel informed, supported, and valued, they consistently deliver better customer experiences. Recent research found that companies with highly engaged employees achieve a 10 percent increase in customer loyalty and engagement and 18 percent higher sales.[2] In addition, 92 percent of executives now agree that employee engagement is directly tied to customer happiness–a link so strong that nearly half of customer-experience leaders are making employee-focused technology their top investment priority.[3]

Consider how AI applications can enhance the employee experience. Imagine a generative AI internal portal that enables employees to answer customer questions quickly. Employees feel more empowered, while customer feedback highlights friendlier, faster, and more knowledgeable customer care. Consider AI-powered training, for instance, which uses AI-created simulations, AI avatars, and gaming experiences to personalize the learning experience for employees, making it more practical and enjoyable. People learn from practice, and AI provides a massive playground for personalized practice, adapting to individual learning styles, pace, and desired outcomes.

AI applications for employee engagement create a virtuous cycle, where technology and meaningful work uplift the workforce experiences, which in turn translates into happier, more loyal customers. When considering how AI enhances customer engagement, remember that AI applications also empower employees to craft exceptional customer experiences.

For example, at DeVry University, one of the early efforts focused on using AI to handle administrative tasks. The goal was to free faculty and advisors from repetitive tasks, enabling them to spend more time with students and have more meaningful interactions, which in turn would improve their experience and learning outcomes. Tom Monahan, DeVry's vice chair and former CEO, told us: "To support student success, especially for adult learners, we need to streamline administrative tasks, so advisors and faculty can focus on higher-order activities. It was important to capture data from conversations and manage those interactions as assets to provide personalized support."

By harnessing AI to deliver predictive, proactive, personalized, and precise experiences, you can build deeper, more meaningful customer relationships.

CUSTOMER ENGAGEMENT CASE STUDIES

The following case studies provide a blueprint for your strategic thinking. We've ordered them to take you on a journey from the heart to the head–starting with a story of pure creative connection, moving to the reinvention of a core sales process, and finally exploring how some of the most complex and regulated industries can benefit from this approach.

First Heritage Mortgage: Spreading joy

For most companies, a mortgage is a transaction. First Heritage Mortgage saw an opportunity to use AI to transform the home-buying process into a relationship, focusing on a specific, deeply human side of home buying: the stress of moving with young children.

"Instead of a generic book, you can create an illustrated children's book in ten minutes with ChatGPT," explained SVP Erica Goodwin in an interview with us. Her team began creating hyper-personalized stories for clients' families, featuring the child's name and favorite toys in a tale about their specific move. Printed in-house, the books create a moment of pure magic during a difficult time.

As Goodwin put it, "We're using AI to spread joy." It's a profound lesson that sometimes the greatest value AI can create is in making a business more human in these small ways that can scale empathy and also help you stand out in a crowded market.

GID: From a single property search to a property vision

In the competitive real estate market, it's not uncommon for apartment seekers to find themselves out of luck, with their first-choice apartment unavailable. GID, a major commercial real estate company, recognized that the traditional transactional approach of leading with market inventory represented a missed opportunity. They used AI to transform the leasing process, shifting the focus from the property to the customer's goals and vision for their dream apartment.

"In the past, our AI would respond with information on just [that] one community," Jamie Gorski, a senior executive at GID, told us. "Now . . . the AI tool is going to surface up anything that's going to meet your need in that search radius." To do this, GID's AI application acts as an intelligent leasing concierge, understanding a prospect's real need (a home in a specific neighborhood) and showing them all relevant properties. The system also optimizes for business goals, prioritizing buildings with higher availability or suggesting a premium penthouse to a qualified customer.

By anticipating needs and personalizing the journey, GID captures revenue that would have been lost and also builds a stronger brand. It's a powerful lesson: Winning with AI often means stopping it from answering the questions customers ask and starting to solve the problems they're experiencing.

Pfizer: Personalizing customer engagement while streamlining compliance

Pfizer, one of the world's leading pharmaceutical companies, exemplifies how AI can create value by transforming engagement with healthcare professionals–an audience where trust, speed, and compliance are critical.

Pfizer faced a classic bottleneck: The enormous volume of medical and promotional content required meticulous review for accuracy and regulatory compliance, slowing their marketing campaigns and adding costs.

To address this, Pfizer built "Charlie," a proprietary AI-driven content platform adapted from the Publicis Groupe's Marcel AI platform.[4] Charlie automates content creation and enhances compliance review through a red/yellow/green risk triage. Previously approved language and claims are automatically cleared (green), while novel or higher-risk messaging is escalated for manual review (red).

This system enabled rapid personalization at scale through AI-analyzed healthcare professionals' interactions, while also streamlining compliance to accelerate time to market. The impact was immediate as AI-curated content increased healthcare professionals' engagement and response rates, decreased approval processes by half, and reduced development costs. The automated safeguards also maintained Pfizer's compliance standards.

Pfizer's approach became a source of differentiation, deepening relationships with crucial healthcare stakeholders while practicing responsible AI use.

EFFICIENCIES: AI AS AN OPERATIONAL EXCELLENCE DRIVER

AI enhances efficiencies in three fundamental ways:

- **Automating repetitive tasks**. AI frees up employees for higher-value work and reduces error rates by automating repetitive manual tasks such as data entry, document summarization, and handling routine calls about simple questions like parking directions or hours of operation.
- **Augmenting decision-making**. By synthesizing vast amounts of data, generative AI extracts takeaways and creates recommendations, which enables faster and better-informed decision-making.
- **Scaling operations without proportional costs**. AI allows companies to expand operations–such as handling more complex customer inquiries, producing personalized content, and generating legal drafts–without increasing expenses.

As AI evolves, we're seeing a shift from AI that assists with tasks to AI agents that can autonomously complete entire workflows.

THE LIMITS OF AUTOMATION

While many organizations salivate at the idea of AI applications driving greater efficiency and productivity, there are limits. Organizations must strike a balance between automation and the potential loss of a human touch that may be much needed.

Take, for example, the hard-earned learnings from Klarna, a financial services company offering payment solutions like "buy now, pay later." In 2024, Klarna laid off seven hundred customer service agents and replaced them with AI-powered systems—an explicit, large-scale staff reduction announced as a move toward efficiency and cost savings.[5] While this slashed costs and sped up routine requests, many customers soon felt frustrated and disconnected. AI struggled with empathy and complex issues, leading to a decline in overall satisfaction.

By mid-2025, Klarna reversed course, publicly admitting the change had hurt service quality.[6] The company began rehiring human customer service agents and testing a flexible, remote-support model to restore the empathy and care that customers valued.

The lesson is that pursuing efficiency with AI too quickly undermines customer experience and brand loyalty if human support disappears.

EFFICIENCY CASE STUDIES

Efficiency is often where businesses start to work with AI, but the most innovative leaders look beyond simply automating tasks. They use efficiency gains to create momentum, where newfound productivity generates capacity for growth and innovation.

AI-driven efficiency gains are appearing across every industry. Professional services giant PwC, for instance, now uses AI to automate complex financial reporting and contract reviews, freeing its experts to focus on client interactions, consulting, and client engagement.[7] Similarly, travel leader Expedia has deployed AI-powered agents to handle millions of customer interactions, saving an estimated eight million hours of human agents' time and reducing operational costs by around $150 million.[8]

AI-driven efficiency isn't just about cutting costs—it's about building a faster, nimbler, more inventive organization. The following examples show a strategic progression of AI-driven efficiency. We'll start with the universal challenge of unlocking trapped internal knowledge, then see how efficiency can become a direct revenue driver, and explore how to empower your entire workforce to become innovators.

AARP: Creating a virtual expert to unlock knowledge

A classic knowledge-access problem was hurting productivity at AARP, a nonprofit organization focused on empowering people age fifty and over. A new automation tool was documented in a massive 250-page PDF training manual that, as Sami Hassanyeh, chief transformation officer at AARP, explained to us, "Nobody reads." Instead, employees repeatedly asked the engineering team for basic help, creating a productivity drain for both the business teams and the engineers.

Driven by a request from the business, AARP's digital team developed an internal bot in just a few days. They fed the 250-page manual into an LLM and created a virtual expert that employees could query using natural language. The impact was immediate: "It's freed up engineers," Hassanyeh explained in an interview. "It's removed frustration from the business unit team members, and they feel they're much more self-sufficient."

SelectQuote: Turning ignored calls into revenue

For years, SelectQuote, a leading insurance broker, faced a persistent challenge: a surge in inbound calls, many of which were low-priority or "disqualified" leads. The organization had deemed these calls unlikely to convert, so they routinely went unanswered due to staffing constraints.[9]

That changed when the company began to implement AI. Rather than ignoring those calls, SelectQuote deployed an AI voice agent. The thinking was simple—this was an experiment. There was no risk of failure, since these calls had already gone unanswered. But if the experiment worked, it could unlock untapped value.

Unlike a chatbot that responds to text-based inquiries, the AI voice agent answered live phone calls and engaged in real-time conversations with prospective customers. It assessed the caller's intent, asked relevant questions, and determined whether an inquiry had potential value. If the AI voice agent identified a promising lead, it seamlessly transferred the caller to a human agent. If not, it gracefully ended the conversation, freeing up people to focus on higher-value interactions.

The impact was instant. Within weeks of launch, the AI voice agent had handled over 163,000 calls and brought in $20,000 in new revenue per day.[10] "That was just found money," said Dan Savino, the former senior vice president of artificial intelligence and innovation at SelectQuote. "We're just now able to service the clients that we were unable to before."[11]

And the benefits didn't stop there. By engaging with callers and resolving low-priority inquiries, the company was able to meet high call volumes during peak periods without resorting to the traditional route of hiring additional staff.

Designing a self-serve platform for employee empowerment

In every large organization, the silent killer of productivity is the mind-numbing manual task of rekeying data from unstructured documents into structured systems. The traditional fix–a formal, centralized IT project–is often too slow and expensive to justify for the hundreds of small processes that need it. Marsh, a global professional services firm, decided to break this bottleneck by creating a system that empowers employees to solve the problem themselves.

"A very common problem is getting a document with data you want to pull out, which we currently do by rekeying," explained Paul Beswick, the chief information and operations officer at Marsh, in an interview with us. "We have hundreds of types of documents and schemas, and I don't want to treat them as individual problems, so we've made it self-serve."

They created an AI application called the Structured Data Extractor, a simple internal tool that allows any employee to upload a document, define the data they need, and let a large language model do the work of finding and formatting it. Instead of waiting in an IT queue, business teams can now build their own lightweight automation in minutes.

This AI application enabled people to solve their own problems at speed, without any dependencies. It shows that one of the most powerful ways to scale efficiency is to put the power to automate directly into the hands of the people doing the work.

REINVENTION: UNLOCKING NEW POTENTIAL WITH AI

What if AI's true purpose isn't to make your current business 10 percent better but to help you invent an entirely new one? This is the essence of reinvention–the most challenging, and most potent, of the three AI value areas. It requires leaders to shift their focus from asking, "How can we do what we do faster or better?" to asking, "What becomes possible now that the old constraints are gone?"

WHAT REINVENTION LOOKS LIKE

Reinvention takes several forms, each representing a different way to tap into AI's transformational potential by asking a fundamentally different question: "What becomes possible when AI removes our current constraints?" Here is how reinvention could look:

- **New business models.** AI enables entirely different ways of creating and capturing value. A traditional service company might use AI to package its expertise as scalable digital products. A manufacturing company might transform from selling products to selling outcomes, using AI to monitor and optimize performance continuously.
- **New revenue streams.** AI can turn internal resources into external offerings. Companies discover that their data, services, or AI-powered processes have value to other organizations, creating new income sources. A professional services firm, for example, could train an AI system on its proprietary data from thousands of past client engagements. It could then package and sell those unique, AI-generated learnings about best practices, successes, and their drivers–for example, as a new, subscription-based digital product, creating a new revenue stream separate from its consulting business.
- **New market opportunities.** AI can enable companies to tap into previously unreachable customer segments. By automating complex analysis or personalizing at scale, companies can expand into markets that were once too costly or complicated to address. For example, a midsize financial advisory firm traditionally served only high-net-worth, usually older, clients due to the high cost of personalized portfolio management. However, it could use generative AI to develop a new,

lower-cost service for young professionals, creating customized starter investment plans, portfolio suggestions, and financial literacy content at scale and lower costs, thereby unlocking a new market.

- **Industry disruption**. The most ambitious reinvention uses AI to fundamentally shift the balance of power and rewrite the rules of competition.[12] This is about dismantling the advantages of incumbents. Consider the pharmaceutical industry, long defined by decade-long, billion-dollar R&D cycles. An AI platform capable of predicting molecular interactions and simulating clinical trials could significantly reduce development time and costs. The advantage then shifts from the companies with the biggest labs and deepest pockets to those with the best algorithms and data, enabling smaller, agile biotech companies to compete on a level they never could before.

Disruption also challenges fundamental assumptions about how an industry works. This might mean eliminating traditional intermediaries by using AI to automate their core functions. For example, an AI platform could disrupt the real estate industry through end-to-end automation, data enrichment, and increased accuracy of property valuations, which in turn would generate marketing, handle buyer inquiries, schedule viewer appointments, narrate property visits, and even negotiate and close on behalf of buyers and sellers. This could lead to a lower-cost, direct-to-consumer real estate service to challenge traditional commission-based agents.

REINVENTION CASE STUDIES

The following case studies showcase this bold thinking by addressing such questions as these: How is AI reinventing how we work and collaborate across industries? How is AI transforming the way we learn from customers and make critical decisions? And how do organizations use AI for generative design to reinvent what we create and build?

Spencer Stuart: Creating new ecosystems of value

Historically, industries have operated within well-defined boundaries. A bank was a bank; a media company was a media company. According to Jason Baumgarten, a senior leader at the executive search firm Spencer Stuart, AI is poised to demolish these silos, acting as a universal translator that enables what he described in an interview with us as "crazy combinations of organizations, knowledge, and data" to create entirely new business ecosystems.

"Imagine," Baumgarten said, "call centers have more voice data than anyone on Earth. You want to feed that into a language model to create better scripts? You need tech people. Want to know what makes a good script? You need Hollywood folks." In the past, the friction and cost of bringing these disparate worlds together would have been prohibitive. But AI drastically lowers that barrier, making it possible to combine their unique assets—data, technology, and creative talent—to develop conversational experiences that no single company could build alone.

This is reinvention at the industry level. The next wave of competitive advantage won't come from what your company does in isolation but from the novel, AI-enabled partnerships you build.

Nestlé: Reinventing how we learn from customers

For decades, consumer research operated on a cruel trade-off: You could go deep or you could go broad, but you couldn't do both. Qualitative research—in-depth interviews with twenty to thirty people—provided rich insights but lacked statistical confidence. Quantitative surveys delivered scale but missed the nuanced "why" behind consumer preferences. Companies stitched together these disparate methods, losing time and coherence in the process.

Nestlé, a company built on product innovation, felt this constraint acutely. Launching a new product could take twelve months or more, with consumer research creating a significant bottleneck. "We needed to both go deep with consumers to understand their feedback, but gather it at real scale," explained Michael Widenmeyer, consumer insights senior manager at Nestlé. "We needed confidence in our findings."[13]

The solution came from rethinking the research process itself. Nestlé partnered with Outset.ai to deploy AI agents that conduct nuanced, dynamic conversations with consumers—at unprecedented scale.[14] The AI moderator presents product concepts, probes for deeper understanding, and synthesizes both quantitative metrics and qualitative reasoning.

This is reinvention, not efficiency. Nestlé didn't just automate the old process; they created a previously impossible and entirely new capability. The AI delivers qualitative depth (participants shared more than twice as much detail as with traditional methods) combined with quantitative scale (ten times more participants). This isn't doing the same research faster; it's doing fundamentally different research that eliminates the century-old trade-off between depth and scale.

Nestlé has deployed this approach across more than one hundred product concepts, seven brands, and five countries. The broader lesson: Reinvention often emerges when you question long-standing constraints in your industry.

Tavistock: Using generative design to build cities of the future

For centuries, the blueprint for designing our physical world–from buildings to entire cities–has followed a simple formula: Rely on experience, then use data to validate the results. Real estate developer Tavistock is flipping that script, using AI to pioneer generative design and reinvent how communities are created from the ground up.

"Right now, experience drives design, and that design is validated by data. There's a gap," Juan Santos, senior vice president for brand experience and innovation at Tavistock, told us in an interview. "If you're able to connect design and data *first*, it will allow us to see blind spots . . . It may give us something completely unexpected."

Instead of relying solely on data to validate predrawn plans, Tavistock is incorporating into AI models real-world data on how people live, work, and move. The goal is for the AI to generate novel designs for living environments that are more efficient, sustainable, and human-centric than any expert could conceive of on their own. This is the reinvention of the creative process itself–moving from a static, experience-based model to a dynamic, data-driven one that has the potential to solve intractable problems like traffic and urban sprawl.

General Electric: Reinventing the playbook for economic development

In many parts of the world, progress is constrained by a massive infrastructure deficit. For developing nations, the traditional path–building more power plants, hospitals, and roads–is incredibly slow and capital-intensive. General Electric (GE) South Africa is demonstrating how AI can reinvent the playbook for economic development, enabling countries to leapfrog these traditional constraints.

"The problem Africa has is an infrastructure deficit in hospitals, roads, energy, and water," explained Nyimpini Mabunda, the former CEO at GE South Africa, in an interview with us. "Generative AI allows us to make the little we have more efficiently distributed."

Rather than focusing on building more, the company uses AI to intelligently manage what already exists. For example, by using AI to analyze real-time grid data, it's possible to see where there is an oversupply of electricity and instantly reallocate it to areas with none. The impact is profound. "We can electrify another 20 percent of Africa without building new power stations," Mabunda noted.

This isn't just an efficiency gain; it's a new, more sustainable model for growth that also demonstrates that AI's most powerful reinvention may be in solving some of the world's most intractable challenges.

BRINGING IT ALL TOGETHER: YOUR ONGOING TRANSFORMATION

Embracing AI means creating the conditions for ongoing transformation. As you've seen throughout this chapter, companies that successfully integrate AI don't just automate existing processes; they rethink how they operate, compete, and create value.

Yet transformation doesn't happen overnight. It's a combination of continuous commitment to discovery, iteration, and scaling what works. The most forward-thinking organizations know they won't have all the answers to start—but that doesn't stop them from moving ahead.

Konecta offers a powerful, distinct blueprint for leading a successful AI transformation, providing an example of how an organization can create value in AI applications that drive customer engagement, efficiency, and reinvention.

KONECTA: THE ALL-IN-ONE REVOLUTION

What happens when a company decides AI isn't just a tool for efficiency but a catalyst for a full-blown revolution? You get a company like Konecta, a global leader in customer management, including call center operations and back-office processes. With 130,000 employees, Konecta could have settled for incremental gains through automation. Instead, its leadership saw a once-in-a-generation opportunity to reinvent its business model.

Konecta asked: How could AI help us move beyond call centers? "Call centers were just the starting point," Massimo Canturi, general manager of Konecta Digital, explained in an interview with us. "Now, we offer AI-driven automation services tailored to industries like finance, healthcare, and legal. We're not just handling calls–we're managing full end-to-end processes."

"We look at the impact of generative AI through three lenses," Canturi continued. "First, there are productivity gains. Second, we focus on product innovation to better serve our customers. And third is developing a competitive advantage that creates a revolution." This strategic clarity provided Konecta with a powerful direction, allowing them to create value across all three areas–engagement, efficiencies, and reinvention–at the same time.

Engagement: Empowering people with AI

Many companies fall into the trap of using AI to simply replace humans with chatbots, often to the detriment of the customer experience. Konecta took a different path. They decided to use AI to augment their workforce, creating an experience that sparked a higher level of customer engagement.

They understood a fundamental truth: Their human call center agents are the heart of their customer experience. The greatest immediate value of AI, therefore, was not to remove the human employees but to empower them. Konecta developed an AI-powered copilot that acts as a real-time assistant for agents during customer calls. The tool handles the heavy lifting–navigating complex processes, pulling up specific information, and suggesting next steps–freeing the human agents to focus on what they do best: applying empathy, navigating nuances, and building relationships.

The result is an engagement model that offers customers the best of both worlds: the speed and accuracy of AI, combined with the irreplaceable value of a focused human expert.

Efficiencies: Streamlining to fuel growth

For Konecta, efficiency isn't just about cutting costs; it's about fueling growth. The company is developing scalable, high-impact AI applications to enhance the productivity of its massive workforce, with plans to reinvest the gains back into the company.

A prime example is their automation of back-office tasks, like complaint management. By applying AI to this complex, multistep process, even Konecta's initial programs delivered staggering results. Within the first year of implementing AI applications, the company saw

- a 25 to 30 percent reduction in the time it took to process a complaint;
- an 85 to 90 percent drop in errors, boosting service quality; and
- a 40 percent decrease in the time needed to train agents on the process.

But here's the crucial point: Konecta isn't interested in shrinking the workforce. Quite the opposite: Konecta plans to grow its workforce by 5 percent by 2028, with a focus on recruiting people who are both tech savvy and empathetic.[15]

Reinvention: Beyond efficiency to new revenue streams

Instead of being satisfied with improving their existing business, Konecta's leadership posed a bigger, bolder question: How could AI enable them to enter entirely new businesses? This is where their reinvention strategy shines.

For example, Konecta serves law firms with back-office processing. Konecta's law firm clients have struggled for years with the handling of nonperforming loans, where the borrower fails to make a scheduled payment for at least ninety days. Traditionally, law firms had to conduct extensive manual legal reviews, combing through thousands of pages of contracts, court rulings, and financial records. Due to time constraints, even the most efficient law firms could only analyze about a quarter of the documentation. Konecta saw an opportunity to use its existing relationships and back-office support for law firms and spin an adjacent, new, AI-powered service and revenue stream.

Konecta deployed an AI system to evaluate all the nonperforming loans, instead of law firms' human employees doing that manually. With AI, Konecta can analyze 100 percent of the loan documents, providing its law firm clients with a significantly more accurate understanding of a loan's actual value and the probability of repayment. "The legal sector doesn't have AI expertise," Canturi noted. "These firms couldn't develop this technology themselves, so they relied on us. This was a huge competitive advantage."

By stepping into this gap, Konecta transformed a traditional back-office outsourcing service into a high-value, AI-driven offering—creating a new revenue stream in the process. With AI, Konecta did more than just optimize its existing operations; it reinvented its business model.

This ongoing transformation through AI will lead to a time, possibly not too long from now, when AI will have penetrated the entirety of businesses and organizations. AI-powered companies will offer an immersive engagement for customers and employees; harness unprecedented efficiencies that, together, compound to a new workplace we can't imagine today; and tackle entirely new opportunities through reinvented business models and revenue streams. This is the natural evolution of emerging tech, a matter of when, not if. AI is inevitable and will be a natural part of business, life, and society. And it will bring value we'll no longer question. Does anyone ask for ROI from the internet? Or Wi-Fi? Or mobile phones? The same is in store for AI, only much faster, given a speed of adoption that outpaces all previous technologies.

We will know AI is delivering value everywhere when people stop asking about return on investment from it. And that time is coming.

YOUR WEEK 4 ACTION PLAN

This week focuses on building a comprehensive view of AI's value potential across your organization. Next week, you will connect your organizational strategy to AI value creation. To prepare, we've examined the three key areas of value that AI can offer.

EXPLORING AI VALUE OPPORTUNITIES

Now it's time to explore how AI can create value across your organization. Your AI leadership or the minimum viable team should lead this exploration, involving key stakeholders from different departments to ensure comprehensive coverage.

The following questions will help you identify AI applications across all three value areas. We'll begin with structured guidance for engagement and efficiencies, followed by a deeper focus on reinvention exercises, as transformational thinking requires the most support.

At the end of these explorations, you'll have a firmer grasp of how AI could create value for your organization. At this stage, resist the urge to delve too deeply, prioritize, or figure out feasibility. The goal this week is to practice curiosity and stoke your imagination. In chapter 5, we'll get deeper into tying these opportunities to your business objectives.

ENGAGEMENT OPPORTUNITIES

Most organizations have experience thinking about customer and employee experience improvements, but AI opens up possibilities that weren't previously feasible. AI can help you dramatically enhance your customer and stakeholder engagement. How do you go about it? Start by mapping your key stakeholder journeys—both customer and employee experiences. Research the steps your customers take, from initial research to consideration and ultimately to making a final buying decision. Identify moments where current limitations hinder your ability to deliver the desired experience.

Here are some questions to help you understand AI's value for your customers, particularly in terms of engagement:

- Where do customers (or employees) face friction, delays, or frustration in their interactions with us? What causes these pain points?
- What information would help them make decisions at key moments in the customer journeys? What do we wish we knew about their context or needs?
- How could we anticipate their needs before customers reach out to us? What patterns in behavior or data could signal upcoming needs?
- Which routine interactions could become more personal and valuable? Where do we currently treat diverse stakeholders with one-size-fits-all approaches?

EFFICIENCY OPPORTUNITIES

Efficiency applications of AI are often the most intuitive, but don't limit yourself to automation. AI can enable new ways of working, not just faster versions of current processes. Look for opportunities to eliminate entire categories of work, not only speed up existing tasks. Here are some questions that can help you determine those:

- What repetitive tasks consume significant time across our organization? Which of these follows predictable patterns versus requiring human creativity?
- Where do bottlenecks slow down processes? What causes bottlenecks: volume, complexity, or coordination challenges?
- What decisions require analyzing large amounts of data manually? Where do people spend time gathering information versus applying judgment?
- Which workflows can we automate? What handoffs between systems or people can we streamline?

REINVENTION OPPORTUNITIES

Reinvention requires a fundamentally different mindset than applying AI to deepen engagement or drive efficiencies. While those build on existing operations, reinvention asks you to imagine what becomes possible without current constraints. How would you envision your business if you were starting from scratch today, with AI on your side? This is often the most challenging area for organizations because it requires stepping outside the current model.

Reinvention is both the most challenging and most rewarding. It's only possible when you break free of current constraints and imagine new possibilities, without considering what's feasible. Instead, focus on what might be possible by considering these options:

- **Breaking the rules.** What bold moves could you make if you had no barriers–no budget limits, no regulations, no operational challenges? What if you can predict market trends or customer needs with near-perfect accuracy? How would that change your approach to products, services, or entire business lines?

- **Taking the 10x leap**. What could make your business ten times faster, more innovative, or more efficient? What fresh opportunities for growth or new customer experiences could you unleash? What new products, services, or business models could you create?
- **Flipping the script**. Could you disrupt your industry before a competitor does? Could you turn a product-based business into a service-driven model, or create a new digital offering? What if you could deliver your core value proposition in a completely different way than you do today?
- **Future-proof fantasies**. In ten years, when AI and other emerging tech have transformed every industry, how would your company offer something no one else can replicate? What new value will you be providing that no one else saw coming?

SUMMARY

You've now finished Week 4 of your 90-day effort to set yourself up for success with AI. This week, you built a comprehensive understanding of how AI can create value across your organization.

In this chapter, you did the following:

- **Strengthened your understanding of AI applications** as business solutions that happen to use AI, rather than AI implementations looking for business problems.
- **Explored the three AI value areas** of engagement, efficiencies, and reinvention, understanding how each contributes to business success.
- **Avoided the efficiency trap** by understanding that competitive advantage typically comes from engagement and reinvention applications of AI.
- **Conducted comprehensive value exploration** across all three areas to understand AI's full potential in your organization.

You're now ready to connect these opportunities to your business strategy and make choices about where to focus your AI efforts.

Use cases are not a strategy.

—George Connolly

Five

GROUNDING AI IN YOUR STRATEGY

WALKING INTO A CANDY STORE is a delightfully overwhelming experience. Shelves overflow with chocolates, gummies, and caramels, tempting you at every turn. Excited by the sheer abundance, you might start grabbing everything in sight. But at some point, reality sets in–you can't eat all the candy in the store, even if you could afford it. So, do you go for your favorites? Try something new? Stick to your budget?

This is the challenge many organizations face when developing their AI roadmap. After working through chapter 4, you likely have a long list of AI applications that could transform parts of your business. But without a clear connection to your business strategy, your AI effort risks becoming a scattered collection of experiments rather than a force for competitive advantage.

Here's the key point that may go against what you hear and read, but it's tried and true: You don't need an AI strategy. You already have a business strategy. What you need is an AI roadmap–a clear path for using AI as a tool to achieve your existing strategic goals (see figure 5-1).

Too often, organizations mistake a laundry list of AI use cases and tools for a strategy, believing that simply implementing AI will make them competitive. But AI is a means to fulfilling your vision; it's not the strategy. For AI to deliver value, it must serve your organization's overall strategy. AI in the service of business strategy will help you achieve your vision, solve the most pressing problems, seize new opportunities, and advance the goals that matter most to leadership.

Figure 5-1: From business strategy to AI roadmap

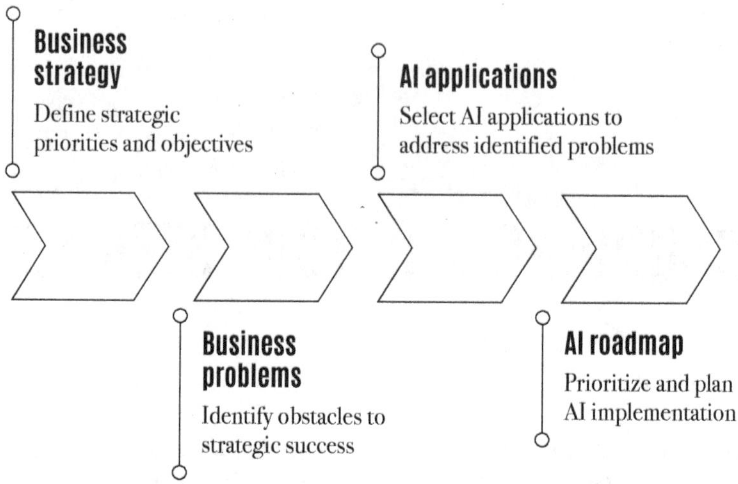

This week is crucial for setting yourself up to create value with AI. You will think through your organization's strategy and its top pillars and priorities, and then map AI applications directly to those priorities. This will ensure your AI efforts support the company's strategic vision and broad business objectives.

This week, you will take these steps:

- **Clarify your organization's top three to five strategic priorities** and identify specific problems that stand in the way of achieving them.
- **Validate your findings** to ensure agreement and build early support.
- **Prioritize AI applications using the Double-S Matrix** (size of value versus speed to value) to identify your highest-value opportunities for AI to tackle.
- **Document the top AI applications** that you will prioritize through this process to accelerate your business strategy.

By the end of this chapter, you'll understand how AI serves your business strategy and develop the discipline to focus only on what drives value. This will prepare you for the next step, creating your AI roadmap, in Week 6.

Although we're presenting this as a linear process, in reality, developing an AI roadmap is iterative–expect to revisit, revise, and refine your approach continuously.

THE USE CASE TRAP: WHY MOST AI STRATEGIES FAIL

Walk into most AI strategy sessions and you'll see the same scene: whiteboards covered with dozens of AI use cases, generated through enthusiastic brainstorming sessions. Automation, call deflection, document processing, sales forecasting, various optimizations . . . the list grows longer by the hour.

This approach feels productive. It's inclusive, democratic, and generates excitement about "the art of the possible," as the jargon goes. The facilitator encourages wild ideas, sticky notes multiply across walls, and participants leave energized by AI's potential. The session concludes with promises to "prioritize and roadmap" the collected ideas.

But we know better.

Walk into that same organization six months later, and you'll find the excitement has faded into frustration. Employees are scattered across dozens of small AI pilots or proofs of concept, none of which deliver meaningful results, let alone transformational value. Budget conversations focus on ROI calculations for individual use cases rather than cumulative strategic impact. The AI initiative feels more like a collection of science projects than a coherent approach to delivering value with transformational technology in service of business strategy.

This conventional approach creates what we call the "use case trap"—the illusion of strategic progress through the accumulation of possibilities. Organizations mistake activity for strategy, confusing a long list of ideas with a clear path to value. They fall into the democratic fallacy that each department's AI ideas deserve equal consideration, regardless of their importance and potential value.

The problems compound quickly. Without strategic anchoring, AI applications float disconnected from what matters to the business. A website chatbot receives the same attention as a potentially transformational customer-experience platform. Technical feasibility becomes the primary filter, ensuring that only manageable use cases with clean data and full stakeholder support advance. In the meantime, breakthrough opportunities that could turn into a competitive advantage fall off the prioritization lists because the data is not perfect or the technical implementation is too challenging.

Perhaps most damaging, this approach spreads resources thin across dozens of marginal improvements rather than concentrating them on initiatives that could fundamentally change competitive position. Teams burn out managing endless project pipelines while leaders grow skeptical about AI's promised impact. The organization ends up with lots of AI activity but little AI value.

Here is the strategic alternative we advocate:

1. **Start with the business strategy.** What are your three to five most critical objectives?
2. **Identify strategic problems.** What prevents you from achieving those objectives?
3. **Connect AI to solutions.** Which AI applications directly address your strategic challenges?
4. **Prioritize by size of value and speed to value.** Focus on applying AI where it will advance strategic goals quickly.
5. **Invest decisively.** Commit resources to strategic AI applications rather than spreading them thin.

This approach produces shorter lists but a bigger impact. Instead of fifty marginally useful AI experiments, you get five to ten applications that could transform your competitive position.

The difference isn't just methodological–it's strategic. One approach treats AI as a collection of interesting tools. The other treats AI as a strategic engine for achieving your vision.

THINK BIG, START SMALL, SCALE FAST

This motto has served us well through multiple AI transformations in global enterprises across industries and geographies. For example, one of us inherited a list of at least fifty AI use cases from an international company seeking to create commercial value with AI. But each use case was episodic, isolated from other AI use cases, and unconnected to business strategy.

Instead of continuing on that path, she turned the approach on its head. She started with the company's overall business strategy and vision to "think big." She then identified concrete AI applications that would deliver value individually at speed and collectively would amount to transformational impact in service of the overall vision. The individual AI application is the "start small" part. Small does not indicate lack of impact; it means focus and ability to deliver.

Speed of delivery leads to "scale fast." It's not difficult to create prototypes. It's challenging to develop sustainable enterprise-grade AI applications that operate at the scale of entire functions, business units, geographies, and companies in a sustainable manner.

But that is where the actual value from AI lies–when it becomes embedded throughout the entirety of an organization. The initial small (or focused) AI applications are similar to the CRISPR gene-editing technique that delivers microinjections of DNA-changing cells, resulting in an overall organism transformational effect. Think big, start small, scale fast is the way to go with deploying AI in a business organization, too, beginning with focused applications, followed by scaling each of them while also connecting their impact for a compound value that transforms the organization.

CASE STUDY: SECURIAN'S SHIFT FROM AI USE CASES TO A STRATEGIC ROADMAP

Securian Financial, a leading provider of insurance and financial services, faced a challenge familiar to many organizations diving into AI: an overwhelming number of potential AI use cases but no guiding strategy. With dozens of AI applications under consideration, the company risked falling into the trap of fragmented experimentation rather than following a focused, strategic approach. George Connolly, Securian's chief strategy officer, stated it plainly at an executive meeting, explaining to us in an interview, "Use cases are not a strategy."

"We had identified 60-plus use cases," said Connolly. "Every week or two, another AI proposal would come in. If someone had asked, 'What's our AI strategy?' the most honest answer at the time would have been, 'We don't have one.'"

Instead of rushing into implementation, Securian took a step back. With the CEO's direct encouragement and Connolly's leadership, the company committed to developing AI to serve its broader corporate strategy. Rather than creating a separate tech initiative, they would integrate AI into the business's core objectives.

From ideating use cases to solving business problems

The first step was to shift the mindset from "What can we do with AI?" to "What can AI do to solve our most important problems?" Connolly emphasized this shift repeatedly, ensuring that AI initiatives would serve the company's long-term priorities.

"We had a governance committee sorting through use cases," Connolly explained. "But what we really needed was a top-down strategic overlay. We began by defining our corporate enterprise strategy–what are we solving for as a business? And equally important, what aren't we solving for?"

To facilitate the shift, Securian gathered sixty leaders from across the company for an AI roadmap forum. They reviewed the organization's overarching strategy and used it as a filter to assess which AI applications were most in line with their long-term goals. By the end of this process, the team had identified three core business challenges that AI could directly address.

Connolly drove home the need for discipline. He emphasized, "A strategy that tries to be all things to all people is not a strategy–it's a Christmas list."

Selecting AI initiatives with strategic impact

Once Securian clarified its top business problems, it narrowed its AI initiatives down to nine high-impact areas of focus, and ultimately prioritized three applications:

1. **Accelerate proposal processes in group insurance.** Securian sought to enhance the speed and efficiency of proposal generation, particularly for its employee benefits business. By using AI, the company aimed to reduce insurance proposal turnaround times from weeks to days, enabling it to respond more quickly to client needs and stay competitive.
2. **Enhance claims processing.** The company sought to streamline claims reviews, ensuring that complex, high-value claims received appropriate scrutiny, while lower-risk ones could be processed more quickly. AI would help categorize and prioritize claims, improving efficiency while maintaining accuracy.

3. **Optimize underwriting for individual life insurance.** Securian sought to reduce the time required to underwrite high-value policies. By incorporating AI-driven requests for quote submissions, document processing, and actuarial analysis, the company planned to significantly reduce underwriting times, Connolly told us, reducing a process that could take seventy-five days to just five.

This disciplined approach ensured that Securian's AI efforts were strategically essential.

The strategic lesson

Securian's experience illustrates a key lesson: AI is not a strategy–it is a means to achieving a strategy. By starting with business problems and applying strategic discipline, Securian turned a long wish list of AI ideas into a focused, high-impact roadmap.

The company's approach also highlights the importance of leadership involvement. The CEO personally encouraged the work and highlighted its importance in company forums at all levels of the organization. AI adoption wasn't the purview of individual teams or departments; it became an enterprise-wide priority with clear executive sponsorship.

"When people ask me how AI fits into strategy," Connolly reflected, "I tell them: AI is not a strategy generator. AI is a toolkit. It has to be connected to people and processes in a way that makes sense for the business. If you use AI in the service of strategy, you can lift up your company, lift performance, and maybe even create new ways of competing."

IDENTIFYING YOUR TOP STRATEGIC PRIORITIES FOR AI

To get out of the use case trap, take the following steps to prioritize your AI applications:

- Step 1: Clarify your strategic priorities.
- Step 2: Validate and connect with domain stakeholders.

- Step 3: Map specific AI applications to business problems.
- Step 4: Prioritize AI applications using the Double-S Matrix, which plots the size of value versus the speed to value.
- Step 5: Document your AI application priorities.

STEP 1: CLARIFY YOUR STRATEGIC PRIORITIES

Start with the big picture—your company's strategic priorities. AI should serve these, not the other way around. Although this may seem obvious, many organizations assume they understand their strategy, yet they haven't taken the time to confirm that their leaders agree. This step ensures that everyone is working toward the same goals and that AI investments will lead to meaningful business impact.

Your MVT should lead this process. If you already have a chief AI officer or equivalent role (as discussed in chapter 3), they should coordinate this effort. Schedule a working session to revisit your company's most important objectives for the coming twelve to thirty-six months. These should be goals that the organization actively focuses on and invests in—objectives that would create significant value or a competitive advantage.

If your company has a well-documented business strategy, use it as your starting point. If not, these materials will provide clues about what leadership sees as the company's most critical focus areas:

- Annual reports and investor presentations
- Company vision and mission statements
- Executive memos or leadership town halls
- Existing annual business plans or transformation roadmaps

At this point, you should have a list of your organization's top strategic priorities. A crucial aspect to consider is how you will gauge and measure the impact of AI applications. Make sure you use strategic business metrics that already matter to the organization.

For each strategic priority, identify either obstacles that stand in the way of achieving your goals or ways in which to accelerate getting there. This isn't about identifying problems that AI can solve—it's about developing a deep understanding of blockers and opportunities for progress first.

Spend some time working through your strategic priorities and asking two simple questions for each: What's preventing us from achieving this goal? What are some ways we could accelerate our progress to achieve this goal? With this deep understanding of the problem, you can then consider how applying AI can address it better, faster, and cheaper than other options.

THREE WAYS TO UNCOVER THE REAL PROBLEMS OR OPPORTUNITIES

Here are three effective methods for identifying your most pressing business challenges and accelerating your progress toward your goals. Choose one or more approaches that work best for you and your organization.

The "Five Whys" approach

This approach helps uncover the root cause of business challenges by repeatedly asking "Why?" until you reach the root cause. Each time you answer a question, ask why until you reach the fundamental issue.

For example, imagine your company's strategic priority is to increase customer retention by 25 percent. You ask these questions:

- Why are customers leaving? → They don't feel engaged.
- Why don't they feel engaged? → We don't personalize their experience.
- Why don't we personalize? → We lack data and tools to do it at scale.
- Root problem: Inability to deliver personalization at scale.

The AI opportunity: Now that you've asked why, you can see that the real problem isn't just "We need AI for customer engagement" but rather a lack of data-driven personalization. AI-powered recommendation engines or transformational customer experiences could be valuable solutions.

The value-obstacle map

How it works: This method helps you assess where AI could add the most value by identifying the main obstacles.

Steps:

1. Write down one of your business priorities.
2. List the two to three barriers or obstacles preventing success.
3. Evaluate which obstacles you believe you should tackle with AI.

For example:

- Strategic priority: Reduce loan processing time from fourteen to two days.
- Obstacle 1: Manual document review takes eight to ten days.
- Obstacle 2: Credit verification requires multiple system checks.
- Obstacle 3: A restrictive sign-off policy creates delays.

This method forces you to separate problems AI can solve from those it can't. While AI is ideal for accelerating the manual document review (obstacle 1), it cannot fix delays caused by the restrictive sign-off policy (obstacle 3). That problem requires a leadership decision to change company rules, not a new technology.

The competitive pressure lens

This approach identifies external threats where AI could help maintain or create a competitive edge. The goal is to develop a clear, specific list of problems whose solutions would directly advance your strategic objectives. For example, a global e-commerce company might observe that competitors are using AI to generate highly personalized product recommendations, which significantly increases conversion rates. To stay competitive, they are exploring the use of AI to match their personalization engines, thereby enhancing customer engagement and sales.

This method ensures that AI is used not only to improve internal operations but also to stay competitive in a rapidly changing landscape. It also identifies which forces are making your strategic priorities more urgent. Some questions to ask include the following:

- What major shifts are happening in our industry (new competitors, regulatory changes, emerging technologies)?

- How are competitors moving faster than we are in key areas?
- Are there new entrants that challenge how we do business today and can disrupt our industry?
- How are customer expectations changing faster than we can adapt?
- How are regulatory or market changes creating new pressure points?

The AI opportunity: Identify one industry trend that could impact your company in the next twelve to thirty-six months. How could AI help you adapt or respond?

STEP 2: VALIDATE AND CONNECT WITH STAKEHOLDERS

At this stage, you've defined your organization's top strategic objectives and identified ways to achieve them faster or the key obstacles preventing success. Before mapping AI applications to these strategic objectives, it's crucial to consult with key stakeholders to confirm that these priorities, problems, and opportunities are the most relevant ones to focus on. This brief validation step prevents downstream misunderstandings and builds executive support for your AI applications. Here is what to cover with stakeholders:

1. Strategic priorities confirmation
   - Are these still our most critical objectives for the next twelve to thirty-six months?
   - Have any priorities shifted due to market changes or new decisions?
   - Do these priorities have broad executive consensus?

2. Problem and opportunity validation
   - Are these the real obstacles preventing us from achieving our strategic goals? Are these realistic ways to accelerate our progress?
   - Are we missing any critical barriers or opportunities that stakeholders see as hindering progress?
   - Which problems feel most urgent to solve first? Which opportunities to seize first?

How to position the conversation

Frame this as a strategic check-in to confirm business priorities, not AI validation. Here are key messages to convey:

- We want to ensure our focus supports the company's strategic priorities.
- These are the problems we see blocking our key objectives.
  These are the opportunities and ways to accelerate progress.
- We're exploring how various tools and approaches could address these challenges.

Keep AI in the background during this conversation. The goal is to achieve business leadership agreement first, then cover AI applications.

Business leaders will naturally want AI applications to deliver measurable value. Still, they may also expect fully developed answers too soon—wanting details on feasibility, costs, or implementation before the foundational strategy is established. It's essential to set expectations that you are simply validating priorities to deploy AI for value creation.

Common executive concerns

Some executives may be wary of AI, viewing its deployment as a technological task rather than a business-driven strategy. The best way to overcome this skepticism is by reinforcing that AI is the means to achieving strategic business priorities. Here are some questions and concerns that you can expect to come up in the conversations, and how to address them:

- **Is this really a priority right now?** Show the direct connection to the overall company objectives.
- **We don't have resources for this.** Emphasize that you're validating problems and opportunities first; AI solutions come later. If it's crucial strategically, you will find a way to support AI work in its service.
- **AI initiatives haven't worked before.** Position the effort as business problem-solving that uses AI tools.

By framing this step as validating business priorities and opportunities rather than pushing AI solutions, you increase the chances of securing support from the top. With leadership validation complete, you're ready to map specific AI applications to your strategic problems.

STEP 3: MAP SPECIFIC AI APPLICATIONS TO BUSINESS PROBLEMS

Now comes the important work of reviewing your validated strategic priorities and key problems and thinking through how AI could address them. Start by reviewing the AI application opportunities you identified across engagement, efficiency, and reinvention in chapter 4. Which of these directly connects to the strategic objectives and problems you've identified? Don't force connections–focus only on the AI applications that could meaningfully advance your organization's strategic goals.

Then, create a table like the one on the next page that shows the strategic priorities and an AI application in support of it. As seen earlier, Securian needed to transition from a lengthy list of isolated use cases–which were unconnected to strategy–to a more focused plan. To do that, they thought through each strategic priority and how AI supported it. Their approach provides a clear model for how to ensure AI serves strategy, not the other way around (see figure 5-2).

Figure 5-2: How Securian mapped AI applications to its strategic priorities

STRATEGIC PRIORITY	AI APPLICATIONS
Increase competitive advantage and revenue in the large-case group insurance market	• **Accelerate proposal generation.** Reduce the turnaround time for complex insurance proposals from weeks to days. The goal is to complete 85 percent of an RFP response within three to four days. • **Manage multiproduct complexity.** Rapidly configure and price sophisticated proposals that bundle core group life insurance with a suite of new voluntary benefits. This capability is essential for becoming a more attractive single-source partner for large clients who increasingly prefer to deal with fewer vendors.
Improve customer experience and operational efficiency in claims processing	• **Nuanced claims review.** Differentiate the level of rigor applied to claims based on their value and risk. A multimillion-dollar benefit requires more scrutiny than a thousand-dollar one. • **Automated processing with human in the loop.** Quickly process lower-risk claims to improve the customer deliverable while flagging complex, high-value claims for human review.
Dramatically reduce time to decision for high-value individual life insurance policies	• **AI-powered document analysis.** Ingest and analyze hundreds of pages of complex medical records to identify and summarize key risk factors for the underwriting team. • **Streamlined data gathering.** Capture information from various sources to prefill applications, reducing the number of questions asked of the potential client and accelerating the initial information-gathering phase.

This list will likely include more applications than you can pursue simultaneously, which is why you need the prioritization framework in step 4.

STEP 4: PRIORITIZE AI APPLICATIONS USING THE DOUBLE-S MATRIX

With your list of strategically connected AI applications in hand, it's time to prioritize using an approach tailored for AI's fast pace. Traditional prioritization methods assume stable conditions and lengthy planning cycles. AI demands a different approach–one that balances strategic impact with speed of value delivery.

There is no way to overstate the importance of moving at speed today. So much is changing and so quickly that speed is nonnegotiable. **Moving fast and creating value** is the only way to go today. You can win with AI, thanks to its speed.

A significant challenge in prioritization is defining the "size of value" in a way that avoids subjective debate. Murli Buluswar, a data and analytics leader in insurance and consumer banking, emphasized the need for very powerful metrics in an interview with us. He advocated for framing value "through the lens of a CEO, CFO, and a head of audit."

This framework translates value into three distinct, measurable categories:

- **CEO (materiality):** Does this application move the needle on the organization's most critical strategic goals?
- **CFO (financials):** What is the tangible, concrete financial impact?
- **Head of audit (traceability):** Can we trace, verify, and govern the process and its outcomes?

When value is defined in terms that are "pragmatic, very tangible, concrete, within a well-defined time frame," the resulting "KPIs . . . are hard to debate with," said Buluswar. This approach anchors prioritization in business reality, ensuring that the organization pursues applications that deliver measurable strategic impact.

Forget feasibility–focus on value and speed

Here's the core point: Feasibility is not the right filter for prioritizing AI applications.

Why? Because feasibility is subjective and constraining. Something that feels impossible to one person might fall into someone else's wheelhouse. A plan that seems unrealistic today might be viable next quarter. If you only prioritize what's immediately feasible with current resources, you'll severely constrain yourself to marginal improvements rather than transformational impact.

Instead, prioritize AI applications based on two strategic questions, which together inform the Double-S Matrix prioritization method:

- **Size of value:** What value will this AI application create in service of our most important business goals?
- **Speed to value:** How quickly can we deliver that value?

This approach is straightforward and strategic. If an AI application truly supports a critical business objective, you'll find ways to make it happen. You'll develop partnerships with vendors, acquire technology, hire expertise, and/or start assembling internal talent. You won't stop because you don't have everything in place you'd need to get going. That's what strategic initiatives require: focus, determination, and not letting current gaps stop you.

Remember: You can borrow, buy, or build what you need to deliver value with AI. But you cannot afford to miss strategic opportunities. Not today. Not at the speed of AI. If you did, you'd fall so far behind that your entire business viability would be at stake.

Using the Double-S Matrix prioritization method

One way to practice this approach is with the Double-S Matrix, which will help to prioritize and categorize AI applications (see figure 5-3).

Momentum makers (bigger size of value, higher speed)

This quadrant is the sweet spot for AI focus. AI applications in this quadrant deliver substantial value quickly. They demonstrate that AI is a tangible force for change, creating internal momentum to fuel further AI progress in the service of your overall strategy.

Quick wins (smaller size of value, higher speed)

This quadrant represents AI applications that are fast to implement and easy to demonstrate. They build credibility and capability. While not strategically transformational, they create the foundation for more ambitious initiatives. Having quick wins doesn't mean you cannot deliver substantial transformational value overall. When you thoughtfully assemble several of these applications that complement each

Figure 5-3: The Double-S Matrix

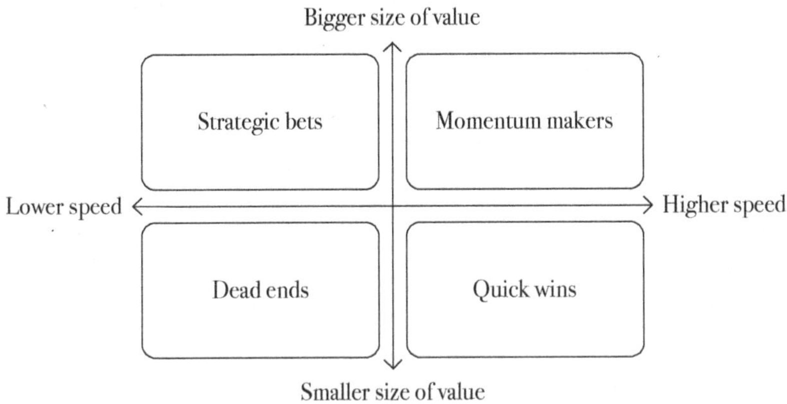

other, you can build a collective transformation engine that can create meaningful value in combination with several quick wins.

Strategic bets (bigger size of value, lower speed)
This quadrant represents some of the most transformative AI applications. They promise substantial value that may take a bit longer to realize but is worth the build-out. They're deeply strategic but may take longer to materialize due to complexity or dependencies. Don't discard these–ask how to accelerate their timeline while recognizing their strategic importance. Note that lower speed does not mean years, as in traditional IT roadmaps. Lower speed means twelve to eighteen months, or three to six months for quick wins.

Dead ends (smaller size of value, lower speed)
This quadrant represents potential AI applications that neither move fast nor deliver significant value. Explicitly categorizing these prevents wasting resources while creating a watch list for future consideration as conditions change.

Strategic AI application prioritization
Here are the steps to take to prioritize your AI applications:

Step 1: Assess each application. For each AI application from Step 4, evaluate these attributes:

- **Size of value:** Will this AI application create higher or lower value for the organization, in service of strategic objectives? For AI applications that seem lower in value, ask if combining some of them could increase their strategic value. For instance, combining several quick wins can transform them into momentum makers.
- **Speed:** How quickly could we deliver and demonstrate meaningful value? For applications that seem lower on speed, ask, "What would it take to accelerate this?" Consider strategies to overcome speed constraints through partnerships, focused resources, or phased approaches.
- **Success criteria:** Develop specific, measurable outcomes for each prioritized AI application. What value do you expect the AI application to deliver, in what time period, against a strategic priority? What are the metrics of success? There are three typical ways to measure value: controlled A/B tests, simple before-and-after comparisons, and counterfactual analysis that models what would have happened without AI.[1]

Step 2: Plot and prioritize. Place each AI application in the appropriate quadrant:

- **Focus first on momentum makers**, which should be your immediate priorities.
- **Include two to three quick wins**, which build capability and credibility.
- **Select one or two strategic bets**, which provide transformation impact in a slightly extended time frame.
- **Document, but defer, dead ends**, which will keep these visible but deprioritized.

CASE STUDY: ALLY BANK

Ally Bank saw AI as a transformational force that went far beyond automation. They recognized it as a catalyst for rethinking their customer service, empowering employees, and positioning themselves for the future. But instead of starting with a fully mapped-out plan, they built a foundation that allowed them to learn, scale, and lead.

"We knew this wasn't just a technology transformation–it was a company transformation," explained Sathish Muthukrishnan, Ally's chief information, data, and digital officer, in an interview with us. To ensure a structured approach, they developed the Ally AI Platform, an internal system that enabled safe AI experimentation while addressing concerns regarding privacy and compliance. Clear guiding principles ensured a responsible rollout: AI would be used for internal-facing applications first, personally identifiable information would never be shared externally, and a human would remain in the loop until the technology could be trusted to work autonomously.

The first major AI application focused on a common challenge: summarizing customer service calls. Before AI, agents had to manually document key points for ten thousand daily calls, a task that required a significant amount of time and effort. AI-generated summaries streamlined the process, reducing documentation time by thirty seconds to two minutes per call, resulting in $1.2 million in annual savings. More importantly, AI improved consistency and accuracy, capturing details that agents might have missed.

What started as skepticism among customer service employees quickly turned into advocacy. "They told us, 'Don't take this away from me,'" Muthukrishnan recalled.

Encouraged by this success, Ally brought AI into other areas, including content production for marketing and predictive analytics to anticipate customer needs. AI-assisted content creation reduced drafting time by 30 percent. Unlike many companies that were discussing and experimenting internally, Ally was executing.

"Everybody is talking about AI—we are actually doing it," Muthukrishnan said.

AI also reshaped leadership dynamics. Ally established a dedicated AI stand-up with the executive committee every three weeks, ensuring that AI remained a top priority and that leadership stayed actively engaged. The company also encouraged employees to embrace AI, not fear it.

"If we don't adopt this technology, we will be left behind," Muthukrishnan emphasized. "So why shouldn't it be us leading the way?"

Ally's AI transformation is a testament to the fact that transformation isn't about having all the answers up front—it's about building the capability to evolve. "Have the courage to create a path," Muthukrishnan advised. "It doesn't have to be perfect. It doesn't have to be straight. But you have to start."

By adopting a portfolio mindset like Ally Bank's, organizations break free from the common trap of treating AI as a collection of one-off projects. Instead, AI becomes a strategic capability–one that Ally Bank continuously evaluates, adjusts, and optimizes to create sustainable, long-term value.

COMMON CHALLENGES IN PRIORITIZING AI APPLICATIONS

As you navigate this strategic process, you can expect to encounter predictable challenges and tensions. We've been there, we know, we empathize. Here is our guidance to maintain momentum while making sound strategic decisions. There are several potential challenges.

THE FORCE-FIT TEMPTATION

- **What you'll encounter:** Pressure to justify every AI application from chapter 4 by connecting it to a business problem, even when the connection is weak or artificial.
- **Why this happens:** People become attached to interesting AI opportunities and don't want to waste their exploration work. In addition, there may be pressure to include everyone's ideas.
- **What to do instead:** Stay disciplined about strategic fit. Not every AI application opportunity identified from chapter 4 will match your top strategic priorities–and that's fine. The goal is to focus on the AI applications that solve your most critical challenges. Set aside applications that don't clearly connect to strategic objectives. They may become relevant later as priorities evolve.

THE OVERCOMPLICATION TRAP

- **What you'll encounter:** The strategic process gets bogged down in its complexity. Discussions often devolve into exhaustive analyses for every possible problem, causing the team to get stuck in endless loops of mapping connections instead of making decisions.
- **Why this happens:** This occurs when teams mistake activity for progress, believing that more analysis automatically leads to better strategic clarity. They fall in love with the intellectual exercise of strategy rather than the practical goal of solving problems.
- **What to do instead:** If the process feels stuck in analysis paralysis, return to your core strategic priorities and use them as a filter. Ask the simple question: "What is *truly* preventing us from achieving our top three to five goals?" This focus forces you to discard secondary issues, maintaining clarity on what matters most.

THE FEASIBILITY-CREEP PROBLEM

- **What you'll encounter:** Despite prioritizing size of value and speed over feasibility, companies tend to gravitate toward projects for which everything is already in place.
- **Why this happens:** It's natural to prefer certainty over uncertainty. People want to succeed, but they worry about overcommitting to ambitious applications.
- **What to do instead:** Remember that if something is truly strategic–if it directly addresses a critical business problem or helps you seize an opportunity–you'll find ways to make it happen. Budget constraints, skill gaps, and technology limitations are challenges to solve, not reasons to avoid strategic AI applications. Ask, "If this fundamentally improves our ability to compete, what would it take to make it work?"

THE ENDLESS IDEATION CYCLE

- **What you'll encounter:** Teams often get stuck in Step 4 (mapping AI use cases), where they continuously generate new ideas without progressing to prioritization and decision-making.
- **Why this happens:** Brainstorming AI potential is energizing and creative. The process feels productive and avoids the more complex work of making strategic choices.
- **What to do instead:** Set clear time boundaries for each step. Once you have fifteen to twenty strategically connected AI applications, move to prioritization. Remember: You can always identify additional AI applications later, but you need to start delivering value at speed. Now.

THE DEPARTMENTAL SILO PROBLEM

- **What you'll encounter:** Resistance to AI applications that require cross-functional coordination, with departments protecting their data, processes, or decision-making authority.
- **Why this happens:** Strategic AI applications often require breaking down silos and sharing resources across organizational boundaries. This threatens existing power structures and comfortable operating models.
- **What to do instead:** Anticipate this resistance and address it directly. Highlight that the most impactful AI applications generate value that benefits multiple departments and the entire organization. Frame cross-functional coordination as a competitive advantage, not an operational burden. Discuss the issue at senior leadership forums to resolve territorial disputes that could limit AI's impact.

BALANCING AMBITION WITH REALISM

- **What you'll encounter:** Tension between visionary thinking and practical execution. Some team members will advocate for big transformational ideas, while others will urge caution and stick to safe incremental changes.

- **Why this happens:** Strategic AI work naturally invites bold thinking. But without a clear decision-making process and a manageable starting point, teams can get stuck debating whether to go big or stay grounded. The result? Momentum stalls.
- **What to do instead:** Channel ambition and practicality into the right steps. Encourage expansive thinking during mapping of AI applications to strategic priorities (Step 3), then prioritize (Step 4) using tools like the Double-S Matrix. Plan for a phased implementation of AI applications to balance shorter-term wins with longer-term transformation, while also continuously developing further AI advancements.

Remember, these challenges are normal. The organizations that succeed with AI are the ones that anticipate, manage effectively, and maintain relentless focus on value creation.

YOUR WEEK 5 ACTION PLAN

This week is about ensuring your AI efforts serve your company's strategic priorities. Guide your team through these essential actions to identify the top AI applications that serve and support your business strategy.

- **Clarify your top three to five business priorities.** Use your existing strategy, leadership discussions, and strategic planning document reviews to identify the most critical strategic goals for your organization over the next twelve to thirty-six months. For each priority, identify the tangible obstacles hindering success and explore ways to accelerate it. Use methods such as the Five Whys, obstacle mapping, and competitive pressure approaches to uncover real business challenges.
- **Validate your findings with stakeholders.** Confirm with executives that you've correctly identified strategic priorities and key problems. This ensures agreement and builds early stakeholder support for AI applications.
- **Map AI applications to strategic problems.** Connect AI applications to your specific business challenges by using examples and problem-solving to identify those that support your priorities.

- **Evaluate AI applications using the Double-S Matrix.** Focus on value over feasibility—if an application serves critical business objectives, you will find ways to make it happen, rather than ruling it out based on current constraints.
- **Document your AI application priorities.** Summarize the connections among business priorities, key problems, and prioritized AI applications. This provides clear guidance for creating your AI roadmap in chapter 6.

SUMMARY

You've now completed Week 5 of your 90-day AI blueprint and have taken a crucial step toward planning to deploy AI in direct service of your business strategy.

In this chapter, you accomplished the following:

- **Shifted from chasing AI use cases** to anchoring AI in your overall strategy and top priorities.
- **Applied a structured process** to identify specific blockers of progress or accelerators of it, using proven methodologies to uncover root causes.
- **Learned to use AI strategically** by focusing on solving high-priority business challenges and seizing strategic opportunities, rather than pursuing isolated use cases or technology for technology's sake.
- **Mapped AI applications to strategic problems and opportunities**, using multiple sources, including real-world examples and creative problem-solving.
- **Prioritized AI applications using the Double-S Matrix**, recognizing that strategic deployment of AI applications warrants creativity and other ways to overcome any shortfalls in data, skills, or infrastructure.
- **Engaged stakeholders early to confirm agreement** and avoid future roadblocks to AI adoption by validating strategic priorities and areas of AI deployment.

With this clarity in place, you're ready to move into Week 6, where you'll transform these prioritized AI applications into a dynamic AI roadmap and an ongoing cadence of agile value delivery.

In preparing for battle, I have always found that plans are useless, but planning is indispensable.

—Dwight D. Eisenhower

Six
CRAFTING A DYNAMIC AI ROADMAP

YOU'VE IDENTIFIED WHERE AI can create value (chapter 4). You've connected AI applications to your business strategy (chapter 5). Now comes the moment of truth: putting timelines and commitments behind your plans.

For many leaders, this feels uncomfortable, even foolish. How can you create an eighteen-month roadmap for a technology that's evolving daily? Won't your plans be obsolete before the ink dries? These concerns are valid, but they miss a crucial point: Without a concrete roadmap, AI remains an intriguing possibility rather than a strategic reality.

The Six-Quarter Walk offers a solution to this dilemma. It's a rolling eighteen-month roadmap that strikes a balance between the need for concrete planning and the reality of constant change. Why eighteen months? Because twelve-month plans too often default to budget exercises rather than value-creation strategies. The bigger, more strategic AI applications—the ones that can transform your business—may require looking further out than twelve months, but still not too far into the future. Speed is key, and we cannot afford to let work drag out. Eighteen months is close enough to reflect more transformational AI work, with realistic assessments about what it would take to deliver and to scale.

Most importantly, your Six-Quarter Walk is written in pencil, not carved in stone. Once the plan is documented, you can debate, challenge, test, and refine it. The roadmap becomes a living document that evolves with both your understanding and the technology itself.

This week, you will continue your strategic planning work, focusing on translating priorities into executable roadmaps. This week, you will focus on these objectives:

- **Understand the Six-Quarter Walk framework** and why eighteen-month planning matters for value creation with AI.
- **Learn to balance ambition with the reality of implementation** and planning for the practicalities of delivering AI applications.
- **Sequence initiatives across six quarters**, balancing quick wins and transformational efforts.
- **Create your first Six-Quarter Walk**, delivering clear value each quarter.
- **Establish adaptive review processes** to keep your roadmap dynamic and relevant.

By the end of this chapter, you'll have a concrete AI roadmap that transforms strategic intent into quarterly value delivery while maintaining the flexibility to adapt as you learn.

WHY SPEED IS YOUR STRATEGIC ADVANTAGE

Speed matters. AI moves fast, too fast for traditional strategic planning. The conventional "waterfall" approach–setting a fixed, multiyear roadmap and executing against it–simply doesn't work when technology, competitors, and your own strengths are advancing by the month. AI demands a new strategy, one that is clear enough to drive action but flexible enough to adapt.

Traditional strategic planning resembles climbing a tidy staircase–sequential steps where you complete one phase before moving on to the next. Build your data foundation first. Then implement AI platforms. Then integrate with business systems. Then develop use cases. Each step waits patiently for the previous one to finish.

AI transformation looks nothing like this orderly progression. It's akin to navigating a bustling Los Angeles freeway, with its multiple winding lanes, intersecting paths, and constant movement in all directions. You're simultaneously building competencies in one lane while delivering value in another and managing governance in a third, all while adapting to rapidly changing conditions around you.

Rather than following sequential steps, you need to balance speed with coordination across multiple parallel efforts to reach your destination safely and efficiently.

The old model assumed you could afford the luxury of linear progress. AI's pace makes that assumption obsolete. Your AI roadmap acknowledges this reality—instead of waiting for perfect readiness, you build and deliver in parallel, switching lanes as conditions change, always moving toward value creation.

"The technology evolves so fast that, by the time you finish planning for one use case, the tools and approaches might already look outdated," said Albert Chow, who oversees AI products at financial services platform Pipe.com, in an interview with us. "Staying flexible isn't just a preference—it's survival. And not just because it's thrilling to move fast, but because it's the best way to learn, adapt, and advance."

Most legacy organizations view speed as a constraint. Organizations that transition from defining AI value to delivering value faster than their competitors create sustainable advantages that compound over time.

To be clear, deploying AI at speed is not about moving recklessly or cutting corners. It's about moving intentionally and with urgency, because speed enables you to do the following:

- **Build credibility**. AI can seem abstract until people see tangible results. It shifts the conversation from "what are you trying to do?" to "how can it help me?" Delivering value quickly makes AI real for your organization.
- **Unlock creativity**. When you give teams a short runway, they're forced to think differently. Speed sharpens focus and pushes people to try new approaches. It encourages problem-solving and continuous learning, both of which are essential for a fast-evolving technology like AI.
- **Learn and adapt faster**. Each quarter of execution provides insights that inform better decisions for subsequent quarters.
- **Outrun tech obsolescence**. By delivering value quickly, you stay ahead of tools and approaches that become outdated. A faster, imperfect rollout will outperform inevitable obsolescence. (This is where your tech platforms can help, too, something we'll cover in chapter 10.)
- **Create momentum that attracts resources**. Success breeds success, and early wins unlock investment for more ambitious initiatives.

This is why the Six-Quarter Walk prioritizes quarterly value delivery over perfect long-term planning. Better to have an imperfect roadmap that delivers results than a perfect plan that never gets executed.

THE SIX-QUARTER WALK

The Six-Quarter Walk provides an eighteen-month horizon to help you think about when and how each AI application will deliver impact. It asks, quarter by quarter, "What's the value we will deliver, and how?"

This time frame provides a medium-term perspective that allows you to envision the transformational value you want to achieve eighteen months from now, then work backward to determine what needs to happen each quarter to make the vision a reality. Some of your most strategic AI applications may require the whole timeline to deliver their intended impact, whether due to technical complexity, organizational change requirements, or the need to build supporting skills or resources first.

The eighteen-month horizon also liberates you from the constraints of traditional twelve-month fiscal year planning cycles. While annual budgets remain important, AI advances more rapidly than yearly planning allows. The Six-Quarter Walk offers flexibility to think beyond current budget cycles while maintaining sufficient specificity to drive quarterly execution and value delivery.

Defining quarterly value outcomes shifts the conversation from tasks and timelines to outcomes and momentum. It encourages you to consider what's visible, meaningful, and will sustain energy. This becomes especially powerful when you consider that some of the biggest wins–the ones that create a competitive advantage–require ongoing refreshment and updates, commensurate with tech advancements, evolving customer expectations, and the changing business environment. The Six-Quarter Walk enables you to continuously and dynamically update your outlook.

Think of it as rebalancing your AI value portfolio, helping you spot gaps and imbalances. If you realize that your next two quarters are heavy on quick wins but light on momentum makers, that may be a signal to adjust. If your high-value AI applications all come later, consider what it would take to accelerate them. The Six-Quarter Walk provides clear visibility into what your current activities are and when the organization can expect to see results.

Three core principles should guide your Six-Quarter Walk:

- **Quarterly value delivery**. Define the value your AI applications deliver each quarter with visible and measurable metrics. This prevents AI applications from becoming endless research projects and ensures stakeholders see continuous progress.
- **Strategic coherence**. Ensure individual quarters connect to your overall long-term strategic objectives as identified in chapter 5. Wins in earlier quarters can support more ambitious AI applications planned for later quarters.
- **Adaptive evolution**. The roadmap evolves based on the ongoing delivery of AI applications, the lessons learned from the work, changing business priorities, and technological advancements. Although your plans for quarter six may change, having a clear direction can still be helpful.

This approach serves several crucial purposes. First, it ensures companies' leadership has visibility into the full scope of AI deployments across the organization and over time. This prevents redundancies and enables the strategic consolidation of several complementary AI applications that, together, achieve a high-value, transformational impact.

Second, it helps coordinate dependencies between AI applications. For example, implementing an AI-powered customer service chatbot that accesses order history and preferences requires first having customer data integration and basic AI governance processes in place. These prerequisite elements enable more sophisticated customer-facing applications to work effectively.

Third, it fosters transparency, preventing departments from duplicating efforts or working in isolation. When teams can see what AI applications others are developing, they can identify opportunities to bundle smaller projects together to create a more substantial impact worthy of enterprise-level investment and support.

CREATING YOUR SIX-QUARTER WALK

Now it's time to translate your strategic priorities into a concrete roadmap. This process combines the prioritized AI applications with decisions about resource development and value-delivery timing. Think of this as building a bridge between your strategic ambitions and quarterly execution. Each step ensures your roadmap is both ambitious enough to drive transformation and realistic enough to deliver.

The moment you write down your six-quarter roadmap, it becomes real–not because it's done, but because it's visible. Writing it down gives your organization something to respond to, challenge, and improve. It turns vague goals into clear priorities. And it gives you something to adapt, which is what we'll explore now.

Your Six-Quarter Walk must be organized by quarter, with specific deliverables and value defined for each three-month period. This quarterly structure fosters accountability, facilitates regular progress reviews, and maintains the pace that AI demands. Once you've documented your initial roadmap, expect to adjust it regularly as you learn, as business priorities evolve, and as AI technology advances.

STEP 1: REVIEW YOUR PRIORITIZED AI APPLICATIONS

Begin with the AI applications you prioritized using the Double-S Matrix in chapter 5. You should have a clear list of momentum makers, quick wins, strategic bets, and documented dead ends, all of which are connected to your top strategic priorities.

Before diving into sequencing and timing, take a moment to review these applications with fresh eyes. Are they still the right priorities? Have any business conditions changed since you completed your chapter 5 work? This will ensure that you're building your roadmap on current realities.

STEP 2: SEQUENCE FOR STRATEGIC IMPACT AND REALISTIC TIMING

The art of roadmap creation lies in balancing strategic priority and execution reality. Your sequencing should be driven primarily by strategic importance, with timing adjusted based on your understanding of organizational readiness and resource needs.

Begin by organizing your applications in order of strategic importance, as determined by your chapter 5 work. Your highest-impact momentum makers should generally come first, followed by supporting applications that enable or amplify their success. Don't let perceived resource constraints override strategic priority at this stage. If something is strategically critical, your job is to find a way to make it happen sooner rather than later.

Once you have established strategic sequencing, consider what foundational work may be required and how it impacts timing. Applications requiring significant new infrastructure may need to have it built first, but don't automatically assume this means long delays. Sometimes you can start applications while building infrastructure in parallel.

Consider a retail company that wants to implement personalized recommendations (strategic bet) but lacks a customer data infrastructure. Rather than delaying recommendations for a year while building infrastructure, they might start with a simple purchase history analysis (a quick win) that begins delivering value immediately, while building the data resources needed for sophisticated personalization later.

Look for opportunities where early applications build foundations that enable later, more ambitious applications. These "progression ladders" will accelerate your overall timeline. A simple customer service chatbot might seem like just an efficiency improvement. Still, if it's well designed, it also builds conversational AI expertise, customer interaction data, and organizational confidence that enables more sophisticated customer-experience applications later. The key is intentionally designing these connections rather than letting them happen accidentally.

STEP 3: NOTE RESOURCE REQUIREMENTS

At this point, you may feel a strong urge to dive deeper into capability assessment before proceeding. This is natural, as you want to understand precisely what you'll need to build, buy, or find a partner for before committing to specific timelines. Resist this instinct for now.

Your job in this step is to note what resources and competencies each quarter will require, rather than determining how you'll acquire them. For each quarter, create a brief list of the human skills, technical infrastructure, and governance processes required for your applications. Don't overthink it. Capture the obvious requirements like "customer data integration for Q2 personalization engine" or "AI training program for Q1 customer service team."

The detailed work of assessing your current strengths, identifying specific gaps, and planning how to close them is the focus of chapter 7. That's where you'll conduct a thorough readiness analysis and create targeted plans to develop your building blocks. If the pull to assess readiness now is overwhelming, go ahead and read chapter 7 to understand what's involved; then, come back here to complete your initial roadmap.

Why finish the roadmap first? Because you need to see how all your strategic applications fit together across six quarters before you can make smart decisions about resource development. The timing and sequencing of your applications will heavily influence which skills to prioritize and how to acquire them. A customer service AI in Q1 might build conversational expertise needed for a sales AI in Q3, fundamentally changing your development approach.

Complete your roadmap, then use chapter 7 to validate and refine it based on detailed building block analysis. Your strategic vision should drive resource development, not the other way around.

STEP 4: DEFINE QUARTERLY VALUE OUTCOMES

For each quarter, you must specify the exact value to be delivered. This isn't just about setting expectations; it's about ensuring every quarter contributes meaningfully to your strategic objectives while building toward longer-term transformation.

Start with quantitative outcomes that directly measure business impact. These include revenue effects, such as new sales generated or revenue protected from churn; cost impacts, such as process-automation savings or reduced error costs; or operational improvements, including faster decision-making or higher-quality outputs. Be specific and measurable. Instead of "improved customer service," specify "reduce average response time from twenty-four hours to two hours" or "increase customer satisfaction scores from 7.2 to 8.0."

Qualitative outcomes capture value that's harder to measure but equally important. These include resource building, such as acquiring new technical skills or implementing improved processes; market positioning gains, including competitive advantages or brand enhancements; and strategic optionality, which creates new possibilities for future quarters. For example, implementing a customer data platform may have a modest immediate impact on revenue. Still, it creates the foundation for personalized marketing, predictive analytics, and customer experience optimization that were previously impossible.

Don't forget learning outcomes–the insights and knowledge gained that inform better decisions in future quarters. Early AI applications often teach you as much about your organization's readiness and customer needs as they do about AI technology itself. A pilot chatbot might reveal that your customers prefer human interaction for complex issues but love AI for simple questions, fundamentally shaping your customer service strategy.

The goal is to ensure every quarter delivers stand-alone value while contributing to your cumulative strategic progress. Each quarter should answer these questions: "What did we accomplish, what did we learn, and how does this position us for even greater success next quarter?"

CASE STUDY: SECURIAN FINANCIAL'S AI SEQUENCING

Securian Financial's approach to its AI roadmap reveals the power of turning experimentation into execution. After narrowing an overwhelming list of sixty-plus use cases to three top strategic applications (as detailed in chapter 5), the company faced its next challenge: how to turn those priorities into a sequenced plan that could deliver value consistently across multiple quarters.

The result was what George Connolly, chief strategy officer and executive sponsor of AI at Securian, referred to as a "first cut" of a strategic AI roadmap. Rather than trying to launch all three AI applications simultaneously, Securian designed what Connolly described as a "horizon" approach, carefully sequencing their work. They used twelve to eighteen months to define each horizon, recognizing that specific early initiatives were necessary stepping stones that would enable more ambitious applications later.

"Some of the activity in Horizon 1 was really in service of being able to do stuff in Horizon 2," Connolly explained in an interview with us. By mid-2025, Connolly expected this sequenced approach to mature into a long-term strategic plan that could extend across several years. But from the outset, the roadmap created a shared understanding across the company: AI wasn't something to dabble in; it was something to deliver with discipline.

This wasn't about achieving perfection in the initial plan; it was about creating enough clarity to move forward with confidence. As Connolly emphasized, "Last year was about learning and exploring. This year, we run."

STEP 5: CREATE YOUR VISUAL ROADMAP

Document your Six-Quarter Walk in a format that communicates clearly to different stakeholders. This step synthesizes and makes visible all the strategic work from Steps 1 to 4—your roadmap doesn't exist as an organizational tool until it's written down and shareable. The visual roadmap transforms your prioritized applications, sequencing decisions, and value outcomes into a format that drives coordinated execution across your organization.

Structure your roadmap around three core elements:

- **When** (quarterly timeline)
- **What** (value outcomes delivered each quarter)
- **How** (specific AI applications that create that value)

Figure 6-1 illustrates this approach with a customer-experience transformation roadmap, mapping just one strategic objective and the AI applications that support it. Notice how each quarter specifics both the measurable business impact (reduced response times, increased satisfaction scores) and the AI applications that deliver those results (chatbot implementation, sentiment analysis, predictive analytics).

The most effective roadmaps balance comprehensive information with stakeholder-specific clarity. Your core roadmap should encompass all three elements, with the option to emphasize different aspects for various audiences. For executive stakeholders, highlight the what—quarterly revenue impacts, cost savings, and strategic positioning gains. For technical teams, emphasize the how—which AI applications launch when, their dependencies, and success metrics. For the broader organization, focus on the when and what—clear timelines for when AI will enhance their work and what benefits they can expect.

Remember that this visual roadmap becomes your organization's shared reference point for AI transformation. It should be detailed enough to drive quarterly execution while remaining accessible to stakeholders who need to understand AI's strategic direction without technical complexity.

Figure 6-1: Sample Six-Quarter Walk for customer-experience transformation

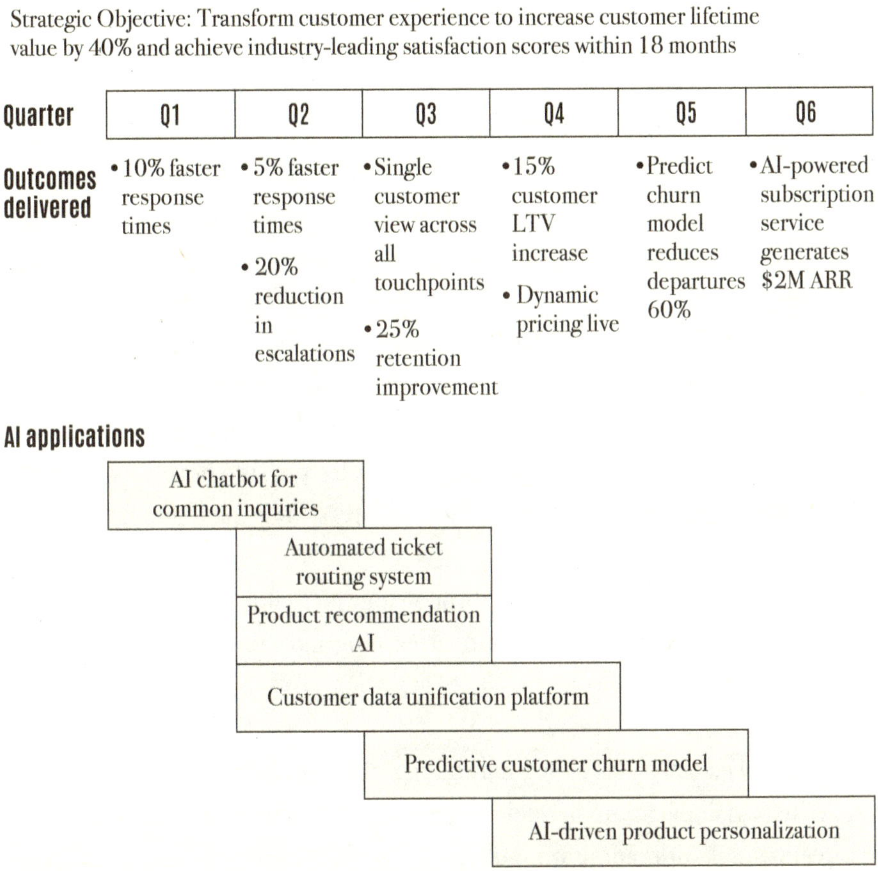

KEEPING YOUR ROADMAP DYNAMIC WITH ADAPTIVE REVIEWS

AI moves fast, and not in straight lines. New models emerge, regulations shift, business priorities evolve. What made sense last quarter might not work today. That's why your plan can't stay static. It needs a rhythm, a way to stay current, adjust course, and keep organizations coordinated over time.

We refer to this practice as adaptive reviews–structured checkpoints that ensure your AI priorities, roadmap, and governance approach remain relevant as the world evolves. They transform scattered information into actionable insights. Done right, adaptive reviews connect strategy with execution, learning with delivery.

The Six-Quarter Walk's power lies not in its initial accuracy, but in its ability to evolve intelligently as you learn. This requires establishing adaptive review processes that ensure your roadmap remains relevant as business priorities, technology advances, and market conditions change.

THE QUARTERLY ADAPTIVE REVIEW PROCESS

The quarterly review process follows a clear pattern that transforms scattered information into actionable insights. Implementing AI applications is demanding as teams work intensively to learn new skills and adapt to new ways of working. Without regular opportunities to pause and assess progress, organizations risk change fatigue, where people become exhausted from working hard without seeing tangible results.

Adaptive reviews combat this fatigue by creating structured moments to take stock, celebrate successes, acknowledge challenges, and reorient efforts based on what has been learned. These quarterly cycles provide both accountability and renewal, ensuring teams can see their progress while maintaining energy for continued change.

Each quarterly cycle progresses through four interconnected phases that build upon one another to foster organizational learning and strategic coordination (see figure 6-2).

1. **Reflect on the current state.** Begin by taking stock of your current situation. Which AI applications are delivering results? Where are people and product teams stuck, or is adoption stalling? What did we learn? Where did things go off course? What collaboration challenges or blind spots emerged?
2. **Revise the six-quarter AI roadmap.** Armed with insights from reflection, recalibrate your forward view. Are your organizational strategic priorities still the same? This quick check is essential because AI often creates new opportunities that shift where competitive advantage can be found. At the same time, emerging customer needs may require different responses, or competitors may have moved in unexpected directions, altering your strategic landscape. This is not a revision of the overall business strategy every quarter, but a revision of your roadmap of AI applications. You need a quick pulse check to continuously validate your organizational strategic priorities to ensure they haven't changed.

Figure 6-2: The quarterly review process

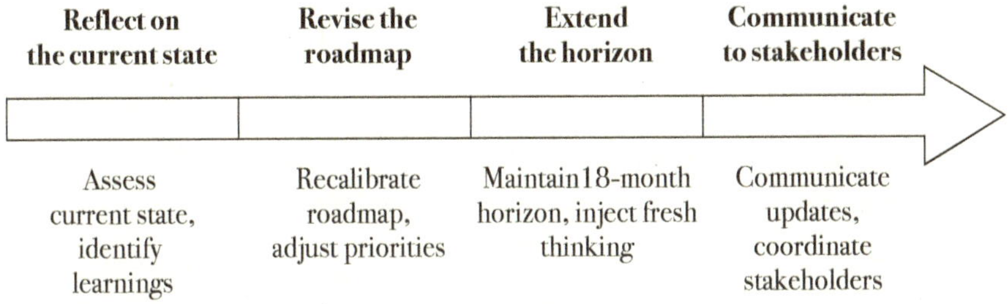

The MVT or AI leader can do that with the company's leadership. Then go back to the prioritized AI applications: Are they still serving the organizational strategic priorities? Should some of the prioritized AI applications be accelerated, paused, or adjusted in focus or scope? This revision process keeps your AI roadmap connected to reality.

3. **Extend the horizon**. Maintain an eighteen-month rolling roadmap, adding new quarters as you complete existing ones. This is also the moment to inject fresh thinking. What's newly possible? What breakthrough opportunities have opened up? How can we adapt our prioritized AI applications to support emerging opportunities?
4. **Communicate the updated roadmap to key internal stakeholders**. Using tailored messaging for different audiences, share the current status of AI applications, what's changing in the AI roadmap, and why. For the board, focus on strategic implications and risk signals. For product and delivery teams, update priorities and timelines. For compliance and ethics, detail any shifts in how you are thinking about risk and how risk oversight needs to change. The goal is to maintain a shared understanding of what's happening and what matters most.

This iterative approach ensures your AI roadmap stays as dynamic as the technology it deploys. Rather than becoming bureaucratic overhead, adaptive reviews evolve into a strategic accelerator that helps you turn AI potential into measurable business impact.

This adaptive rhythm serves as the operating model for AI initiatives. For example, McKinsey & Company intentionally designed the development of their internal generative AI platform, Lilli, as a dynamic, evolving system. Erik Roth, a senior partner who helped lead the initiative, described it in an interview with us as a complex but coordinated effort:

"I created a new operating model with thirteen different work streams that go horizontally, working toward different outcomes and goals. My job . . . is to encourage the progress of each independent work stream while simultaneously facilitating the interdependencies among them. Putting in that operating model was challenging, but now it's in place, it works beautifully, and I can increasingly focus my energy on our forward-looking goalposts."

This structure embodies an adaptive strategy. It's not a static plan but a living system designed to manage the complexity of a firm-wide AI application and continuously incorporate frontier technology. "It is 1,000 percent adaptive, because it has to be, given the nature of the team's management challenge, the technology evolution, and how we're envisioning our business model adapting to all of it," Roth said. For McKinsey, the review process isn't a periodic check-in; it is the core mechanism for driving the entire AI strategy forward.

MAKING AI ROADMAP REVIEWS ACTIONABLE

The test of your adaptive review process is your ability to translate the inevitable, ongoing business, technology, and strategic changes into updates to your AI roadmap, keeping it current and relevant. Many organizations conduct thorough reviews but struggle to ensure their roadmaps accurately reflect changing conditions.

Effective adaptive roadmap reviews create a clear path to planning the subsequent actions. When your Q1 customer service chatbot exceeds expectations, that success should trigger immediate decisions about mobilizing further resource reallocation and accelerating timelines. You could shift the budget from a lower-performing AI application (or from other business initiatives) to expand the chatbot to additional departments ahead of schedule. You could consider accelerating the timeline for your Q3 advanced customer analytics project, given that the chatbot has already established organizational confidence and the necessary technical infrastructure.

If the delivery of AI applications encounters unexpected challenges, your review process should facilitate swift course corrections rather than prolonged analysis. For instance, if work on one of your Q2 AI applications reveals serious data quality issues that weren't apparent during planning, you need to adapt. The change may include adjustments to both timing and workload, incorporating data usability efforts into Q3 more quickly while shifting the AI application's delivery to Q4. The goal is to address setbacks dynamically and maintain overall momentum on the roadmap.

A crucial point to note is that an AI roadmap should be flexible. If AI is delivering clear value faster than other work in the organization, why not allocate more resources to it? Instead of treating department budgets as static and unconnected, consider your budgets through an overall organizational lens and reallocate resources across departments and initiatives based on strategic priorities and the probability of success.

The most successful organizations treat their quarterly reviews as strategic investment decisions. They're constantly asking, "Based on what we've learned, where should we invest our next dollar and our next hour of organizational attention?" This might mean doubling down on successful AI applications and redirecting resources from struggling projects, AI or not, to high-potential opportunities. Alternatively, it can also mean investing in additional tools, personnel, data, and other resources that may have emerged as bottlenecks for an otherwise likely-to-succeed AI application. The key is maintaining a portfolio mindset that optimizes for overall strategic value, rather than protecting individual AI applications or, for that matter, other business initiatives.

PORTFOLIO VERSUS SWIM LANE MINDSET

Organizations managing multiple AI applications face a fundamental choice: treat each as an isolated project (swim lane approach) or manage them as an interconnected portfolio.

The swim lane approach assigns dedicated resources and boundaries to each AI application. This feels organizationally cleaner because it reduces coordination complexity and creates clear accountability. However, it locks resources into predetermined allocations, regardless of performance, prevents learning transfer between applications, and misses opportunities for applications to build upon one another.

The portfolio approach views AI applications as interconnected investments that can mutually reinforce one another. This enables dynamic resource reallocation, which accelerates successful applications while adjusting those that struggle. Applications can be sequenced to build foundations for more ambitious initiatives in the future. Data quality improvements, infrastructure investments, and lessons from organizational change are applied across the entire portfolio.

Most importantly, the portfolio approach prioritizes enterprise-level value over departmental success. Instead of asking, "How is each application performing individually?" you ask, "How is our overall AI investment creating strategic value?" This perspective reveals opportunities to combine applications, adjust timelines, or reallocate resources for greater collective impact.

While the portfolio approach requires stronger governance and coordination, it's essential for creating transformational value rather than a collection of marginal improvements. Organizations that default to swim lanes typically miss the compound competitive advantages that strategic AI deployment can deliver.

COMMUNICATING YOUR SIX-QUARTER WALK

A roadmap that lives only in planning documents will never drive value creation from AI. Your Six-Quarter Walk should become an integral part of your organization's shared language. This common reference point helps everyone understand where AI is headed and how their work contributes to that roadmap.

The communication challenge arises because different internal stakeholders and functions require fundamentally different information from the same roadmap. Your executive team wants to see how AI applications connect to business objectives and what investment levels will help you achieve desired outcomes. Your AI delivery and engineering teams require operational details in order to understand precisely what they're building, when it needs to be delivered, and how success will be measured.

Your board and governance (compliance, risk, legal) stakeholders need confidence that AI initiatives serve the overall business strategy while maintaining appropriate levels of risk and ensuring compliance with relevant regulations.

Meanwhile, the broader organization seeks to understand the impact of AI on their daily work, the new opportunities AI presents for professional development, and the potential contributions of people to AI's success.

Rather than creating separate roadmaps for each audience, a core roadmap can be customized as needed to share through different lenses. Begin with your comprehensive Six-Quarter Walk, then create customized views that highlight the information most relevant to each stakeholder group. For executives, highlight quarterly business impact and resource allocation. For engineering and delivery teams, focus on specific timelines and technical dependencies. For the broader organization, highlight how AI will enhance employees' work experience by allowing them to dedicate time to strategic and less mundane work than in the past.

The key to effective communication is maintaining consistency in your core messages while varying the details and emphasis. Every conversation about your roadmap should reinforce that AI serves business strategy, not technology exploration; that value delivery is continuous while building toward transformation; that everyone has a role in creating AI value; and that adaptation based on learning is expected and healthy.

Your communication approach should also evolve as your roadmap progresses. Early communications focus on vision and possibility to help stakeholders understand AI's potential and their role in realizing it. As you begin delivering AI applications, communications will shift toward progress and learning–sharing success stories, addressing challenges, and demonstrating continuous value delivery. Over time, your communications will shift to focus on sustained value, transformation and future opportunities, and demonstrating AI's role in driving organizational success and competitive advantage.

Remember that communication about your roadmap isn't just about sharing information; it's about organizational change management. Every conversation is an opportunity to build confidence in AI's value, reinforce strategic priorities, and unify an organization around shared objectives. The quality of your roadmap communication often determines whether AI creates value in your organization or remains a collection of interesting but disconnected experiments. We will go deeper into communications and change management in chapter 9.

YOUR WEEK 6 ACTION PLAN

This week focuses on translating your prioritized AI applications into a concrete, actionable roadmap for delivery and ongoing value creation. Complete these activities to create your Six-Quarter Walk and establish the foundation for dynamic AI execution.

- **Create your initial Six-Quarter Walk.** Using your prioritized AI applications from chapter 5, sequence actions and work across six quarters using the step-by-step process in this chapter. Focus on quarterly value delivery to build compound value throughout the year.
- **Define quarterly value outcomes.** Specify the quantitative and qualitative outcomes each quarter will deliver. Ensure every quarter contributes meaningfully to your strategic objectives.
- **Establish your adaptive review process.** Set up quarterly review sessions using this framework: Reflect → Revise → Extend the horizon → Communicate the updated roadmap. Don't wait. Plan for and schedule the first AI roadmap review for thc end of your first quarter of delivery.
- **Develop a stakeholder communication approach.** Create tailored views of your roadmap for different audiences. Prepare initial communication materials that explain the Six-Quarter Walk approach and its strategic importance.

SUMMARY

You've now completed Week 6 of your 90-day AI blueprint and created the strategic backbone for AI value creation in your organization.

In this chapter, you accomplished these objectives:

- **Grasped why speed creates strategic advantage** in AI, learning how quarterly value delivery compounds over time.
- **Mastered the Six-Quarter Walk framework** for balancing strategic ambition with reality through rolling eighteen-month planning.
- **Learned to sequence AI applications** for ongoing impact that compounds and builds on itself over time.
- **Created a dynamic planning process** through adaptive reviews that keep your roadmap relevant as conditions change.

- **Developed stakeholder communication approaches** that maintain strategic coherence while serving different information needs.

You now have a concrete roadmap that delivers clear benefits and momentum every quarter while also building compound value for transformational impact over time.

With your roadmap complete, you're ready to move on to chapter 7, where you'll begin to assemble the building blocks your AI roadmap will need to turn a plan into concrete deliverables.

A goal without a plan is just a wish. A plan without foundations is just a dream.

—Adapted from Antoine de Saint-Exupéry

Seven

FOCUSING ON AI'S BUILDING BLOCKS

CHRIS STARED at her ambitious AI roadmap with equal parts excitement and anxiety. As CEO at a midsize financial services firm, she'd spent weeks identifying high-impact AI opportunities with her team and building a compelling AI roadmap. Routine transaction automation, customer service enhancement through an AI voice agent, AI-powered investment research and market insights—the possibilities seemed endless.

But late at night, questions kept her awake: "Do we have what it takes to make this happen? How will this work when our data is scattered across dozens of systems? Why does half of our senior team still think AI is hype? Can we proceed when our processes take months for even simple technology changes?"

Chris's dilemma is universal. Every organization seeking to deploy AI for value creation faces a common reality check: a gap between its strategy and the ability to deliver on its roadmap. You can have the world's most brilliant AI vision, but it cannot become a reality without the right building blocks. This week combines strategic planning with assembly of the building blocks to deliver on your AI roadmap.

Here are your objectives for this week:

- **Discover the four building blocks** for AI that you must establish to deliver on your roadmap.
- **Conduct strategic assessments** of your organization's readiness across each building block.
- **Identify critical gaps** that could slow your roadmap delivery.

- **Develop a targeted plan** for strengthening expertise while maintaining momentum.
- **Prepare for the following four chapters**, each focused on building one of these essential foundations.

This isn't about whether you're ready enough to start with AI—you are as ready as you'll ever be. It's about identifying what you need to start delivering value from AI, recognizing existing gaps, and planning how to address those gaps. Think of it as a preflight systems check. You're cleared for takeoff, but ensuring all systems function optimally is the key to a smooth flight, avoiding turbulence or delays.

THE FOUR BUILDING BLOCKS OF AI VALUE CREATION

Four building blocks are essential to deliver AI applications that create value (see figure 7-1):

- **Mindset:** The organizational culture and behaviors that enable AI adoption, including the speed, focus, experimentation, customer-centricity, and learning orientation that AI adoption and value creation require.
- **Skill set:** The human talent and ability to create, scale, grow, manage, and use AI, from AI fluency to collaboration skills that turn employees into effective AI partners to the sophistication required for developing AI systems.
- **Toolset:** The way in which you assemble the components of AI systems, the data and models that make AI possible, and the orchestration and consumption layers that make it usable. This encompasses how you think, now and in the future, about the systems that power AI, the data that fuels it, the models that help make sense of it, the ability to coordinate various AI components, and the interface for use, maintenance, and deriving value.
- **Decision set:** The governance frameworks and processes for making AI choices quickly and responsibly, including decision-making speed, authority, clarity, and cross-functional coordination that enables innovation while managing risk.

Figure 7-1: The four building blocks of AI value creation

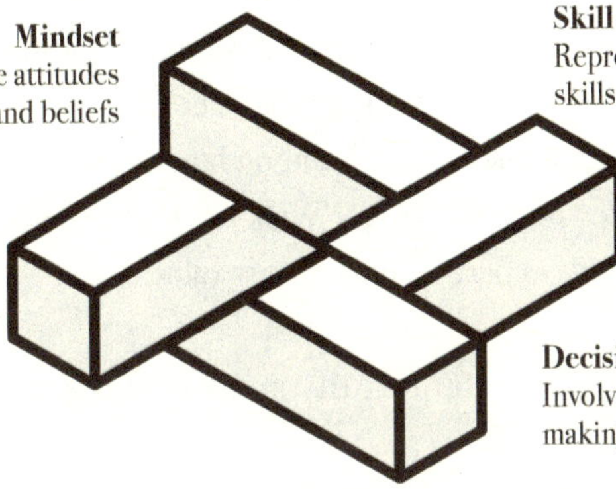

These building blocks support and reinforce one another. AI skill sets enable value-driving mindsets, which create future-proof toolsets that support decision-making for greater value, ultimately accelerating and amplifying skill set development.

We'll go into greater detail about how to develop each of the building blocks in chapters 8 through 11. The purpose of this week is to understand how each building block supports your roadmap of AI applications, determine whether you have them in place, and if not, what it would take to implement them and add their development to your AI roadmap.

ASSESSING YOUR AI BUILDING BLOCKS: A THREE-PHASE APPROACH

This week, you'll conduct a focused diagnostic of your organization's readiness to deliver on your AI roadmap. This isn't a comprehensive readiness assessment–it's a targeted evaluation designed to identify gaps that could slow your roadmap delivery.

The approach includes three phases:

- **Phase 1: Building blocks assessments and conversations**. Conduct focused assessments and use them in conversation with your team to discuss building blocks. These conversations reveal where your organization currently stands in terms of mindset, skill set, toolset, and decision set strengths.

- **Phase 2: Gap analysis**. Map your current state against the requirements of your prioritized AI applications. Categorize each building block element as ready, developing, or gap to identify where targeted investment is needed.
- **Phase 3: Integration planning**. Weave building block development into your Six-Quarter Walk to create a unified roadmap that builds expertise and delivers value.

This diagnostic helps you identify areas needing attention and maintain momentum.

BUILDING BLOCK 1: THE AI MINDSET

Mindset represents your organization's cultural ability to create value with AI—the leadership behaviors, risk tolerance, and learning orientation that determine whether AI initiatives thrive or stall. This building block shapes how quickly you can move, how well you handle AI's inherent uncertainty, and whether employees feel safe and encouraged to experiment with new approaches.

Here are key indicators of an AI-ready mindset:

- Leadership moves quickly from identifying AI opportunities to developing and delivering AI applications.
- Employees view AI setbacks as learning opportunities, not failures.
- The organization naturally prioritizes customer value over departmental silos.

AI value creation is particularly dependent on breaking down silos. Without that, the value from AI would remain narrow and unable to reach its full potential across an organization, its customers, and its stakeholders.

Here are key indicators of mindset challenges:

- Decision-making cycles take months rather than days.
- Failures often trigger blame and finger-pointing rather than serving as opportunities for learning.

- Departments often prioritize protecting their data and processes over collaboration, which can hinder their ability to benefit customers and drive overall AI value creation for the organization.

It's important to have a conversation with colleagues, including team members, to help you assess whether mindset—a critical AI building block—is in place in your organization, and if not, what it would take to get there.

The mindset assessment: How does culture enable us to create value with AI? Your mindset assessment examines whether your organizational beliefs, behaviors, and leadership approaches support what AI value creation depends on—namely, speed, focus, experimentation, customer value, and continuous learning.

Consider speed first. AI evolves rapidly, and competitive advantages can either vanish or emerge overnight. Ask your leadership and team members, "How fast can we move from planning an AI application to having it ready to serve customers at scale?" If the answer involves multiple quarters of planning, approval, and implementation cycles, your culture is foreign to the AI mindset and needs to change.

Next, examine how your organization approaches uncertainty, a characteristic of the pace of AI development and change. AI models develop, evolve, and swap places, performing differently than expected. Breakthroughs often emerge from unexpected directions. How does your organizational culture handle this kind of uncertainty? Is there an understanding that it's there, and so plans and roadmaps include built-in flexibility? Or does your organization demand detailed, rigid, up-front plans with stagnant timelines and guaranteed, unchangeable outcomes?

In addition to uncertainty, consider how your organization handles failure and learning. The development and deployment of AI will inevitably produce setbacks—AI applications that, at scale, do not meet the expectations of prototypes, models that don't perform as expected, and implementations that require course corrections. Do leaders and employees treat setbacks as learning opportunities or as evidence that AI initiatives are problematic? Is there sufficient psychological safety for employees to take calculated risks in pursuit of innovative solutions? The answers to these questions will indicate whether you have an AI mindset that prioritizes speed, focus, experimentation, customer value, and continuous learning.

Customer value, or centricity, deserves special attention in your mindset assessment. AI's ability to create value requires breaking down silos, sharing data across departments, and thinking through the lens of a customer, not an individual department or product. Does your culture naturally organize around customer value, or do departmental boundaries create friction that could limit the impact of AI? If the latter, how can you establish the mindset building block for creating AI value?

BUILDING BLOCK 2: THE AI SKILL SET

Skill set encompasses your employees' ability to work effectively with AI, including everything from leaders who understand the strategic implications to frontline employees who collaborate confidently with AI tools. Skill sets aren't just about coding skills or deep technical expertise; they encompass pragmatic knowledge and the practical application of AI in everyday workflows, as well as collaboration with nonhuman tools such as AI agents.

Key indicators of a strong skill set include the following:

- Employees know when and how to use AI tools, which AI recommendations to trust, and how to maximize the benefits of AI for customer benefit and across the full scope of their organization.
- Leaders evaluate their companies' strategies and understand how AI can help achieve them, solve top problems, and seize opportunities that were previously impossible.
- Tech teams strike a balance between buying and building with AI vendors, staying as up-to-date as possible in the face of the rapid pace of technological evolution.

Key indicators of skill set gaps include the following:

- Employees tend to avoid or use AI tools sparingly, outside of their everyday workflow, missing the opportunity to learn from them.
- Training initiatives struggle with low adoption or fail to translate into practical skills.

- Leaders are often swayed by competitive pressure, news headlines, or board expectations and push their people to develop lengthy lists of AI use cases without a cohesive unification around their business strategy and top priorities.
- Or worse, leaders wait on the sidelines, expecting others to figure it out before they even get started.

The fundamental challenge isn't technical complexity–it's fear. Employees worry about job security, question whether they can develop AI fluency, and lack confidence in their ability to work effectively with AI systems. Without addressing these human concerns and building AI fluency across the organization, a company will struggle to create value with even the most sophisticated AI roadmap.

As with mindset, it's essential to discuss this with your colleagues and team members to help you understand if the skill set block is in place within your organization, and if not, what it would take to achieve it.

The skill set assessment: How can our people deliver on this roadmap?
Begin by assessing your workforce's ability to deliver on your AI priorities, specifically asking whether they can effectively use AI tools in their everyday work.

Begin by asking your leadership team, "When we look at our top AI priorities, do our senior leaders understand AI's strategic implications well enough to guide decisions, allocate resources, and navigate inevitable challenges?" A CEO who cannot effectively integrate AI applications into their company's strategy, a CIO who can't competently evaluate AI vendor proposals, or a department head who doesn't understand AI's limitations is a clear indicator of skill set gaps in critical areas of the organization.

Next, examine workforce readiness through the lens of your prioritized AI applications. If customer care enhancement is a key initiative for your AI deployment, does the customer service team understand how to work effectively with AI tools? Can they evaluate AI-generated responses for quality and appropriateness? Do they know when to override AI recommendations in favor of human judgment?

The conversation with your leadership or other team members around the AI skill set should surface specific gaps. For example, your customer-experience team might consider deploying an AI assistant for technical support. Still, they can't distinguish between accurate AI responses and plausible-sounding errors that, if not curbed, could damage customer relationships. Or, your salespeople may be eager to use AI for proposal writing. Still, the reality is that they struggle to guide AI in capturing your company's unique value proposition, resulting in generic industry content.

Your skill set assessment reveals not just current gaps but also learning velocity–how quickly your organization can develop AI fluency and AI value-creation skills. An organization with strong learning systems and high employee engagement will close skill gaps more rapidly than one where training initiatives typically struggle with adoption. (We will dive deeper into this in chapter 9.)

BUILDING BLOCK 3: THE AI TOOLSET

The AI toolset encompasses your technical foundation for AI value creation–the data, models, coordination and orchestration of models, and user interfaces that make it all accessible. This is where the skill set and mindset also play significant roles.

The AI toolset requires flexibility to scale effectively and sustainably, despite the rapid pace of technological change. In short, your AI toolset is a flexible system of assembled, swappable components rather than a monolithic platform that the organization cannot easily disassemble and reassemble as new technological developments emerge.

Key indicators of a strong AI toolset include the following:

- Your organization captures and reveres data as a strategic asset, making it available and usable for AI models.
- AI applications can quickly access relevant data from multiple sources across the organization, regardless of departmental boundaries.
- You can easily swap AI models and features as they become available and improve.
- New components to the toolset integrate seamlessly into existing workflows, rather than requiring massive, lengthy, and expensive changes.

Key indicators of toolset gaps include the following:

- Data exists but remains trapped in departmental silos or is unusable due to poor formats and a lack of consistency in basic data elements.
- Traditional monolithic IT systems architecture decisions lock you into inflexible tech infrastructure.
- AI implementations require heavy integrations rather than microservice connectivity, or employees need to access AI tools outside of their everyday workflows, which slows down use and harms user adoption.

Again, conversations with your colleagues and team members are key to understanding whether the toolset is in place in your organization, and if not, what it would take to implement it.

The toolset assessment: How can data and systems support AI value creation? Your toolset assessment evaluates whether your existing data and technology systems can support your AI roadmap both today and as it scales. This assessment extends beyond verifying that you have sufficient storage and computing power to build flexible systems that can adapt to rapidly advancing technology.

Start with data. Data availability and quality are integral to creating value with AI. Does your organization capture the data that your prioritized AI applications would need? For example, building AI applications to prevent customer churn is impossible without capturing data on customer behavior. If you do capture the data, is it current? Are key data elements defined and accessible in technology systems? Perhaps more importantly, can you quickly source and use different data when new AI opportunities emerge?

Next, consider AI system flexibility. AI models, tools, and approaches advance monthly, if not daily. Your internal AI system architecture should enable you to swap components–models, algorithms, and software frameworks–without requiring rebuilds. Organizations locked into inflexible technology system architectures struggle to capitalize on AI advances or face costly migrations or rebuilds from scratch.

Next, examine how you deploy AI tools and whether they are accessible in employees' daily workflows. The most successful AI applications seamlessly integrate into existing workflows, eliminating the need for users to learn new systems, follow different processes, or take lengthy steps to access the tools. Can AI applications integrate seamlessly within or adjacent to your current systems? Or will AI deployment take employees so far from their current workflows that adoption stalls and value fails to materialize?

Next, think about scalability. As AI adoption expands organization-wide, can your infrastructure support increased use without performance degradation? Can your technical people manage more complex AI systems without becoming bottlenecks? However, scalability is not only a technical capacity but an organization's ability to absorb and embrace change. This is where the mindset and skill set building blocks come into play again.

BUILDING BLOCK 4: THE AI DECISION SET

This building block encompasses your organization's ability to make AI-related choices with appropriate speed and oversight using governance processes, authority structures, and coordination mechanisms that determine whether AI will create value.

Key indicators of an effective AI decision set include the following:

- Low-risk AI decisions typically occur within hours or days.
- Decision-making authority is apparent for different types of AI choices.
- Cross-functional teams can quickly make choices around shared AI priorities without lengthy approval processes. There is no drawn-out consensus-building process or bureaucratic structure in place.
- At the same time, a clear mechanism is in place to control and minimize risk exposure, ensuring that the company's data, customers, employees, and reputation are protected.

Key indicators of decision set challenges include the following:

- Even simple AI decisions require weeks or months of deliberation.
- The decision-making authority for AI choices is unclear or constantly shifting.

- Different departments struggle to coordinate effectively, leading to bottlenecks that hinder AI initiatives.
- Excessive governance stifles even the slightest attempt at a new approach or test of new tools.
- In contrast to the above, there is no mechanism for controlling the use of AI tools or the development of AI models. Without it, the company's data, customers, employees, and reputation are unprotected.

Conversations with colleagues will help you understand if the decision set is in place in your organization, and if not, what it would take to get there.

The decision set assessment: How can we make AI choices quickly and responsibly?

Your decision set assessment evaluates your organization's ability to make AI-related decisions with the necessary speed while maintaining appropriate oversight. This building block often determines whether AI initiatives gain momentum or get trapped in analysis paralysis.

Start by understanding how your organization makes decisions regarding various AI choices. Low-risk decisions–such as adopting proven productivity tools within established security guidelines–should receive a green light quickly, often within a few days. Higher-risk decisions–like implementing AI systems that directly impact customers or involve sensitive data–require more deliberation but shouldn't take months. The decision could be a "no" or "not now," but it should not drag out and take attention away from other, perhaps more worthwhile AI opportunities for value creation.

Next, examine the clarity of decision-making authority across your organization. For every type of AI decision your roadmap will require, someone should have clear accountability. This person needs not just decision-making authority but sufficient resources and organizational support to implement them effectively. A lack of clarity around accountability can lead to delays, even for simple choices.

Then, consider cross-functional coordination, especially for AI applications that span multiple departments. Can cross-domain groups–such as technology, legal, compliance, and individual business units–rally quickly around shared priorities for AI value creation? Do you have processes that efficiently bring together different perspectives rather than create serial approval bottlenecks?

Next, assess your organization's ability to strike a balance between innovation and the responsible and ethical use of AI. Effective AI governance sifts through various categories of risk, enabling the identification of smart risks. Does your decision-making approach help people understand boundaries within which they can use and deploy AI quickly, or does it default to lengthy review processes? With the pace of AI today, the greatest risk of all is failing to keep up with the speed of change.

Lastly, consider how your board is involved in providing appropriate guidance in a highly dynamic and transformative space. Boards do not typically become operational, but they do need to be aware of the organization's deployment of revolutionary technology such as AI.

YOUR BUILDING BLOCKS DIAGNOSTIC

Now that you understand what each building block encompasses and have the frameworks to assess them, it's time to determine where your organization stands. The goal is to identify specific gaps that could slow delivery of your prioritized AI applications, allowing you to address them while maintaining momentum.

Consider this a focused diagnostic rather than a comprehensive organizational assessment. You're looking for practical answers to practical questions: Can we deliver our Q1 customer service AI using our current skill set? Do our decision-making processes support the speed our roadmap requires? Will our data systems enable the personalization engine we've planned for Q3?

This diagnostic reveals where targeted investment will have the most significant impact on your ability to create value with AI. Some gaps can be addressed quickly, while establishing a governance framework may take weeks. Others require longer-term development; building AI literacy across your workforce could take quarters. The key is understanding what you need, when you need it, and how to sequence development alongside value delivery.

Have the conversations. Use the frameworks from each building block section above to understand your organization's current standing. Don't overthink this–schedule ninety minutes with your MVT or AI leader and work through all four building blocks. Focus on two simple questions for each: Where do we stand today? What gaps could slow delivery of our prioritized AI applications?

The assessments and conversations will provide you with the insights you need to act. Perhaps your leadership makes decisions quickly, but employees are concerned that AI will replace them. Or you have strong technical expertise but weak AI literacy among the people who'll actually use these tools. Document what you discover—you'll need these insights for the next step.

Spot the gaps. Create a simple diagnostic summary that indicates what's ready, what's in development, and what is still missing (see figure 7-2). Pay special attention to timing. If your Q2 application requires trained staff and governance processes that take twelve weeks to develop, you should start immediately.

Look for investments that serve multiple AI applications. For instance, data integration challenges affecting three initiatives take precedence over the skills needed for a single application. These shared investments create value across your entire roadmap.

Update your roadmap. Add building block development to your Six-Quarter Walk to build capacity while delivering value (see figure 7-3). Some development can happen alongside AI applications, such as training customer service staff while piloting the chatbot. Other foundations, such as data governance, must be ready first before implementing customer analytics.

Consider whether successful AI applications should trigger the reallocation of resources from other business initiatives. If your Q1 customer service AI exceeds expectations, should you accelerate expansion rather than sticking to predetermined budgets? Your building block development should be as dynamic as your AI applications.

Focus on the one or two building blocks where targeted investment will have the most direct impact on enabling your strategic AI applications to succeed. Don't try to strengthen everything at once. Use early wins to build momentum for broader building block development, and remember: You're not waiting for perfect readiness. You're building what you need while creating value, which is the only approach that works at AI's speed.

You'll now have a single integrated roadmap—your master plan that both puts in place the building blocks of AI and starts to deliver value from prioritized AI

Figure 7-2: Building blocks gap analysis example: AI chatbot for common inquiries

BUILDING BLOCK	CURRENT STATE	REQUIRED BY	DEVELOPMENT TIME	START BY	SHARED NEED?
Skill set					
Customer service AI training	Gap	Q2 launch	6 weeks	Late Q1	Yes, affects Q3 voice agent
Conversational design skills	Ready	Q2 launch	N/A	N/A	No
Escalation management	Ready	Q2 launch	N/A	N/A	No
Mindset					
Openness to AI assistance	Ready	Q2 launch	N/A	N/A	No
Customer-first culture	Ready	Q2 launch	N/A	N/A	Yes, affects all applications

Comfort with automation	Developing	Q2 launch	4 weeks	Q1	Yes, affects Q4 analytics
Toolset					
Customer data integration	Gap	Q1 pilot	12 weeks	Start now	Yes, enables Q3 personalization
Conversational AI platform	Gap	Q2 launch	8 weeks	Late Q1	No
Performance monitoring	Ready	Q2 launch	N/A	N/A	Yes, needed for all AI apps
Decision set					
Privacy agreements	Gap	Q1 pilot	4 weeks	Start now	Yes, covers all customer data AI
Tool approval process	Gap	Q2 launch	6 weeks	Late Q1	Yes, needed for all AI tools
Quality assurance workflow	Gap	Q2 launch	3 weeks	Mid Q2	No

applications. Traditional approaches require that you do these essential types of work sequentially, building the foundation first, and only then starting work on use cases to build upon. But that's not how it works with AI. Linear and stepwise thinking no longer apply.

AI transformation doesn't follow the consultants' neat PowerPoint slides with their tidy, sequential steps. It's messier. Coordination occurs across lanes, not in a lockstep sequence.

Understanding these building blocks conceptually is one thing; seeing how they work together in practice is another. The reality is that successful AI transformation requires simultaneous progress across all four building blocks, each reinforcing the others within real-world constraints and competitive pressures.

CASE STUDY: ONE BANK'S INTEGRATED APPROACH TO AI BUILDING BLOCKS

A large pan-European banking group, which asked not to be named, demonstrates how the four AI building blocks must work together. Their experience reveals both the interdependencies between building blocks and the real-world constraints that shape AI transformation in highly regulated industries.

The chief data and analytics officer (CDAO) described in an interview with us a transformation that required simultaneous progress across multiple fronts: "The big benefits of AI don't come from the technology department. They come from the business. But the business needs to understand its processes deeply to identify where AI can truly transform them."

BUILDING MINDSET AND SKILL SET TOGETHER

The bank faced overwhelming demand for AI training, far exceeding its technical team's capacity. "It's too sexy for everybody to jump onto the bandwagon even if they don't understand what it is," the CDAO explained to us. And senior leadership needed time to grasp that AI transformation wouldn't happen overnight and required substantial foundational work.

Their solution illustrates the interconnected nature of AI building blocks. Unable to scale technical training fast enough, they developed

Figure 7-3: Example: Integrating building block development into the AI roadmap

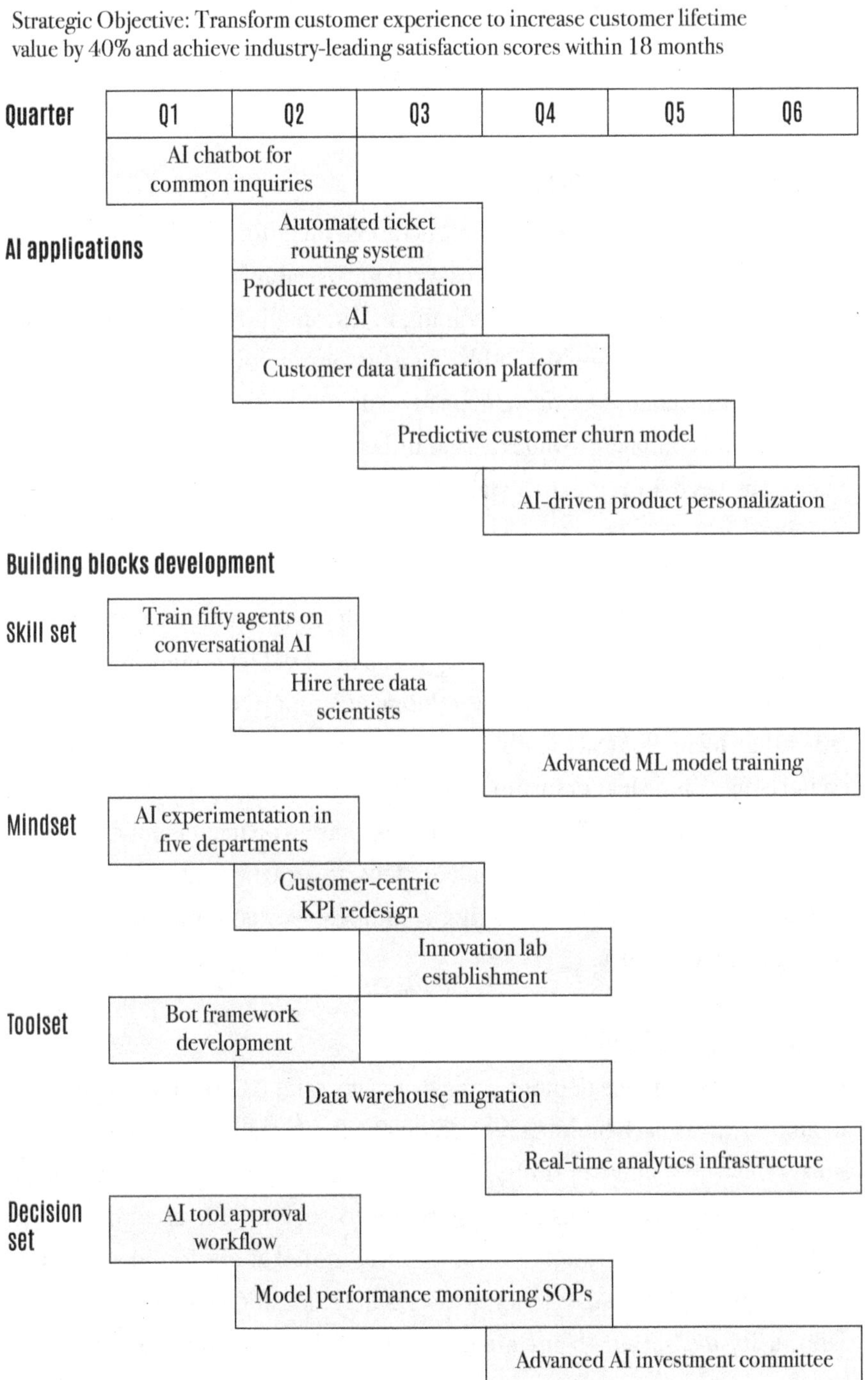

multiplicators—business experts who could translate AI capabilities within their domains. This approach revealed that effective business translators naturally specialize, leading the bank to focus initially on three core areas: risk, finance, and technology.

TOOLSET CONSTRAINED BY DECISION SET

Operating under strict European regulations, including GDPR and the EU AI Act, the bank's technical choices were inextricably linked to governance requirements. "With the AI Act coming in Europe, it is unthinkable to use large language models on the public domain for our company information," the CDAO explained. This drove them toward private cloud deployment—more expensive but compliant—while constantly balancing cutting-edge capabilities against the need for regulatory stability.

GOVERNANCE ENABLING ALL FOUR BUILDING BLOCKS

The bank established a formal AI program with cross-functional governance, led by the CDO, CFO, head of strategy, and head of technology. This structure ensured that their resource development supported strategic priorities rather than technological possibilities. They established a steering committee comprising senior leaders from across business, technology, and strategy functions, supported by five working groups focused on implementation, risk, ethics, legal, and people development. This governance structure enabled systematic progress while managing complexity across multiple countries and regulatory regimes.

THE INTEGRATION LESSON

The bank's experience demonstrates that successful AI transformation isn't about perfecting each building block individually—it's about creating a coherent system where mindset shifts, skill development, technical infrastructure, and governance frameworks work together to enable value creation within real-world constraints. As the bank's CDAO noted about foundational requirements, "Just because generative AI is here doesn't mean we can ignore data quality and lineage. If anything, these issues become even more critical."

Their approach demonstrates that building blocks develop through use, rather than in preparation for use. Each AI application they deployed strengthened multiple building blocks simultaneously, creating compound benefits that accelerated their overall ability to implement AI.

YOUR WEEK 7 ACTION PLAN

This week focuses on assessing your organization's readiness to deliver on your AI roadmap and integrating building block development into your strategic plan. Your goal is to identify where targeted investment will have the most significant impact on your ability to create value with AI.

- **Conduct your building blocks conversations.** Use the assessment frameworks provided in each building block section to evaluate your organization's strengths and weaknesses across mindset, skill set, toolset, and decision set. Schedule ninety minutes with your MVT or AI leader to work through all four areas, focusing on current readiness and potential gaps.
- **Create your diagnostic summary.** Map your current state against your prioritized AI applications using the ready/developing/gap framework in figure 7-2. Include timing requirements and identify shared investments that serve multiple initiatives.
- **Identify integration opportunities.** Focus on building block development that can happen alongside AI application delivery rather than developing infrastructure that must be ready beforehand. Focus on shared resources that create value across your roadmap.
- **Update your Six-Quarter Walk.** Integrate building block development requirements into your AI roadmap to create a unified plan that builds expertise while delivering value.
- **Determine your immediate priorities.** Based on your diagnosis, identify the one or two building blocks where targeted investment will most directly enable your strategic AI applications to succeed.

SUMMARY

You've now completed Week 7 of your 90-day AI blueprint and established a clear understanding of what your organization needs to deliver on its AI roadmap.

In this chapter, you accomplished the following:

- **Identified the four building blocks** essential for AI value creation: mindset (organizational culture), skill set (human expertise), toolset (technical foundation), and decision set (governance processes).
- **Conducted a focused diagnostic** to assess current readiness against your specific AI roadmap requirements rather than pursuing generic AI readiness.
- **Learned to integrate building block development** into your AI roadmap, enabling simultaneous capability building and value delivery instead of sequential foundation-then-application work.
- **Understood the interconnected nature** of building blocks through real-world examples, learning that successful AI transformation requires coordinated progress across all four areas.
- **Established priorities for immediate action** based on which building blocks will most directly enable your strategic AI applications to succeed.

You now have a comprehensive roadmap that addresses both AI application delivery and the foundations needed to support sustained AI value creation. This integrated approach ensures you're building what you need while creating value, which is the only approach that works at AI's speed.

Now that your building blocks assessment is complete, you're ready to dive deep into developing each building block. The following four chapters will provide detailed guidance on strengthening your organization's mindset, skill set, toolset, and decision set to accelerate AI value creation.

Culture eats strategy for breakfast.

–Attributed to Peter Drucker

Eight
ESTABLISHING THE AI MINDSET

AT A LARGE REGIONAL BANK, the customer service department just finished testing an AI prototype. The results were stunning: Hold times dropped by 40 percent, reps were resolving issues faster with AI support tools that pulled up relevant data in seconds, and customer satisfaction surged.

But in the weekly leadership meeting, tension crackled.

"It's not scalable," said Sam, the head of operations. "The testing team was unusually tech savvy. Our other call centers will never adopt this so smoothly."

Across the table, Lee from HR added, "People are already anxious. You bring this in too fast, and you'll have walkouts. We need to slow this way down."

The AI team lead looked stunned. "But the pilot team *loved* it. They said it made their jobs easier, not harder."

Silence.

Finally, the CEO spoke. "We keep saying we want transformation. But every time we get a win, we protect the status quo. Are we thinking about this the right way?"

That's a moment every organization reaches when it tries to transition from AI exploration to adoption. It's not the technology that gets in the way. It's the mindset. Not just among customer-facing employees or operational staff but also in leadership, middle management, and the very structures meant to support change.

Developing skills without the right mindset is like planting seeds on barren ground. We've repeatedly seen companies hire skilled people and launch promising AI initiatives, only to watch momentum stall as organizational thinking resists change. A study from MIT found that 95 percent of AI initiatives fail.[1] Legacy processes, internal politics, and confusion about priorities block progress.

It wasn't the tech that failed. Or the people. It was the mindset.

Here are some actions to take this week:

- See how AI transformation creates unique mindset challenges that require new approaches.
- Learn three essential actions to shift organizational thinking and ensure AI execution success.
- Apply a systematic approach to changing entrenched beliefs and behaviors.
- Create practices that reinforce AI-ready mindsets across your organization.

The greater your ambitions for value from AI and the more transformation you need, the more your mindset must change. If you're paving the future, your thinking can't remain stuck in the past.

WHY TRANSFORMATION IS HARD—ESPECIALLY WITH AI

We've been here before. In 1999, the idea of buying shoes online, much less on a mobile device, seemed absurd to most people. "Who would trust sizing without trying them on?" skeptics asked. However, by 2004, e-commerce had transformed retail and created new customer expectations, forcing every business to think digitally first.

The companies that succeeded during that transformation weren't necessarily those with the best technology; they were the ones that completely changed their approach to business. They reimagined customer relationships, operational processes, and the very concept of value creation.

The same resistance patterns that have repeated across twenty-five years of digital transformation efforts have surfaced with AI: People and organizations often use excuses such as industry complexity, uncertainty, and a lack of existing behavior to justify their resistance to adoption, when in fact they are actually resisting the new technology. The same adoption challenges arise: Technical expertise outpaces organizational readiness. The same cultural barriers surface: Existing ways of working are protected, even when processes become outdated. The same inertia settles: We stick to what we know, even when it's holding us back.

But emerging tech requires a leap of faith. The winners in these transformations are the companies and people who make that leap, reimagine behaviors, reinvent themselves, and revolutionize what they do and how they do it.

LEGO: A CASE STUDY IN CULTURAL AND MINDSET TRANSFORMATION

The LEGO Group's journey provides a vivid illustration of how a deeply rooted culture and collective mindset can make–or break–a company's strategic ambitions. Over the past two decades, LEGO has undergone two remarkable transformations, each anchored not simply in leadership or technology but in a fundamental shift in how the organization thinks and behaves.

By 2003, LEGO was teetering on the edge of bankruptcy.[2] Years of overexpansion and organizational silos had clouded its purpose and eroded profitability. The crisis required more than financial restructuring; it demanded a complete recalibration of culture and mindset. Under new leadership, LEGO rejected distraction and complexity to refocus on its core–the creative play facilitated by the humble brick. The company encouraged employees to reconnect with the organization's legacy of imagination and quality, thereby fostering a sense of pride and responsibility. Cross-functional collaboration returned, operational discipline took hold, and the organization relearned to listen to its customers.

This turnaround didn't just stabilize LEGO; it established the cultural DNA for innovation, community engagement, and customer-centricity, laying a solid foundation for future growth and resilience.

Two decades later, LEGO faced new challenges from digital disruption, evolving consumer expectations, and the need for sustainable practices. Instead of a top-down overhaul, LEGO engineered a bottom-up cultural movement.[3] Cross-functional "playground builders" championed curiosity, bravery, and a sense of purpose throughout the organization. Technology became a driving force as cloud platforms, agile teams, real-time data, and digital customer engagement transformed ways of working, product design, and the brand's iconic connection with families and growing minds. Sustainability and social responsibility became central to KPIs and daily processes, reflecting a broader evolution of mindset around stewardship and global impact.

Both of LEGO's transformations demonstrate that a successful enterprise strategy, whether AI-driven or otherwise, relies on a collective willingness to rethink core values, embrace change, and cultivate cross-company curiosity and collaboration. For LEGO, culture and mindset weren't an afterthought; they were, and are, the engine for enduring success in a world of speeding technological and market upheaval.

THE FIVE CULTURAL TRAITS OF AN AI-READY ORGANIZATION

The transformation that organizations need to undergo to create value with AI presents unique psychological barriers, unlike those of previous technology changes. Unlike earlier digital shifts, AI challenges people's fundamental sense of worth at work, evolves too rapidly for traditional change management, and triggers perfectionist paralysis when speed is essential. These dynamics reveal why successful AI adoption demands a systematic shift in organizational mindset.

The companies that navigate these challenges successfully cultivate five interconnected traits that eradicate resistance: speed, focus, continuous reinvention, lifelong learning, and customer-centricity (see figure 8-1). These traits overlap and reinforce one another–speed relies on focus, focus enables continuous reinvention, which drives learning, and everything must serve customer needs.

TRAIT 1: SPEED

In AI, speed matters because the technology evolves rapidly, competitive advantages emerge and evaporate in days rather than years, and learning occurs through hands-on experience. Organizations that move quickly with AI face fewer barriers to testing, learning, and adapting their strategies. Every day of delay means falling further behind competitors and failing to meet customer expectations.

Speed involves a certain degree of friction and the willingness to live with it in the interest of driving value with AI. In many organizations, entrenched cultures often justify the lack of speed by citing the need for alignment. But, in our experience, "alignment" is usually code for resistance. There is a key difference between alignment and the processes of engaging, encouraging, and inspiring organizations. The latter occurs when speed is present, as it drives results, and these results help

Figure 8-1: The five traits of an AI-ready culture

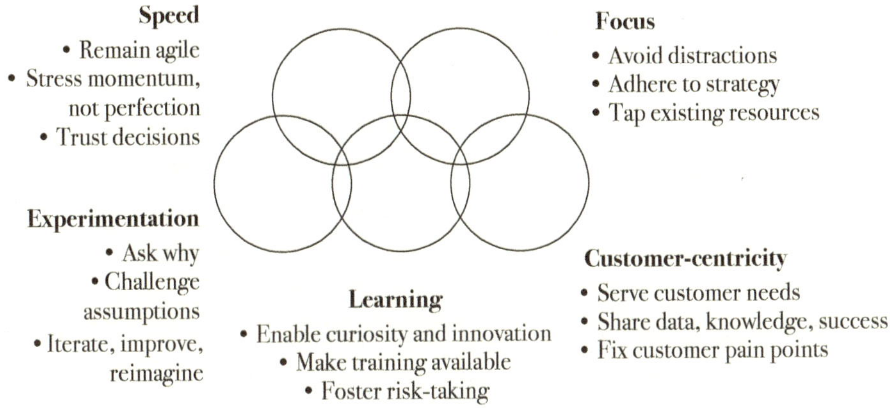

transformations gain momentum.

However, achieving a complete organizational consensus is unrealistic when inherently disruptive technologies enter the workplace. The reality is that not everyone will be on board, as not everyone will see things the same way or be supportive. Visionary leaders committed to creating value with AI do the essential work of communicating to win hearts and minds.

This communication goes beyond sharing information; it's about making AI feel human and accessible. Leaders who succeed at winning hearts and minds focus on three key elements: humanizing the technology by sharing relatable stories of how AI helps real people solve real problems; amplifying the positive by consistently highlighting AI's transformative potential rather than dwelling on disruption; and creating visibility for early wins and advocates who can demonstrate value to skeptical colleagues. Successful leaders understand that fear of AI often stems from its perceived complexity and threat. Hence, they deliberately craft messages that position AI as an empowering tool that enhances humans rather than replaces them.

Organizations that create value with AI are intentional about speed. They don't wait for funding for AI projects or for consensus, because it will never come, or for perfect data, because data is dynamic and transformations are messy. They don't explore every possible tool, vendor, or option for execution; they don't wait for more information, options, use cases, or support. If in life fortune favors the brave, in AI value favors the fast.

In companies, speed manifests in three key behaviors:

- **Choosing iteration over perfection**. Rather than waiting to launch the perfect AI solution, successful organizations embrace an adaptive approach. They start with a minimum viable concept that solves a problem, conduct rapid prototyping, move to deployment, incorporate user feedback throughout, and practice ongoing scaling with real-world performance. This agile mindset prioritizes learning and recognizes that the best AI applications emerge through cycles of building, testing, and refining.
- **Making decisions with incomplete information**. AI solutions rarely come with perfect data or guaranteed outcomes. Organizations acting with speed become comfortable making decisions with, say, 70 percent of the information, rather than waiting for 100 percent. They learn to assess risk, make informed bets, and adjust their course quickly based on new information. Analysis paralysis is particularly dangerous when faced with the unprecedented pace of technology change. While leaders should always strive to gather as much data as possible to make informed decisions, they must also streamline decision-making, reach a decision, and proceed with execution. Chances are, there are only a few wrong decisions and many more right ones. The odds are in favor of those who move fast. And even if they've made a wrong decision, they can course-correct fast because the environment will change anyway, forcing adaptation.
- **Empowering people**. Because everyone rallies around the same priorities (see the "Trait 5" section), there's trust in employees' ability to make sensible choices. This trust enables faster decision-making throughout the organization, eliminates bottlenecks, and allows organizations to move at the speed of opportunity rather than the speed of approval processes. Empowering people has always been a tenet of a healthy organizational culture. In value creation with AI, it's a must. Without that empowerment, decision-making stalls, doubts linger, and people protect themselves but jeopardize their organization's future. It doesn't have to be this way. Instead of centralizing decision-making and emasculating employees, you can win by empowering people through decentralized decision-making.

For example, at GE South Africa, former CEO Nyimpini Mabunda emphasized the need for structural agility to keep pace with transformation. "We need to structure ourselves in a way that we are navigating and moving and course-correcting as we go," Mabunda explained to us in an interview. Instead of static org charts and lengthy decision cycles, he said, GE South Africa organized around flexible squads that enabled faster learning loops and empowered local action.

TRAIT 2: FOCUS

An AI truism: "The good thing about AI is you can do so much with it. The bad thing about AI is . . . you can do so much with it."

Organizations that win with AI singularly focus on delivering what matters most, avoiding distractions from tangential ideas or individual stakeholders' pet projects. This is why the prioritization we covered in chapter 5 and elsewhere is critical. You don't need to gather hundreds of ideas and AI use cases across the organization. Instead, mobilize AI to address your key business challenges and strategic priorities.

Focus helps answer critical questions: What's worth solving? What can wait? What should we say no to, even if it seems interesting or innovative? Without this clarity, organizations scatter their energy across too many initiatives, resulting in exhaustion without achieving breakthroughs.

Here's what focus means:

- **Directing AI to serve top organizational priorities.** Your AI roadmap should directly address the most significant business challenges and opportunities rather than chase novelty, create side projects, or pursue a lab approach that may not address top business needs.
- **Repurposing existing budgets.** Do not fall into the trap of treating AI as a new expense. When you deploy it to solve your top challenges and priorities, the budget you've set aside for them will be there for AI. Remember that AI is not a separate project. It is a technology tool, and it is up to you to use it in the best way you see fit. When you channel AI to address your top challenges and priorities, you will find the budget, resources, and attention to make things happen.

- **Creating effective mechanisms to say no.** Focus involves not just what you do but what you choose not to do. One company we interviewed required people proposing a new AI project to identify an existing project they would stop or eliminate. This focus creates intentional choices about resource allocation and prevents endless accumulation of competing priorities.

TRAIT 3: CONTINUOUS REINVENTION

Organizational transformation begins with reinvention, stemming from the question *Why*? When you ask why, you learn the truth about a company's culture. If the answer you receive is "Because that's how we've always done it," then you know it's time to change. Relentless questioning challenges current thinking in a healthy way, unearths opportunities for reinvention, and formulates the vision for value creation.

In our experience, the questions *why* and *why not* are the keys to reinvention and the roots of AI for value creation. For example, at a venerable financial services firm, the key question was this: "Why can't customers find what they need, even though we have the products, services, and people to help?" The answers led to aggregating and analyzing the customer data of all business entities, gaining insights from the combined dataset that were not possible with siloed data, and developing transformational, customer-centric AI solutions.

Similarly, at a global mobile company, the question became this: "Why can't people live without their phones but so easily switch providers, the very companies that make those devices come to life?" From there came the vision to make the company as indispensable to its customers as the devices it connected for them. At yet other organizations with which we've worked, we frequently heard this question: "Why isn't the business as big as the brand?" This question unearthed the opportunity to focus AI solutions on driving business growth.

Organizations that cultivate continuous reinvention and relentless questioning tap into three critical areas:

- **Challenge assumptions.** Just because a thought has always been there doesn't mean it should continue that way. Questioning surfaces irrelevant vestiges of the past, reminds us of customer needs and wants, and identifies opportunities for transformation.

- **Reveal inconsistencies**. There is often a gap between an organization's stated goals and reality. For example, a company may claim to prioritize customer-first values, yet still require customers to navigate five different departments to resolve a simple issue. AI can bridge these gaps by creating unified customer experiences that deliver on stated promises. When you map stated values against actual customer journeys, the disconnects become obvious opportunities for AI-powered solutions.
- **Refine the metrics**. Traditional metrics often measure internal efficiency rather than customer value. AI enables organizations to track what really matters—for example, customer effort scores instead of call resolution times, or predictive satisfaction indicators rather than lagging complaint volumes. Predictive AI identifies patterns in customer interactions, revealing which metrics correlate with business outcomes and customer loyalty. This enables organizations to optimize for what drives value that matters, rather than what's easy to measure.

Do not confuse this reinvention with traditional research and development efforts, which aim to explore future possibilities and may yield results in the distant future. Reinvention involves taking a deliberate critical look to determine how to deliver value most effectively every day.

TRAIT 4: LIFELONG LEARNING

With the mainstreaming of AI, the shelf life of specific skills continues to shrink, but the ability to learn continuously becomes the ultimate skill. Organizations that thrive with AI create cultures where learning becomes as natural as breathing. This involves more than developing AI fluency training programs, which we'll address in the next chapter. This is about rewiring how people approach knowledge, adaptation, and growth.

The mindset of lifelong learning recognizes that today's expertise may become tomorrow's limitation. It also fosters intellectual humility, recognizing the limits of one's own knowledge and being open to revising one's mind when confronted with new information.

Organizations that encourage lifelong learning focus on building an environment with these foundational behaviors:

- **Normalize not knowing**. Create a psychologically safe environment that encourages admitting knowledge gaps and asking questions. When leaders say, "I don't understand this yet" or "Help me learn," they permit everyone else to do the same. This removes the intimidation that prevents people from engaging with new technologies and ideas.
- **Embed reflection into work rhythms**. Establish regular moments for teams to step back and assess their learning, identify what's working, and determine what needs to change. This could be weekly debriefs after project milestones or monthly sessions where teams share discoveries and course corrections. The goal is to make reflection a habit.
- **Reward curiosity over certainty**. Recognize and promote individuals who ask questions, think critically, and adapt quickly to new information and insights. Create advancement criteria that value learning agility alongside technical competence. When organizations reward those who embrace uncertainty and continuous growth, they signal that adaptation is more valuable than expertise in yesterday's methods.
- **Connect learning to purpose**. Help people understand how their lifelong learning serves larger goals, such as achieving better customer outcomes, unlocking innovation opportunities, or gaining strategic advantages. When employees feel the connection between learning and meaningful work, motivation grows, engagement rises, and performance soars.

This mindset shift transforms learning from a periodic activity into a core organizational capability. Chapter 9 will detail the specific AI skills people need, but remember that the mindset of lifelong learning ensures that they'll continue to grow long after formal training ends.

TRAIT 5: CUSTOMER-CENTRICITY

When organizations fail to create value with AI, it's invariably due to internal dynamics and losing sight of customer needs. Company politics can undermine even the most focused and thoughtful AI plans and deployments. That's because corporate politics are inherently internal and myopic, diverting attention from customers.

Customer-centricity is the hallmark of some of the most successful businesses. Companies such as Amazon, USAA, and Fidelity Investments have built their competitive advantage by obsessively focusing on delivering value to their customer and embodying customer advocacy.[4] Creating value with AI requires thinking from the customer's perspective first, then organizing people, processes, and technology to deliver that value.

Customers don't care–nor should they–about the internal workings of your company. They are unaware of individual departments, siloed functions, and isolated structures or systems. Yet most organizations design AI solutions around internal structures and processes rather than external value creation. Leaders can shift this by making customer-value creation a key filter for AI investment decisions and recognizing employees who surface, emphasize, and advocate for customer needs.

Customer-centric thinking requires the following:

- **Organizing around customer journeys**. Instead of using traditional silos, structure teams and processes around complete customer experiences that cut across conventional boundaries and departments. For example, instead of using separate AI tools for marketing, sales, and service, consider implementing unified and comprehensive customer-view systems. These systems follow customers from awareness to purchase to support and further engagement, ensuring seamless experiences regardless of the department or individual process with which customers interact.
- **Shared metrics tied to customer success**. When everyone's incentives reward customer success, collaboration becomes natural and grows. For example, we've had the good fortune to work in customer-centric organizations where the key customer metric was as prominent as the company's stock price. This set the tone to always put the customer first and think and act in the customer's best interest.
- **Cross-functional collaboration mechanisms**. Create explicit channels for departments to share data, insights, and AI tools in the service of addressing customer needs. This involves establishing regular forums where various departments can identify customer pain points, share

relevant data, and coordinate AI solutions that require collaboration across multiple teams to deliver effective results. Without these mechanisms, even customer-focused teams end up working in isolation.

THE FOUR DRIVERS OF AI CHANGE MANAGEMENT

Understanding these five traits is essential, but knowing what an AI-ready culture looks like is different from actually building one. The gap between aspiration and reality is where most AI efforts stall.[5] Shifting an organization's mindset requires deliberate intervention–specific actions that make the abstract traits concrete and inevitable.

Based on the most successful AI transformations we've led, experienced, and studied, four strategic drivers consistently separate winners from strugglers:

- **Leadership mandate:** Making AI nonnegotiable
- **Performance integration:** Making AI adoption measurable
- **Universal access:** Putting AI tools in every employee's hands
- **Strategic communication:** Winning hearts and minds through deliberate messaging and dialogue

These four drivers work together synergistically, not sequentially (see figure 8-2). Think of them as interlocking forces that reinforce one another: Mandates create urgency, performance systems sustain behavior change, tool access enables practice, and communication builds understanding and buy-in. Remove any driver, and the entire transformation becomes unstable.

DRIVER 1: LEADERSHIP MANDATE–MAKING AI NONNEGOTIABLE

The most successful AI transformations begin with unambiguous leadership declarations that make it clear AI adoption is not optional. A mandate does three critical things: It creates urgency, signals organizational commitment, and provides permission for employees to prioritize learning new ways of working. In 2025, a wave of CEO mandates demonstrated the power of this approach.

Shopify's CEO, Tobi Lütke, declared to his organization, "Reflexive AI usage is now a baseline expectation at Shopify."[6] But he didn't stop at inspiration. Lütke established a concrete policy: Employees must prove that AI cannot perform a

Figure 8-2: The four drivers of AI change management

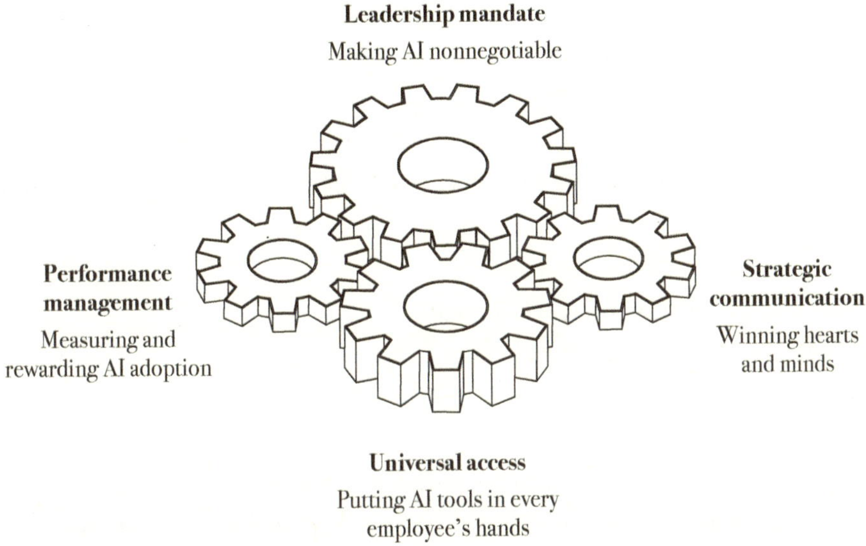

given task before requesting additional resources or hiring staff. The expectation is that AI is to be used daily by everyone, with AI exploration becoming a job requirement included in peer reviews. The results have been dramatic. Some Shopify teams report productivity increases up to one hundred times, and the company has achieved a cultural shift where AI competence has become a requisite skill.[7]

Box CEO Aaron Levie positioned their AI-first approach as tapping new value streams that were previously unfeasible due to cost or resource constraints.[8] He envisions AI agents that run 24/7 across the enterprise, handling routine work while unlocking opportunities for entirely new types of knowledge work.

At Norway's sovereign wealth fund, CEO Nicolai Tangen took perhaps the most direct approach, making AI use mandatory across Norges Bank Investment Management.[9] Tangen framed AI fluency as essential to remaining competitive in global financial markets, telling staff that using AI "is a must." Early implementations have already delivered a 15 percent productivity boost, validating his approach. His directive reframes AI not as an innovation perk but as a core competency that all investment professionals must master to stay relevant in managing the world's largest sovereign wealth fund.

And in mid-2025, Amazon CEO Andy Jassy declared in a message to employees that AI must be central to all of Amazon's operations in order to reduce rote work and free employees for strategic, creative work.[10] Jassy pointed to the potential of AI agents to change the scope and speed at which they innovate on behalf of customers. He also added that over the next few years, Amazon expected to reduce its total corporate workforce as it gained efficiency from using AI extensively across the company.

What makes these mandates effective

These leadership approaches share several critical characteristics that make them effective:

- **Imperative drives adoption**. Each organization ties AI usage directly to business and employee performance rather than treating it as optional innovation. The message is clear: AI adoption is essential for the organization's future and is not just a technological upgrade.
- **Enforcement focuses on creating fluency**. Rather than penalizing nonuse, these mandates typically include training, resources, and support. For example, the CEO mandates include compulsory upskilling programs, the integration of AI fluency into performance metrics, and inclusion in professional development plans.
- **Expectations are clear**. In companies driving AI adoption, leadership mandates that policies don't explicitly state "No AI, no job." But they do establish unmistakable expectations: AI fluency is not optional for future-ready contributors in these organizations.

Why do these declarations work? Because they create new organizational norms. When leadership clearly states that working with AI is a baseline expectation, it not only permits but also requires employees to prioritize a new way of working. Moreover, it makes it clear that the old way of working is no longer sufficient.

Building competency alongside the mandate

Mandates without support become dictates that breed resentment. The most effective mandates include comprehensive training and support systems that help employees succeed rather than just demanding compliance. This includes:

- Compulsory training programs that build AI fluency across the organization.
- Integration of AI fluency into professional development plans.
- Clear timelines and milestones for skill development.
- Access to learning resources, internal communities of practice, and expert guidance.
- Protected time for experimentation and learning.

The message must be clear: "We expect you to become AI-fluent, and we're investing in your success." We go into more depth about AI fluency training in chapter 9.

DRIVER 2: PERFORMANCE INTEGRATION—MAKING AI ADOPTION MEASURABLE

Declarations without measurement become suggestions. To make AI adoption stick, organizations must integrate it into their performance management systems, making AI fluency a quantifiable component of professional success.

The measurement principle is simple: "What gets measured gets managed" is a saying frequently attributed to Peter Drucker and V. F. Ridgeway. To achieve an AI-integrated workforce, you must measure the effectiveness of AI use and reward those who exemplify the new ways of working.

At Walmart, employees receive a weekly report detailing their usage of Walmart's AI tools and the estimated time saved. The report also compares the employee's usage with others in the same position as well as with others on their team.[11]

Performance metrics create accountability and reinforcement. Here are specific metrics you might include:

- **AI tool use**. This chart illustrates the frequency of AI tool adoption across various roles. Track login frequency, use of advanced features, and time spent using AI tools through built-in analytics dashboards. Create monthly use reports that show which teams and individuals are actively engaging with AI tools versus those who aren't. Launch internal competitions that reward employees for the most successful prompts, innovative tool usage, process streamlining, or for teaching others and driving further adoption.

- **Participating in AI transformation.** This is the willingness to engage in new ways of working. Measure participation in AI training sessions, contribution to internal AI knowledge-sharing forums, and involvement in pilot projects. Include peer nominations for colleagues who demonstrate enthusiasm for AI-enhanced workflows and help others adopt new approaches.
- **Learning milestones.** This refers to rites of passage, such as completing AI training, obtaining AI certifications, or demonstrating proficiency with AI tools. Establish AI certification programs with competency benchmarks, track completion rates of required and additional AI courses, and implement hands-on assessments where employees demonstrate their ability to use AI tools effectively in their work areas.

Manager accountability is crucial. Include AI adoption metrics in management dashboards that track both business outcomes and tool usage, enabling informed decision-making. A sales manager might monitor how AI-assisted lead qualifications improve conversion rates, while a marketing manager measures AI content creation's impact on campaigns. When managers treat AI proficiency like any other team member skill, it naturally becomes part of career development conversations and advancement considerations.

The reinforcement cycle works by building AI fluency into existing review processes, promotion criteria, and recognition programs. Quarterly reviews include AI productivity sections where promotion committees consider AI fluency alongside traditional qualifications, and recognition programs highlight measurable, AI-enabled employee performance results. When AI adoption influences career advancement, employee recognition, and rewards, people deliberately change their behaviors, with, you guessed it, speed and focus.

Creating accountability at every level

Performance integration works best when it creates mutual accountability. Employees are accountable for engaging with AI tools and demonstrating growth in AI fluency. Managers are responsible for supporting their teams' AI development and integrating AI skill development into team objectives. The organization is accountable for providing the resources, time, and support systems that make success possible.

DRIVER 3: UNIVERSAL ACCESS–PUTTING AI TOOLS IN EVERY EMPLOYEE'S HANDS

People don't truly understand AI until they use it. Abstract presentations and training sessions can build awareness, but personal experience creates believers. Universal access serves two critical functions: It builds practical AI fluency, and it transforms abstract fears into concrete understanding.

This broad exposure strategy complements the focused prioritization discussed earlier in this book. Think of it this way: Focused applications represent the *what*–the specific business challenges your organization mobilizes around to create value. Broad exposure provides the *how*–building the AI fluency and comfort level that enables employees to contribute effectively to those priority initiatives. Without broad exposure, even the best-chosen priorities will struggle because people lack the foundational skills to participate. Without focused priorities, broad exposure becomes unfocused experimentation, dissipating energy and resources. You need both strategic focus on what matters most and widespread AI fluency to execute effectively.

Paul Beswick, the chief information and operations officer at Marsh, understood this principle when he put AI into the hands of ninety-five thousand employees worldwide. Rather than waiting for a formal AI strategy or lengthy approval processes, he assembled a secure AI knowledge system and encouraged all employees to use it.

"We didn't ban or block AI at the beginning," Beswick explained to us in an interview. "The message we sent to the organization was: 'This is going to be important. It's good for you to know it. Start thinking about how it could play.'"

In addition to enabling and encouraging exposure to AI via the company's proprietary AI tool, LenAI, for everyone, Beswick's approach was psychologically astute. "This came in with no threat," Beswick noted. "It was provided to people right from the beginning as a sort of, here's a cool tool. It's not great for everything. Use it. Hopefully, it'll make you a bit more productive."

The results exceeded expectations. By the end of the first year, employees had launched over three hundred AI applications, with the platform handling twenty-five million requests annually at a cost of only a few hundred thousand dollars. Beswick estimates the tool saves at least one million hours per year. Beyond productivity gains, employees discovered unexpected applications, from company research preparation to natural language data querying, with 25 to 30 percent of the workforce using the tool weekly. The shift from discussing AI to using it created a feedback loop where increased usage led to a greater understanding of its value, which in turn drove further hands-on use for additional value.

Why exposure overcomes fear

The biggest obstacle to AI adoption is psychological. The Stanford *AI Index Report* found that only 39 percent of people in the US believe that AI will be more beneficial than harmful.[12] In comparison, 83 percent of people in China share the same view, more than twice as many as in the US. Recent research reveals that 33 percent of workers fear AI in the workplace and want it banned, while 45 percent worry about job security.[13] But here's what leaders need to understand: People aren't afraid of the technology. They're afraid of losing their identity and sense of purpose at work.

Exposure addresses this fear directly by transforming abstract anxieties into concrete experiences. When people use AI tools personally, several things happen:

- **Demystification**. People see firsthand what the experience is like, and AI becomes a valuable tool rather than an existential threat.
- **Empowerment**. Employees discover ways AI can make their work more interesting, not just more efficient.
- **Confidence building**. Hands-on interactions with AI show that people remain essential for judgment, creativity, and relationship building, among many other human traits.

Principles for broad exposure success

Based on successful broad deployments of AI in large organizations, several principles emerge for companies to follow:

- **Make adoption visible and fun**. Publicize employee adoption of AI tools because adopters become internal advocates who demonstrate value to skeptical colleagues. Some companies use gamification and competitions to boost visibility and add a fun element to potentially intimidating processes. At Marsh, the internal AI system, LenAI, incorporated fun elements, such as changing the user interface based on the season and creating a mascot–a plush toy named Len–to humanize and democratize AI use.
- **Start with enhancement, not replacement**. Position AI as a tool that makes existing work better, not as a threat to job security. Focus on removing drudgery, replacing manual repetitive tasks, and enabling higher-value activities.
- **Remove friction**. The easier it is to access and use AI tools, the more employees will explore and experiment with them. Integrate AI tools in existing company intranets, shared systems, and go-to tools. The less they have to change their behavior to access the new tools, the more seamless the access, the easier the adoption, and the faster the use.
- **Address concerns directly**. Acknowledge that AI will change how people work. However, it is essential to emphasize that change creates opportunities for employees. Be honest about not knowing how the future will unfold while demonstrating your commitment to helping people adapt.
- **Encourage knowledge sharing**. Create communication channels and shared knowledge systems and spaces for employees to post discoveries, effective prompts, and best practices for using AI that benefit their work. As we described earlier in this chapter, knowledge sharing accelerates organization-wide learning–a key trait of the AI-ready mindset.
- **Accommodate private learning**. Ensure employees have the opportunity to learn AI independently and privately. This means not tracking the prompts people use or the topics on which they engage with AI tools. While metrics like use frequency can be helpful, the nature of individual employees' specific interactions with AI tools should remain private. Marsh's Paul

Beswick exemplified this when he provided a safe AI space and made it clear to employees that the content of their interactions would be for their eyes only and that they did not have to use the tool for work only; he also encouraged use for personal needs and questions as part of everyday life, from cooking recipes to weather forecasts and driving directions.

These principles work together to create an environment where curiosity drives adoption and use. The goal is to give access and let people demonstrate value to themselves and others through discoveries, specific tasks, and ongoing learning with peers.

Organizations have multiple paths to provide broad AI access to employees, each with distinct advantages and implementation requirements (see figure 8-3). The choice depends on organization size, technical resources, and time constraints.

- **Path 1: Off-the-shelf AI tools**. Deploy enterprise-grade tools like ChatGPT Enterprise or Claude Enterprise that providc for immediate access with built-in security, user management, and compliance features. These solutions require minimal IT involvement and can be deployed in a matter of days, making them ideal for organizations that prioritize speed or lack technical resources.
- **Path 2: Turnkey AI platforms**. Use cloud platforms like Amazon Bedrock, Azure AI, or Google Vertex AI for secure and scalable access to multiple AI models via managed infrastructure. These platforms handle the underlying complexity while offering pay-as-you-go pricing and enterprise-level security, although they require moderate IT support and technical expertise for setup.
- **Path 3: Direct API integration**. Build custom connections directly to AI model providers (OpenAI, Anthropic) with your own management systems, security implementations, and user interfaces. This approach offers maximum flexibility in switching between models based on task requirements and cost optimization, but it requires significant technical expertise and infrastructure development.

Figure 8-3: Comparison of the three paths for AI exposure

APPROACH	DESCRIPTION	PROS	CONS	BEST FOR
Path 1: Off-the-shelf enterprise AI tools	Deploy enterprise-grade AI tools (ChatGPT Enterprise, Claude Enterprise) with built-in security features and user management	• Fastest deployment (days/weeks) • Built-in security and compliance • No technical expertise required • Immediate access to the latest models	• Higher per-user licensing costs • Limited customization options • Restricted document upload capacity • Single-vendor dependency	Organizations needing immediate access or lacking technical resources
Path 2: Turnkey AI platform	Use cloud platforms (Amazon Bedrock, Azure AI, Google Vertex AI) that provide secure, scalable access to multiple AI models through managed infrastructure	• Cost-effective scaling with pay-as-you-go pricing • Access to multiple models from different providers • Cloud security infrastructure included • Faster than custom development	• Requires moderate technical knowledge for setup • Cloud platform dependency • Limited to the platform's model selection • Less flexibility than custom solutions	Organizations seeking a balance of cost, security, and model variety with moderate technical resources
Path 3: Direct AIP integration	Build customer connections directly to AI model providers (OpenAI, Anthropic, etc.) with your own management systems, security implementation, and user interfaces	• Complete control over architecture and user experience • Maximum flexibility in model selection and routing • Lowest per-request costs at scale • Custom feature development is possible	• Requires sophisticated technical expertise and infrastructure • Complex security implementation and ongoing maintenance • Higher up-front development costs • Full responsibility for compliance and monitoring	Organizations with strong technical teams and unique requirements needing maximum flexibility; rare cases seeking competitive differentiation

The path you choose should prioritize the speed of rolling out AI tools across your organization, reinforcing the critical speed trait discussed earlier in this chapter. Unless your organization has a strong technical team with available capacity, we recommend rapid deployment with Path 1 or Path 2, depending on your user scale and budget constraints. Path 3 is a custom technical build, which may be right, but only in rare cases. We cover the buy-versus-build question in greater detail in chapter 10.

DRIVER 4: STRATEGIC COMMUNICATION—WINNING HEARTS AND MINDS

AI implementations often fail because the value created is too hard to see.

Without strategic communication, transformative wins can become isolated successes that don't scale. Communication transforms individual experiments into organizational learning and skeptical observers into engaged participants.

Traditional corporate communication approaches often fail in AI transformation contexts. One-way announcements don't build fluency. Sporadic updates don't create momentum. Technical jargon fails to connect with business impact. Instead, effective AI communication treats messaging as a core component of mindset change, not an afterthought to technical implementation.

Making communication strategic, not overwhelming

Rather than adding new communication burdens, integrate AI content into existing organizational rhythms. Replace routine updates with AI-relevant content instead of creating parallel streams. Augment weekly team meetings by dedicating five minutes to sharing a single concrete AI win. Use existing all-hands meetings to showcase AI progress rather than scheduling separate AI town halls. Let results set the communication rhythm—when teams discover breakthrough applications or hit unexpected roadblocks, those moments become immediate communication opportunities.

Predictable communication creates anticipation and signals that AI transformation is ongoing, not episodic. Design your cadence around:

- continuous learning updates that keep AI top-of-mind without overwhelming inboxes;
- progress visibility through existing communication channels and gatherings;

- team-level reflection that encourages sharing and learning from experience; and
- company-wide recognition that celebrates milestones and builds momentum.

Start with what feels sustainable for your organization, then adjust as needed based on engagement and feedback.

Building credibility through concrete demonstration

Changing minds requires evidence, not just enthusiasm. The most effective communication shows rather than tells by sharing specific examples of AI creating measurable value. Include employee testimonials that demonstrate how AI enhances human potential rather than replaces people. Make success visible and replicable across the organization. When a marketing team reduces content creation time by 40 percent using AI assistance, share not just the metric but the story of how it happened and what it meant for the people involved.

Equally important is transforming communication from a one-way broadcast to a two-way conversation. Create explicit channels where employees can share discoveries, voice concerns, and offer suggestions. When their input influences decisions, clearly communicate that connection using "you said/we did" responses. This approach empowers employees to become cocreators of the transformation rather than passive recipients of change, thereby fundamentally shifting the dynamic from a top-down mandate to a collaborative evolution.

Changing hearts with emotional connection and transparency

Open communication about both successes and challenges builds credibility and demonstrates that AI transformation is a learning process, not a perfect execution. Transparency includes these elements:

- Open updates with specific examples of what's working and what isn't. Share monthly metrics that highlight both successes, such as "AI reduced proposal writing time by 40 percent," and setbacks, like "our chatbot project was paused after accuracy fell below acceptable levels."

- A positive tone from leaders. Since executives set the tone, it's beneficial if their communication is more than orders and directives. Organizations will follow mandates because they must, but positive messaging will make them feel inspired.
- "You said/we did" feedback loops that show how input influences AI strategy and implementation. For example, when employees request better document-processing resources, follow up with something like this: "Based on your feedback, we've added PDF analysis tools to our AI platform." Then show the impact of the upgrade.

This approach normalizes the messiness of transformation and encourages continued engagement rather than striving for perfection.

Humanizing the technology

Leaders must model vulnerability and learning. The guidance to expose leader vulnerability is a much-discussed topic, so we won't cover it here. But executives may struggle as they learn and master AI tools. It would help to humanize this by publicly sharing their experiences. Others feel validated when they hear their boss chuckling in self-deprecation while explaining, "I tried to use AI for a financial forecast and got terrible results before learning it works better for data analysis preparation."

Using stories to drive understanding

Abstract explanations rarely stick, while concrete stories create lasting understanding and emotional connection to AI's possibilities. The most effective communication approach involves storytelling that demonstrates how AI transformation benefits people.

Here are four powerful story formats to use:

- Day-in-the-life scenarios illustrating how AI impacts real-world work experiences.
- Cross-functional libraries of AI value examples that help teams see applications beyond their immediate experience.
- Stories about learning that celebrate both successes and setbacks as valuable learning experiences.

- Employee-hero narratives that position workers as the protagonists who use AI to solve problems, serve customers better, or achieve goals they couldn't reach before. These stories follow the classic hero's journey: Employees face a challenge, discover how AI helps them overcome it, and emerge as more capable contributors to organizational success.

Stories humanize an otherwise intimidating technology, making AI's value relatable and within reach. They are the ultimate tool for winning hearts and minds. Powerful stories replace concern with excitement, anxiety with determination, and fear with a sense of advocacy.

Rather than relying on abstract promises about AI's potential, successful organizations demonstrate value through carefully chosen initial implementations that build trust and credibility.

Making communications stick: The tough conversations

One of the most critical change-management challenges involves directly addressing the impact of AI on jobs. This is the conversation most leaders avoid, but the one that employees most need.

The promise framework: What you can and cannot commit to

Rather than making vague reassurances that could create false expectations, effective leaders use precise language to communicate what they can realistically promise during an AI transformation. The key insight is that employees don't need false certainty–they need transparency and concrete support.

During uncertain times, the instinct is to provide maximum reassurance to anxious employees. However, making promises you cannot keep destroys credibility precisely when trust is most essential. The framework below helps leaders navigate this challenge by clearly distinguishing between commitments that are impossible to guarantee and those that demonstrate genuine investment in people's success (see figure 8-4).

When leaders acknowledge what they cannot control while making specific commitments about what they can influence, they build the trust necessary for successful transformation.

Figure 8-4: Communicating the promises you can keep

PROMISES YOU CANNOT MAKE	PROMISES YOU CAN AND SHOULD MAKE
No one will lose their job because of AI.	We will invest significantly in your professional development and AI fluency training.
AI will never replace human tasks in our organization.	You will receive at least X days' advance notice of any role changes, along with transition support.
Your role will remain the same.	We will aim to create new opportunities that empower people as the human in the loop or that help people apply uniquely human skills–creativity, empathy, complex problem-solving.
Career advancement paths won't change.	We will be transparent about how our AI adoption may impact the timeline and how it affects different roles.
AI will guarantee your future employment with us.	We will help you build skills that increase your value both here and in the broader job market.

This framework provides leaders with specific language they can use during all-hands meetings, team discussions, and individual conversations. The left column represents the tempting–but ultimately damaging–promises that seem reassuring but cannot be guaranteed. The right column offers realistic commitments that acknowledge uncertainty while demonstrating concrete support for employee success and growth.

The direct conversation script

When addressing groups about AI's workforce impact, effective leaders use language like this:

"I want to be direct with you about what AI means for our work. This technology will change how we operate. Some tasks that people do today will be automated. Some roles will evolve significantly. This is happening across our industry, not just at our company.

"Here's what I can promise you: We believe our people are our greatest asset, and that won't change. We're committed to helping everyone in this room build skills that will serve you well in an AI-augmented workplace. We'll provide training, time to learn, and support for career development. We'll be transparent about changes as we understand them ourselves.

"We can't tell you that your job will not change. However, we can promise that we'll invest in your learning and provide you with tools to help you succeed."

CASE STUDY: HOW ALLY BANK TURNED SKEPTICS INTO ADVOCATES

When generative AI first emerged, the general mindset at Ally Bank was one of apprehension. "The narrative was around fear," acknowledged Sathish Muthukrishnan, Ally's chief information, data, and digital officer, in an interview with us.

Rather than fight this fear head-on with presentations or mandates, Muthukrishnan's team chose a different path: They would let results tell their story. But first, they needed to create the conditions for trust. They established simple, understandable principles that addressed employees' core concerns: AI would be used for internal applications first, no personally identifiable information would be shared externally, and a human would always remain in the loop.

These weren't just policies–they were promises that acknowledged employee fears while creating guardrails for safe experimentation.

But the real masterstroke came with their choice of a first project. Instead of targeting a high-stakes, client-facing system, they focused on a problem every employee could relate to: the tedious process of summarizing thousands of daily customer care calls. Critically, they chose the people most likely to resist change–the customer service agents who were, as Muthukrishnan put it, "in the human business."

"If you think about our customer care associates, you cannot blame them for being the last adopters of tech because they are in the human business," Muthukrishnan explained. "But now, we are making the conversation singularly focused, relieving them of the burden of capturing the conversation, multitasking, and they've now become vociferous supporters of this technology saying, 'Do not take this away from me, because I find so much value in it.'"

The transformation was remarkable. The story this single project told was more powerful than any slide deck: AI was here to remove burden, not replace people. When the people most resistant to technology became its most passionate advocates, the message resonated throughout the organization.

The lesson was clear: Winning hearts and minds isn't about convincing people AI is good–it's about showing them how AI makes their work better.

But mindset transformation alone wasn't enough. Ally Bank's success required systematic capability building, organizational infrastructure, and deliberate approaches to ensure this cultural shift could scale across all eleven thousand employees. We'll explore how they built that foundation in chapter 9.

YOUR WEEK 8 ACTION PLAN

This week focuses on addressing the cultural barriers that separate the organization from the value AI can bring. Take these steps to establish an AI-ready culture:

- **Draft the CEO mandate establishing AI as essential work.** Collaborate with your leadership team to develop and draft a company-wide message that declares AI adoption as a baseline expectation for your organization. Use the examples from Shopify, Amazon, or Norway's sovereign wealth fund as templates, but customize the message to reflect your specific business challenges and competitive environment. The memo should specify that AI fluency is now a core competency, not an optional skill, and tie AI adoption directly to remaining competitive in your industry.
- **Integrate AI adoption into your performance system.** Add AI competency measures to your existing performance review templates before your next review cycle. Include specific metrics like frequency of AI

tool usage, participation in AI-related training, and demonstrated ability to apply AI in daily work. Brief your managers on how to have performance conversations that encourage AI adoption rather than penalize early struggles with the technology.

- **Provide hands-on AI access to your employees.** Choose your AI access path based on your technical resources and speed requirements. Deploy your chosen solution within thirty days.
- **Prepare leadership and managers for workforce impact conversations.** Equip your executive team and managers with the promise framework and conversation scripts from this chapter. These conversations are most effective when they occur naturally—in response to employee questions, concerns, or after successful AI implementations demonstrate value. The key is to ensure that your leadership team is prepared to consistently and transparently address these concerns whenever they arise.

SUMMARY

You've now completed Week 8 of your 90-day preparation to create value with AI. This week focused on the culture change that determines whether AI initiatives succeed or stall. In this chapter, you accomplished the following:

- **Recognized that AI initiatives fail** when organizations focus on technology while ignoring mindset and cultural barriers that prevent adoption and value creation.
- **Learned the five essential traits** of an AI-ready culture: speed, focus, continuous reinvention, lifelong learning, and customer-centricity, which work together to enable the transformation required to drive value with AI.
- **Discovered three levers** that shift organizational thinking: making AI use a baseline expectation through leadership mandates, providing broad hands-on exposure to AI tools, and communicating transparently and strategically through the power of stories to win hearts and minds.
- **Created practical approaches** for addressing employee concerns about AI through transparent communication frameworks that build trust while setting realistic expectations.

With your AI mindset now growing, you're ready for Week 9. In it, we'll focus on upskilling your people in AI so they transition from mindset readiness to practical AI application.

Technology is nothing. What's important is that you have a faith in people, that they're basically good and smart, and if you give them tools, they'll do wonderful things with them.

—Steve Jobs

Nine
DEVELOPING AN AI-FLUENT WORKFORCE

PAT, A MARKETING MANAGER, stared at the screen in disbelief. The AI-generated campaign concept wasn't just good; it was exceptional–attention grabbing, imaginative, and on message. But Pat's reaction wasn't excitement; it was fear: "What happens to my job now?"

Down the hall, Alex, a marketing data analyst, used AI to analyze a complex dataset in minutes rather than days. Unlike Pat, Alex felt energized. "This changes everything. Now I can focus on the actions we need to take, based on the numbers."

Same company. Same department. Same technology. Opposite reactions.

That's the paradox of AI: As it automates, it demands more human effort than ever to understand, shape, and work alongside it. The organizations that win with AI will be those with the most capable employees–those who use AI to move faster, drive desired outcomes, and create more value.

Building on the mindset you established in chapter 8, this chapter is about helping your workforce develop AI fluency. Value with AI can only materialize when AI augments and empowers people to achieve things they never could before.

Here are some actions to take this week:

- **Recognize why universal AI fluency is nonnegotiable** for every employee in your organization and understand how to move your workforce from fear to trust.

- **Design your AI training program** using the hub-and-spokes model to develop both general and domain-specific capability at scale.
- **Build your AI talent strategy** by identifying core AI roles your organization needs and determining when to develop expertise internally versus accessing it through partnerships.
- **Transform HR's role** from reactive support to strategic orchestrator of work, redesigning job descriptions, performance management, and career paths for human + AI collaboration.

Building these foundations starts with understanding the fundamental human challenges that every AI transformation creates.

THE HUMAN CHALLENGE OF AI

AI is a catalyst that will change the nature of work. The World Economic Forum's *Future of Jobs Report 2025* predicts that technological advancements will disrupt 22 percent of jobs by 2030.[1] However, the report also expects this disruption to create approximately 170 million new roles, resulting in a net increase of 78 million jobs.[2]

The organizations that win with AI are those that can navigate this transition. They understand that AI adoption is about maximizing *human* value, the potential for people to create value for themselves and their organizations. This balanced perspective recognizes that, while AI will eliminate some roles, it simultaneously creates new opportunities and enhances existing work in ways that can benefit both employees and organizations.

SENIOR LEADERSHIP'S CRITICAL ROLE IN AI VALUE CREATION

The most successful way to AI value creation starts at the top. For AI to take root and bear fruit across your organization, leaders must play a dual role. First, champion AI's strategic importance. Second, at the same time, thoughtfully guide the human transition it necessitates. This applies to all top executives, not just the C-suite.

As we saw in chapter 8, companies such as Amazon and Shopify have publicly committed to being "AI-ready" organizations, with their CEOs actively demonstrating this mindset. However, these announcements matter less than what happens next: executives integrating AI into their daily work, role-modeling the process of becoming AI-fluent, and making decisions with more data than ever before.

The top two levels of your leadership should set direction, allocate resources, and make the highest-impact decisions. When they embrace AI in visible, meaningful ways, it signals to the entire organization that this is a fundamental shift in the organization's ways of working.

Top executives also bear the responsibility to communicate openly about the impact of AI on people and their roles. This means having difficult conversations about how jobs will change, which skills will retain or gain value, what new skills will be needed, and what career paths might look like in the future. When leaders can articulate both the opportunities and challenges with clarity and empathy, they create the psychological safety employees need to embrace change.

FROM FEAR TO TRUST

The number one barrier to workforce adoption of AI isn't complexity–it's fear. The technology advances at mind-boggling speed, everyone is talking about it, and even the typical terminology can intimidate.[3] Employees worry about how they can keep up. They see the headlines and wonder what to believe and what it all means. They fret about whether they'll have a job next year. And many fear the potential harmful effects of AI on society. For example, as mentioned in the previous chapter, at the time of this writing, only 39 percent of people in the US believe that AI will be more beneficial than harmful.[4]

As long as fear is a person's main reaction to AI, no amount of information or training will make a difference in opening them to AI's possibilities. The key to overcoming fear is trust. Trust is built by human connection and leadership. People trust the leaders and their peers who speak plainly about what is changing, what is not, and what they're still figuring out. Admitting uncertainty–while offering a path forward–creates the psychological safety needed for change.

CASE STUDY: PUSHING PAST FEAR TO AI FLUENCY

A Fortune 100 legacy energy company recognized that employee fears–not technical gaps–were the most significant barrier to the adoption of AI. Instead of simply announcing new tools, the company developed employee training programs to demystify generative AI. The company's HR leader told us, "The more they [employees] know what AI is and how it's being used in the business setting, the more the fear factors go away because people don't know what they don't know."

The company developed four modules of on-demand AI training and rolled them out by location to create a critical mass of learners who could support one another. Module 1 was an introduction to explain what generative AI is and address employee questions, concerns, and fears. The purpose was to initiate the conversation and establish expectations that AI would be an integral part of working at the company.

Module 2 introduced employees to potential applications of AI. The course encouraged individuals to explore new ways to apply AI in their daily work by integrating it into existing workflows. Examples ranged from relying on AI to summarize team meetings and action points to developing emails, content, and presentations. Employees attended practical, hands-on training, both virtually and in person, with ample time for questions. The company offered additional courses to hone skills and delve deeper into specific topics, such as how to use Microsoft Copilot in Word or Copilot in Teams.

Module 3 covered responsible and ethical use of AI, reviewing the company's AI policies. That prepared employees for Module 4, training on best practices for interacting with generative AI tools, writing basic prompts that would lead to desired outputs, and developing more advanced skills, for example, specific types of prompts.

While the organizers expected this training to enhance productivity and deliver business value, they recognized that this was just the beginning. The HR leader said, "Our longer-term view is that AI will change and evolve jobs, and we'll have to develop our workforce capabilities. However, the first step is currently to educate people about how to use and adopt AI so that it isn't perceived as a significant threat. We started small to help people reframe AI so that it will become much easier to tackle bigger issues in the future."

GETTING EXECUTIVES TO DRIVE ACTION

It's not easy to spring people into action, even when they recognize the importance of AI fluency. We've personally seen countless organizations struggle with how to get already overextended executives to adopt new technologies.

But there are ways to give leaders a head start. Some organizations host "AI Days" where executives can view AI demonstrations. Some businesses assign "AI ninjas," typically, but not always, young, tech-savvy employees, to demonstrate and help the (usually older) executives learn about and start using various AI tools. Some companies organize immersion trips for executive teams to travel to Silicon Valley, where they meet with tech giants and AI startups to see them in action.

All of these are valid ways to educate and energize executives. But even when executives get excited by what they see, their organizations haven't taken action. And time is not on their side.

To advance from excitement to action, executives need to see AI as a way to meet the top strategic objectives for which they are personally accountable. Steal a page from the chapter about deploying AI in the service of business strategy. Take that same relentless focus on what is most essential and frame the technology as a means to achieve it. Just as with the AI roadmap work, mobilize executives across the organization to rally around AI in direct service of top priorities. We used this approach to craft the AI roadmap; we should do the same for executives. Confirm the business strategy and top objectives, then explain how AI will help achieve them and accelerate their outcomes.

In response, you want them to ask, "How quickly can we do this?"

DEVELOPING AN AI-FLUENT WORKFORCE

Organizations that rapidly develop AI skills across their workforce gain a competitive advantage. Consider that over 77 percent of US workers anticipate that AI will influence their jobs or careers in the next three to five years, but only 31 percent say their employer provides AI training.[5]

To overcome this, all employers must act now. The goal is for everyone to develop AI fluency, which we define as the combination of three skills:

- Understanding what AI can do, and also its limitations
- Using AI in a responsible and ethical way
- Using AI to get your work done

Everyone in your organization needs to become AI-fluent, starting now. This will help your people become confident, effective AI users capable of creating value with it.

WHY WE URGENTLY NEED UNIVERSAL AI FLUENCY

We adamantly believe a sense of urgency must be instilled around AI. The technology is sprinting so far ahead that anyone who does not get going now risks falling woefully behind. Every day a worker doesn't learn how to use the technology, they fall behind. Every day they fall behind sets back their growth prospects.

There is also an organizational cost and reward for AI fluency. When employees use AI confidently, strategically, and proactively, they not only complete their work but also redesign and reinvent workflows and envision new ways to capture value. In chapter 8, we discussed the importance of having a mandate to integrate AI into everyday work. Training focuses on helping your workforce develop that fluency.

The essentials of AI fluency training

We often receive questions about the timing of AI fluency training. Many companies we work with, even tech ones, are not sure how soon they can start training people, especially against the backdrop of what they see as other priorities. They talk about starting in six months, and about phasing and sequencing, prioritizing training of certain employees over others.

Let us be very clear:

- **The timing is now.** Many of your employees are likely already using AI tools, including in the workplace. We know a consultant who asked their client about the proportion of employees who used AI tools at work. The client said very few employees did. But when a group of the firm's employees answered the same question, hands shot up–most employees were in fact using AI tools.

- **Training is for all employees at once.** You cannot justify training a specific group first at the expense of another. Organizations owe it to all their employees to offer AI training. The kind of training may vary by role and domain to ensure relevance, as we discuss below. But general training must roll out to everyone at the same time. And AI can even provide the training through platforms that remove any constraints associated with the limits in numbers compared to a traditional human trainer. And what better way to learn about the technology than to experience it in action during training?
- **Blending mandates and certifications works.** The training must be mandatory. Employees routinely take compulsory training on compliance, cybersecurity, data protection, harassment prevention, and more. We know of one large consulting company with thirty-three thousand global employees that offers a comprehensive AI training curriculum, most of it mandatory. If employees do not complete it, they lose their email access! There is no clearer message on the importance of AI than mandating that all employees participate in AI training. To make it a source of pride, rather than a checkmark, employers could offer certifications and additional modules for continuous learning.
- **Employees must own their AI fluency.** Employers have the responsibility to provide access to tools and training, but employees own the responsibility for their AI fluency. It is inevitable that some employees will go further and deeper than others and will attain a higher level of fluency. But if you provide the access, the training, and the incentives, your best employees will thank you and reward you with loyalty as well as work improvements, innovations, and gains. Other employees will not; that's where the performance management tactics from chapter 8 can help.

DRIVING AI FLUENCY AS A NONNEGOTIABLE

One midsized company CEO took a straightforward approach. After declaring, "We are going to be an AI-ready organization," he created a dashboard that displayed every employee's name with a traffic light indicator: green for active AI users, yellow for those in the learning phase, and red for nonadopters. His message was clear: "In six months, our goal is to have everyone at least in the yellow zone–actively learning and developing AI skills. We'll provide you with all of the training support to get there. And for those who find this transformation doesn't fit with their career goals, we'll work together to help them find opportunities that are a better fit."

HOW TO BUILD BASELINE AI FLUENCY FOR EVERYONE

AI fluency training involves two broad categories of learning: (1) general tool use and (2) adaptation to specialized needs and tasks, usually associated with specific needs, like working with patients' health records, or domains, like finance, marketing, or legal. This includes introducing the enterprise-grade tool that the company makes available to its employees for mass adoption and use.

Training programs need to include four core elements:

- **A general overview of how AI works**. This should be presented from a layperson's perspective, in nontechnical and practical language, regarding how it can be helpful in the workplace and how and why it's essential to use the tools that the company makes available.
- **Effective chat and context prompting**. This means knowing how to phrase requests or questions to guide AI toward producing valid and reliable outputs. Practical sessions teach employees to craft clear instructions, provide relevant context, and refine their requests to achieve better results.
- **Output evaluation**. This involves teaching critical thinking to assess AI responses. Employees learn to evaluate AI outputs for accuracy, tone, completeness, and usefulness. They master the habit of demanding sources and references and cross-checking validity. Overall, employees learn to treat AI outputs as starting points, rather than finished products. They iterate with AI, from generating first drafts to refining them, building on drafts, adjusting tone, and sharpening insights.
- **Responsible and ethical AI use**. This covers core safety protocols around data privacy and security–the nonnegotiables that protect the organization while enabling rapid adoption. Training includes scrutinizing AI outputs for potential bias, understanding the reasoning behind AI decisions, and practicing skills that treat AI outputs as aids rather than the final product. This also includes the company's specific policies and governance.

With this foundation in place, employees become confident in working with general-purpose AI tools and integrating them into their daily work through hands-on practice.

Domain-specific skills

In addition to the general tool training, organizations need tailored, hands-on, and ongoing learning that reflects the daily work associated with specific roles. This can be about specific applications of a general-purpose AI tool, like ChatGPT or Gemini, for individual tasks, or specialized enterprise tools such as Claude's Financial Analysis Solution or Harvey AI for legal contract reviews. Given the rapid advances in AI, we are deliberately not listing many specific tools because they are likely to change. But the point is to train employees to customize the use of general tools to their specific needs and also learn to work with AI tools that provide deeper support for their specialized areas of work.

To help employees master role-specific AI use, programs must define what it means to be AI-fluent for different roles and functions. For example, teams that process large amounts of content–such as finance, HR, and legal–have different AI needs compared to teams that generate content, like sales or marketing. Engineering teams have even more specialized requirements. It's important to create specific tasks and exercises for each domain (see figure 9-1).

Regardless of whether for general or specialized use, there are ways to enhance the relevance and success of the training, as we have discovered from working with various organizations deploying AI fluency programs.

HOW TO DEPLOY AI TRAINING

In our research, several practices emerged as most effective in building AI fluency:

- **Practice hands-on use, not theoretical input.** Focus on concrete tasks and AI applications that matter to employees. Pilot hands-on training with practical exercises tied to real work. Let people experiment with AI tools on real projects like drafting actual emails, analyzing data, or creating presentations. This immediate relevance accelerates learning and builds confidence.

Figure 9-1: Defining AI fluency by role—Domain-specific training

DOMAIN/ DEPARTMENT	DOMAIN-SPECIFIC TRAINING IN AI FLUENCY SKILLS
Marketing	• Generate content tailored to the target audience, analyzing data to optimize it. • Create automated multichannel campaigns that adapt messaging based on audience engagement patterns.
Finance	• Use AI to conduct scenario planning and stress tests based on simulated market shifts or regulatory changes. • Perform financial forecasting, interpreting and validating AI outputs for strategic planning.
Human resources	• Suggest personalized learning and development paths for employees, while critically evaluating the underlying data for inclusivity and fairness. • Develop AI tools that automate frequently asked questions for employee self-service, covering benefits, policies, and procedures.
Sales	• Generate sales presentations and proposals, using client data, preferences, and history. • Personalize follow-ups after customer engagements. • Analyze sales calls transcripts for self-coaching, identifying best practices and refining sales techniques.

- **Measure and keep lifting the bar.** At the beginning, at least, it's important to measure adoption, usage, and, when possible, effectiveness. Soon, as AI penetrates the entirety of our daily lives and work, we will not need to measure that, just as we do not measure mobile phone use, Google searches, or social media consumption. But, for now, to stimulate adoption, organizations will find it beneficial to capture, track, and publicize key metrics:

    - **Adoption:** Percent of employees per organization, department, or group using AI tools every day.

- **Engagement:** This could include frequency of usage, number of interaction sessions, queries per session, or average interaction length.
- **Workflow integration:** AI-assisted task completion rates.

- **Understand AI use metrics.** All these metrics are behavioral, quantitative, readily available from system logs, and objective. Effectiveness and value are harder to measure objectively. Currently, organizations are using surveys and interviews with users who reflect on their work and outcomes, often citing the number of hours saved; new insights and additional perspectives gained; or holistic end-to-end work, from question to output, in a presentable form. While these can be informative in the absence of other value metrics, they are self-reported and are not as objective and reliable as behavioral measures. Some companies are developing software that plugs into or integrates with AI tools and tracks their usage to connect it to value creation and calculate effectiveness or return on investment.
- **Support peer mentoring and knowledge sharing.** Supplement formal programs with informal learning opportunities, especially peer-based sharing. Empower internal AI champions to support and mentor others. Remember our opening example of Alex, who uses AI to analyze datasets? Employees like Alex quickly surface new best practices that can be integrated back into formal training. Alex can coach others more effectively and faster than a formal training program alone. You can create structured opportunities for knowledge sharing through lunch-and-learns, internal AI showcase sessions, and cross-departmental collaboration projects.
- **Introduce healthy competition and gamification.** Research consistently shows that an element of fun enhances and accelerates learning. Some of the companies we work with have launched competitions for the highest use of AI tools, best prompts, most insightful outputs, and deepest integration within daily workflows. You know best what will work in your organization. The point is to infuse enthusiasm for learning and a healthy dose of peer pressure–then watch for results!

- **Encourage continuous learning and experimentation.** Because AI is constantly evolving, fluency requirements change rapidly. Provide regular opportunities to acquire and practice new skills through webinars, certifications, and cross-departmental projects. Encourage experimentation by creating "AI sandbox" environments where employees can test new tools without affecting production systems. Normalize learning curves by celebrating improvements and sharing failure stories alongside success stories. Consider implementing "AI Friday" sessions, where teams dedicate time to experimenting with new AI tools or techniques; "innovation challenges," where employees compete to find the most creative AI applications for their work; and regular "failure parties," where teams share what didn't work and what they learned from unsuccessful AI experiments.

These practices work because they recognize that AI fluency develops through practice, not just instruction.

THE PROGRAM STRUCTURE

The program could include these components:

- General tool training.
- Domain-specific training (finance, HR, legal, marketing, sales, operations, engineering, and more).
- Competitions for best, most creative, most value-yielding use—whatever works in the specific company's context and culture.
- Demonstrations of how teams are using the tools and their outcomes and learnings. Exposing the entire organization to employees who can inspire others is beneficial to all; presenters get visibility, and the audience learns new things.
- Webinars on various topics, such as how the industry is using these tools, ethics, security, and what's next.
- Speakers on AI value—bringing in external thought leaders to share ongoing trends and applications.

INTEGRATING AI FLUENCY IN DAILY INTERACTIONS

Beyond formal training, companies need to drive personal accountability for AI adoption–and an element of fun–by starting meetings with simple questions: How did you use AI over the weekend? How did you use AI to prepare for this meeting? What are some of the ways in which you've used AI lately? This will help normalize AI as a standard tool for work and life. It represents a vital leadership practice that is a forcing mechanism for learning and sets expectations for ongoing practice of AI use as part of daily work.

If the response is unsatisfactory, set the expectation for next time and personally start every meeting by sharing how you have used AI lately and what your results were. In a recent encounter, the most senior executive in the room pulled out his phone, checked his entire ChatGPT history, and told us about the numerous ways in which he used the tool for his personal and professional life, from checking whether his car needed an oil change to starting a draft for a speech. This highlights the role of modeling and transparency in providing a benchmark and accelerating organizational learning.

CASE STUDY: MAKING A COMPANY AI-FLUENT

One Fortune 500 global financial services company partnered with a major AI provider to roll out AI tools to all employees with a company-issued device. The chief digital officer initially faced resistance from some executives who questioned the cost of providing a license for an AI tool to that many employees.

"People still don't understand that this is not optional," explained the chief digital officer to us in an interview. "We had to help them see that using AI is becoming like using Google search. The question isn't whether to provide access–it's how to ensure people get the training to start using the tools immediately."

The effort aimed to solve five critical challenges at once:

- **Eliminating risk.** Providing secure, enterprise-grade AI tools addressed the security risk that occurs when employees use consumer AI tools for work tasks. Banning AI tools in the workplace is not the answer; making safe tools available is.

- **Enabling universal access.** All employees gained access to the same AI tools simultaneously. This encouraged people to turn to AI naturally, with the added peer pressure and expectations that they should use AI, with no excuse for not doing so.
- **Integrating AI training.** The company planned and rolled out comprehensive training programs. The programs covered general training on the tool itself, as well as domain-specific areas, including use for finance, HR, and legal (functions that process high volumes of information); sales, marketing, and product management (functions that generate high volumes of information); and coding for engineering teams.
- **Championing AI across the enterprise.** The partnership also created a movement of AI champions across the organization. To roll out the tool and training, the company designated AI champions centrally and for each function. These champions served as the main point of contact for all things AI within their domain, advised on the training, identified top areas of use, and rallied their coworkers to join and enjoy.
- **Energizing the culture around AI.** The final element of this simultaneous adoption was to infuse gamification and energize the organization around AI rather than maintaining it as a mandatory tool. The AI champions designed competitions for the most frequent AI usage, best prompts, and most creative applications of AI and publicly recognized their peers for such achievements with small but meaningful rewards.

Initial results revealed that employees were saving significant hours in what used to be mundane, manual, repetitive output creation. While the effort is still being implemented, expectations are that employee engagement scores will also improve, and client-facing operations will start seeing value as well.

UNIVERSAL ACCESS WITH PRACTICAL RELEVANCE

As the above case study shows, while every person needs AI training, practical implementation also requires specific domain-relevant training. That's why general-purpose tool training needs to be complemented with functional training. For example, marketing departments would find it helpful to learn to use the variety of AI tools for image, video, and copy generation, like Midjourney.ai. Legal departments would benefit from mastering specialized tools, like Harvey.ai. Product management teams could enjoy learning and using a variety of tools, from roadmapping and prioritization to prototyping and analytics, and engineering teams would need to get deep into specialized coding tools.

WHO OWNS AI TRAINING? THE HUB-AND-SPOKES MODEL

The goal of AI fluency training is to establish a baseline understanding common across the entire company. This typically comes through centrally organized programs that benefit from consistency of design and delivery. One critical question organizations face is: Who owns AI training and capability development across the company? The most effective approach we've seen is the hub-and-spokes model, which we introduced in chapter 3.

We've seen centralized models, where a single entity controls all the training, but it's slow to develop training that meets the needs of different departments and roles. In contrast, decentralized models that rely on each department creating bespoke training lack the necessary knowledge and expertise to ensure security and compliance.

Following is an overview of how the AI hub and department spokes work together to create AI fluency training.

The AI hub

The central AI lead (or AI team) owns overall training for the whole company, working closely with these departments:

- **HR:** To incorporate best practices from learning and development programs and, for additional motivation, to link tool use and training to employee rewards and recognition.

- **Technology** (applies to AI leaders separate from technology): To ensure security, connectivity, and embedding in existing tools and platforms.
- **Strategy and business functions:** To ensure that any training and use are directed toward practical business goals and value creation.
- **Communications:** To ensure a steady drumbeat of internal communications, competitions, and promotion of best AI tool use, most creative and innovative examples, and ways to create value.

The AI hub, together with HR, strategy, and communications, develops an organization-wide program with curriculum, structure, learning modules, incentives, gamification, and ways to showcase what works and cautions about what doesn't. The program also includes overall guidance on safe, ethical, and responsible AI use. The hub designs metrics of success and tracks value creation. They own any integration with business and technology systems, performance management cycles and processes, and corporate communications. Essential responsibilities of the hub are to steadfastly promote the importance, successes, and ongoing value of training; showcase concrete and practical examples; and plan and advance further training for continuous learning.

The program, in most cases, includes both general and domain-specific training. For domain-specific needs, the hub works with the spokes–embedding the necessary customization for specific functions such as creative tools for marketing campaigns, analysis and summary tools for finance, or customer profile tools for service and operations.

The spokes

The spokes are AI experts embedded in each function or geographic unit who work on AI applications. These individuals serve as conduits for disseminating AI training in their specific domains.

These experts are part of the AI organization and represent what we call "bilingual" resources–they have both technical AI expertise and deep domain knowledge. They work with the hub to inform and enable general training and serve as subject matter experts and product owners for AI applications in their specific domains.

It's important to distinguish these AI experts from "AI champions," who are typically employees whose primary job isn't AI-specific, but who have enthusiasm and rudimentary AI skills to help propagate adoption within their departments. The AI experts in the spokes, however, are formally part of the AI organization with professional AI responsibilities.

These functional AI experts collaborate with the hub to ensure success metrics apply across various domains. They provide business knowledge for the hub to customize training and examples, making programs more relevant to specific functions. They support their departments with technical AI expertise as needed, and they gather feedback from their teams and share it back to the AI hub.

HOW TO GET STARTED

Developing AI training for everyone doesn't need to start from scratch. An abundance of tools that can serve as a starting point already exists. Organizations typically choose between two approaches, each with distinct advantages and trade-offs.

Enterprise AI platform partnerships

Some organizations are partnering directly with AI platform providers to deliver enterprise-wide access and training simultaneously. This approach ensures every employee with a company device can develop AI fluency on a specific platform. The primary advantage is seamless integration–if you're already using the platform for work, the training is directly applicable. The limitation is that training focuses on that specific platform and may not prepare employees to use other AI tools.

Major enterprise AI platform partnerships include the following:

- **OpenAI for Enterprise.** OpenAI provides comprehensive training through OpenAI Academy, offering courses ranging from ChatGPT Fundamentals to advanced integration for engineers, with industry-specific options like AI for Non-profits: Prompting 101.[6] The company has launched partnerships with organizations such as Walmart and federal government agencies to provide ChatGPT Enterprise access combined with AI Academy training for all employees and plans to expand with AI certifications for different levels of fluency starting in late 2025.[7]

- **Anthropic for Enterprise**. Anthropic Academy offers courses on prompting best practices for Claude.ai and function-specific training, such as Use Claude for Human Resources and Use Claude for Sales.[8] The company has expanded its Academy through partnerships with Amazon Web Services, Google Cloud, and Deloitte.[9] Deloitte announced a certification program in April 2025 targeting fifteen thousand professionals globally, combining generative AI training with specialized instruction on Anthropic's advanced AI models.
- **Microsoft Copilot for Enterprise**. Microsoft integrates AI training directly into existing Microsoft 365 workflows through Microsoft Learn, providing both tools and learning within familiar environments.[10] The platform offers structured learning paths covering Microsoft 365 Copilot basics, practical usage across Microsoft 365 apps, and best practices for maximizing its potential, with training designed for all professionals requiring no previous AI expertise.

These partnerships typically include baseline training modules, domain-specific curricula, and ongoing support structures that make universal deployment more feasible for organizations of all sizes. The training is tightly integrated with the actual tools your organization uses, making adoption more natural and immediate.

Comprehensive learning platforms

An alternative approach uses tool-agnostic learning platforms that provide broader AI education across multiple tools and concepts. These platforms offer greater flexibility and prepare employees to work with various AI systems, though they require organizations to supplement with platform-specific training for the tools they've actually deployed.

These are the two most prominent comprehensive learning platforms:

- **Coursera**. Coursera partners with top universities like Yale and Stanford and companies like Google and IBM to offer AI courses. The platform provides accredited certificates upon completion that are recognized by employers and can be shared on LinkedIn profiles, featuring university or company branding. Coursera excels at academic-style, in-depth learning with structured courses that follow traditional academic formats, including weekly assignments, quizzes, and peer-reviewed projects.

- **LinkedIn Learning**. LinkedIn Learning offers AI training taught by industry experts in software, creative, and business skills. The platform provides certificates upon course completion, which can be displayed directly on LinkedIn profiles, though unlike Coursera's certificates, these are not accredited. LinkedIn Learning focuses on shorter, more practical courses designed for immediate workplace application, making it ideal for professionals seeking quick skill development rather than academic credentials.

These learning platforms provide flexible, self-paced options for building broad AI literacy and give employees exposure to multiple AI approaches and tools. However, organizations will still need to provide specific training on the platforms they've actually deployed for day-to-day work.

CASE STUDY: IKEA'S UNIVERSAL AI FLUENCY EFFORTS

The transition to AI presents leaders with a stark choice. As Sami Hassanyeh, chief transformation officer at AARP, told us, "The transition to leveraging these AI tools is a people problem. Either you can get rid of your people, or you can bring your people along and really turbocharge your business. I prefer the latter."

IKEA's strategic integration of AI provides a powerful example of the latter, demonstrating how organizations can build universal fluency while creating new value. For example, IKEA introduced "Billie," an AI chatbot that successfully managed 47 percent of customer interactions, streamlining service and allowing human employees to focus on more complex tasks.[11]

Rather than reducing its workforce, IKEA took a proactive approach by training 8,500 call center employees to become interior design advisors. The company built on its existing customer service skills while teaching them new competencies in design and sales. This move yielded impressive results. The newly trained interior design advisors contributed to a $1.4 billion increase in revenue through remote consultation services.[12]

Beyond this specific role transformation, IKEA committed to enhancing AI fluency across its organization. The company launched comprehensive training programs for approximately thirty thousand coworkers and five hundred leaders with four targeted segments[13]:

- **General coworkers** begin with a mandatory AI Fundamentals course that covers generative AI applications for daily tasks, ethical boundaries, and critical evaluation of these applications.
- **Specialized roles** receive targeted courses, such as Responsible AI and Mastering Gen AI, tailored to their specific functions and responsibilities.
- **Leadership** participates in AI Exploration Days to understand AI's potential and incorporate AI into strategic objectives.
- **Tech teams** receive advanced instruction in configuring AI tools and integrating them into existing systems.

IKEA's approach demonstrates that technological advancement and workforce empowerment can work together, leading to both operational efficiency and revenue growth. The key was viewing AI as an enhancement to human expertise rather than a replacement.

USING AI TO TEACH AI: A META-APPROACH TO BUILDING FLUENCY

One of the most effective ways to educate your workforce about AI is to let AI do some of the teaching. AI can serve as a content generator, conversational coach, and personalized tutor, making training more engaging and accelerating learning.

Here are practical ways organizations are using AI to teach AI:

- **AI-powered onboarding tutors.** Teams train internal chatbots on company AI guidelines, tools, and tasks. New hires can ask questions like "How do we use generative AI in our marketing team?" and get real-time, context-specific answers. This creates consistent onboarding while allowing for personalized learning paths.

- **Custom GPTs and copilots.** Using tools like ChatGPT's custom GPTs or Microsoft Copilot, teams build role-specific AI mentors. A sales team might create an assistant that explains how to write AI-augmented outreach emails and offers instant coaching on tone, format, and data use. Finance teams can build AI tutors that guide employees through AI-powered forecasting techniques.
- **Scenario-based learning.** Learning and development teams use generative AI simulations for immersive and realistic skill practice. Employees can interact with AI environments to role-play ethical dilemmas, troubleshoot implementation challenges, or explore consequences of AI bias in decision-making. This creates safe spaces to practice critical thinking about AI outputs.
- **Prompt libraries as learning tools.** Treat your prompts like valuable intellectual property. Rather than just showing examples, organizations turn their prompt libraries into interactive resources. Employees can test and tweak prompts, observing how small changes impact outputs to build fluency through experimentation.
- **Real-time micro-coaching.** Organizations use AI tools to deliver personalized, contextually relevant feedback. A project manager drafting a team update might receive AI suggestions not just for grammar but for clarity, tone, or potential misinterpretations. This micro-coaching teaches people in small bursts, in the moment, during actual work.

This meta-approach to building AI fluency accelerates learning because employees learn by doing, while AI provides immediate, personalized feedback. The result is faster skill development and more confident AI users.

BUILDING YOUR AI TALENT STRATEGY

The technical complexity of modern AI systems creates skill gaps that extend beyond what traditional IT teams can handle. Building custom AI applications, integrating multiple AI models, and maintaining AI systems at scale requires expertise in algorithms, neural network architectures, and specialized programming frameworks that takes years to develop.

Speed also matters. While your organization invests in training programs, competitors may move faster by bringing in experienced AI talent who can immediately contribute to strategic initiatives.

While developing employees into AI-capable contributors is a must, most organizations will also need to add at least some select, deeply specialized AI talent. This talent is critical to organizations' ability to deliver on their AI-value roadmaps. The reality is that some AI skills require years of focused training and experience that internal development programs cannot provide quickly enough. There are several core AI roles that organizations need.

CORE AI ROLES: UNDERSTANDING WHAT DRIVES AI SUCCESS

Before deciding who you may need to hire or partner with, it's helpful to understand what specialized AI work entails. Here are the five core AI roles that drive successful implementation for value from AI:

- **The AI product manager** connects AI with business needs, translating between technical possibilities and strategic objectives. This role requires a unique combination of technical expertise and business acumen.
- **The AI architect** designs and oversees the implementation of scalable AI solutions and their integration with the organization's existing systems for impact across the enterprise. This requires mastery of algorithms and a deep understanding of AI model architectures.
- **The AI engineer** develops, tests, and deploys AI models into business applications, ensuring they function reliably at scale. These roles demand sophisticated programming skills and machine learning knowledge.
- **The data scientist** analyzes large datasets to uncover patterns to develop models that enable AI systems to learn from data. AI-focused data science requires specialized skills in algorithm development and model training that go far beyond traditional business analysis.
- **The MLOps (machine learning operations) engineer** scales AI models from development into production enterprise systems and maintains them over time. This relatively new specialization combines software engineering with specialized knowledge of AI model management.

PRACTICAL CONSIDERATIONS FOR DIFFERENT ORGANIZATION SIZES

Now that you understand what these roles entail, here's how to think about acquiring these skills based on your organization's context:

- **Large organizations** (1,000+ employees) often benefit from hiring core AI roles internally while using external partners for specialized needs. They have the scale to justify full-time positions and can offer career development paths that attract top talent. However, even large organizations frequently start with consulting partnerships to validate their AI strategy before committing to full-time hires.
- **Midsize organizations** (100 to 1,000 employees) typically find success hiring one or two core roles—usually an AI product manager and an AI engineer—while partnering with consulting firms or cloud providers for specialized expertise like MLOps or advanced data science. This hybrid approach provides essential internal skills while accessing specialized expertise as needed.
- **Smaller organizations** (under 100 employees) usually achieve the best outcomes with a consulting-first approach, relying on external expertise to establish initial value from AI while training internal staff to maintain and refine AI solutions. Most successful smaller organizations never hire internal AI specialists; instead, they build strong partnerships with external providers who can fulfill all five functions as needed.

No matter what size your organization is, to get going at speed, start by using contractors or consultants for initial AI applications while beginning the hiring process at the same time.

FINDING TALENT: A STRATEGIC APPROACH

The most effective approach combines internal development with targeted external resources. Begin by assessing the existing talent within your organization. Some employees may have transferable skills, such as software engineers who can master machine learning, statisticians who can transition into data science, or product managers who can develop AI fluency.

Marsh discovered engineers in Dublin with foundational skills to build AI applications. Paul Beswick, Marsh's chief information and operations officer, took the approach of looking internally first, enabling quick movement without external hiring delays. An added bonus was that these internal engineers understood business challenges in ways external hires might not.

However, even Marsh recognized limits to this approach. As their AI applications expanded, they hired additional engineers, data scientists, and product managers to support broader adoption. The key was starting with available internal talent while being realistic about the need for external expertise.

"We started with a small team in Dublin–many were early in their careers–but as AI adoption grew, we expanded," Beswick explained to us in an interview. "Some came from our innovation center, others from existing teams, and we recruited externally when needed. The key was getting started with the talent we had and scaling as we learned."

CASE STUDY: LEVI STRAUSS'S BOOT CAMP APPROACH

Even before ChatGPT gained mainstream awareness, retailer Levi Strauss launched machine learning boot camps for its employees.[14] (Coauthor Katia Walsh launched and led the Levi's Machine Learning boot camps in 2021.) While this example predates the current generative AI era, it demonstrates the power of intensive, hands-on capability development that organizations can adapt for today's AI landscape.

The goals were ambitious: train employees, offer access to all, and enable them to take responsibility for their learning. Hundreds of people around the world participated–most with no computer science background, some without college degrees, and many who had never seen code. However, they took responsibility for their learning. They persevered through eight weeks of hands-on, intensive practical training in machine learning, Python, and agile ways of working, using Levi's data to solve Levi's problems.

Consider Michael Buchanan's transformation. Starting as a stock clerk and working up to store manager over fifteen years, Michael was one of 350 employees who applied for the intensive program. He was selected based on his problem-solving skills, with no requirement for a college degree or prior analytical training. For two months, he left his store role to attend the boot camp, studying Python and machine learning for nine hours a day. By the program's end, at the age of thirty-eight, he had become a data scientist with a job in the Levi Strauss & Co.'s Strategy and AI organization.

Approximately a quarter of boot camp participants transitioned into new roles; others returned to their positions with enhanced skills. Inventory planners automated data processes, design employees developed generative AI models for new products, and distribution center workers used predictive AI for proactive maintenance. All positioned themselves for opportunities they wouldn't have had otherwise.

In late 2025, Buchanan's experience came full circle when Levi's launched STITCH, an AI super assistant to help Levi's store employees answer any questions they may encounter.[15] Tapping his experience as a store manager, Buchanan developed the idea at an internal hackathon and guided the rollout to an initial fifty stores with plans to expand to all stores in 2026.

Buchanan reflected on what the boot camp did for his career, sharing in an interview with us, "The boot camp touched on maybe 10 percent of what I would be doing. The learning never stops. That boot camp was the start of what has been a five-year learning experience because of how rapidly technology changes. The learning continues, it never ends." He pointed out that mindset is the key to successful reskilling. "I do think that anyone can do [reskilling]," Buchanan explained. "But they need the mindset of being able to take that risk and see it as a challenge and opportunity and not a threat."

Modern applications: Today's organizations can apply similar intensive development approaches using current generative AI tools and enterprise training partnerships. The principle remains the same: With sufficient commitment and structured learning, organizations can develop sophisticated AI expertise internally, even starting from nontechnical backgrounds. The difference is that modern AI tools make this type of capability development faster and more accessible than ever before.

Levi's has positioned itself as an employer of choice while garnering value from the practical work that employees completed during the boot camp. This approach demonstrates how intensive internal development can create AI talent while building organizational capability.

REDESIGNING WORK AND THE ROLE OF HR

As AI changes how we work, it's also changing what work *is*. Job descriptions are no longer neat lists of clearly defined tasks. Roles are evolving from static positions into dynamic skill sets. And workflows, once supporting handoffs from person to person, now loop through systems where agents, automations, and people cocreate outcomes.

At the center of all this change is the employee, who is now working with both other people and AI. This is more than a productivity story; it's a transformation story, and no group is more central to building that transformation than HR.

Barbara Cominelli, the executive chairman of Spindox, a publicly listed IT services and AI consulting firm, understands the importance of HR's involvement. "We often start with productivity and customer experience, but the risk is sticking there," she said in an interview with us. The real work is reimagining roles and fixing the skill mismatch—and that means HR must be in the room designing how people and AI will work together.

"AI is the new coworker," Cominelli added, so managers should expect to coach differently—as if "having an intern . . . who knows everything." In a prior transformation, her team made dignity explicit: They renamed call center "reps" to "consultants," reframed the job as consultative, and upskilled to match. People embraced the change because they could see the personal benefit—and they felt proud of their work again.

When we talk about creating a "superhuman" workforce, we're describing the transformation that occurs when AI augments human abilities in ways that empower people to achieve things they could not have before. This transformation requires intentional support and a clear understanding of what employees experience during the transition.

The path from AI-anxious to AI-empowered follows a predictable arc. Initially, employees face the fundamental question "What happens to my job?" This fear is rational—AI does automate tasks, and some roles will indeed change dramatically or disappear entirely. But for those who successfully make the transition, the transformation is profound.

This transformation reveals what becoming superhuman means: It's the ability to focus on uniquely human qualities—empathy, creative problem-solving, strategic thinking—while AI handles routine, administrative, or computational work. The result is employees who can deliver far more value than either humans or AI could achieve independently. We'll explore the topic of how to lead superhumans in chapter 12.

CASE STUDY: MODERNA'S HR EVOLUTION

Consider how Moderna's CHRO Tracey Franklin has integrated AI into strategic planning.[16] Rather than replacing human insight, AI helps analyze workforce trends, predict skill gaps, and model different organizational scenarios. Franklin uses these AI-powered insights to make more informed decisions about talent strategy, while applying human judgment to interpret the results and consider factors that AI might overlook. As Franklin explained, this shift allows the organization to move toward "work planning" rather than traditional "workforce planning," taking a holistic view of what work is being done and creating the most optimal workflows and resources to match.[17]

In a notable organizational move, Moderna placed Franklin, their former CHRO, in charge of both people and technology functions as chief people and digital technology officer. This means IT now reports through HR leadership—a reversal of the more common pattern where HR reports to IT or operations. The structure indicates that Moderna prioritizes the human element in managing AI transformation and human-AI collaboration.

This represents transformation, not replacement. The CHRO's role has expanded to include AI collaboration, but core human skills such as strategic thinking, relationship building, and organizational intuition remain central. This pattern appears across successful AI implementations: humans and AI working together to achieve outcomes neither could accomplish alone. However, Moderna's approach represents an advanced integration that many organizations haven't reached—the company has deployed over three thousand custom GPTs across its functions and merged HR and IT under unified leadership.[18]

This requires more than access to AI tools and training. Employees need a sense of psychological safety to learn and grow continuously, with ongoing support as both the technology and their roles continue to evolve.

HOW HR MUST TRANSFORM TO SUPPORT SUPERHUMAN WORKERS

This shift to human plus AI collaboration fundamentally changes what HR teams need to do. Traditional HR processes—designed around fixed job descriptions, predictable career paths, and human-only performance metrics—become inadequate when work flows dynamically between humans and AI systems.

Forward-thinking organizations recognize that effective AI adoption requires HR to evolve into a strategic orchestrator of work. This transformation spans four critical dimensions:

- **From reactive support to proactive workforce intelligence.** Traditional HR responds to business needs with historical data and backward-looking analytics. In the AI era, HR becomes predictive and proactive, using AI to maintain dynamic skill inventories, predict workforce needs, and optimize team compositions. This involves transitioning from annual performance reviews to continuous capability assessments, and from intuition-based hiring decisions to data-driven talent matching.
- **From fixed job roles to fluid work design.** The traditional model of static job descriptions becomes obsolete when work flows dynamically between humans and AI systems. Instead of predetermined task lists, HR should develop flexible, skills-based work allocation systems that define roles by expertise and outcomes. This requires rethinking fundamental HR processes so that job postings focus on skills rather than titles, performance evaluations measure collaboration with AI systems, and career progression becomes multidirectional based on skill acquisition rather than vertical promotion ladders.
- **From individual performance to human plus AI team management.** Performance management systems designed for individual human performance

become inadequate when work involves human plus AI partnerships. HR should create new frameworks for evaluating collaboration competency, quality evaluation skills, and delegation expertise. This includes developing performance metrics that account for human plus AI team outcomes, creating manager training programs for leading blended teams and designing feedback systems that improve both human performance and AI system effectiveness.

- **From productivity to purpose.** Beyond productivity gains, AI offers HR the more strategic opportunity to reduce the specific repetitive tasks that drain energy. Instead of claiming AI will "transform" work, start tactically: What if your sales team spent 30 percent less time on data entry? What if customer service reps handled fewer password resets? HR can identify these high-drain, low-value activities through employee surveys, prioritize them for automation, and measure whether people feel more engaged in their remaining work—what some companies are calling "joy at work" metrics.

CASE STUDY: ALLY BANK'S HUMAN AND BUSINESS VALUE WITH AI

Ally Bank offers a compelling example of how an entire organization can benefit from AI-powered work redesign. Their approach demonstrates how AI fluency, individual transformation, work redesign, and HR change combine to create sustainable transformation.

Ally's approach began with acknowledging employee fears directly. "You cannot lie or sugarcoat the reality," explained Sathish Muthukrishnan, chief information and digital officer, in an interview with us. "If we do not adopt technology, we will be left behind." Rather than dismissing concerns, leadership positioned AI fluency as essential for future growth.

The bank invested in comprehensive education for all eleven thousand employees, creating, as Muthukrishnan called it, a common language around AI. They developed an AI playbook that served as an interpreter for employees learning to work with AI. As employees became more proficient, they stopped needing the playbook and started contributing to it—becoming internal experts and champions.

Ally's first large-scale AI application exemplified thoughtful work redesign. Before AI, customer care associates had to multitask between listening to customers and taking detailed notes for compliance and training purposes. This attention splitting often meant missing essential details or providing suboptimal service.

With AI, customer care associates focus entirely on problem-solving and relationship building. The AI solution converts voice conversations to transcripts and generates comprehensive summaries, capturing details that human notetakers might miss while being more articulate and consistent.

Ally Bank's transformation extended beyond individual roles to reshape the entire organization's operations. Leadership established regular AI standups with the executive committee every three weeks, creating accountability systems that keep AI adoption moving forward. The bank made an "AI P&L" to track value from every AI implementation, ensuring that business impact, not technological sophistication, drives decisions.

Most importantly, they made every employee responsible for their own AI fluency, while providing the necessary support to succeed. This combination of individual accountability and organizational support created what Muthukrishnan described as "amplifying our open mindset and growth mindset" across the company.

AI adoption at Ally Bank delivered both business and human value, reimagining how humans and AI can work together to create value that neither could achieve alone. The future belongs to employees who become AI-fluent and organizations that redesign work to support these new capabilities.

YOUR WEEK 9 ACTION PLAN

This week focuses on ensuring your organization has the expertise to execute your AI roadmap. Here are some actions to take this week:

- **Think through your AI fluency program.** Select one department critical to your AI applications and begin planning a focused training "soft launch" with three to five early adopters as peer mentors. Work with the AI leader and HR to create or adopt a simple learning guide for one high-impact AI task and plan to start the training in two weeks.

- **Establish your AI fluency hub-and-spokes model.** Identify your central AI learning hub leader and designate AI champions across key functions. Schedule initial planning meetings to design your six-month capability development program.
- **Address workforce fears directly.** Initiate transparent conversations about how AI will change work, emphasizing AI augmentation rather than replacement. Focus on building trust through open communication about uncertainties and opportunities.
- **Assess your AI talent strategy.** Inventory existing talent and identify critical gaps in AI product management, engineering, data science, and MLOps. Determine which skills to develop internally versus acquiring through partnerships or consulting arrangements based on your organization's size and resources.
- **Begin HR transformation planning.** Meet with HR leadership to discuss how job descriptions, performance management, and career paths need to evolve to support human-AI collaboration. Identify one HR process that can be redesigned for skills-based work allocation.

SUMMARY

You've now completed Week 9 of your 90-day preparation for AI value creation. In this chapter, you accomplished the following:

- **Established the fundamental principle: Everyone in your organization needs to learn AI, and everyone needs to start now.** Rather than debating who needs training first, the focus is simple: Universal AI capability development is not optional; it's essential for organizational survival and competitive advantage.
- **Explored domain-specific approaches to AI expertise** that go beyond generic training to develop competencies tailored to how different departments use AI in their work.
- **Adopted the hub-and-spokes organizational model** for developing AI fluency across your entire organization, ensuring coordinated training and support.

- **Identified size-appropriate strategies for AI talent sourcing**, with specific guidance on core AI roles and whether to develop skills internally or access them through partnerships.
- **Understood how HR must transform into a strategic orchestrator** of all work, redesigning job descriptions, performance management, and career paths around dynamic human plus AI partnerships.
- **Learned from real-world examples** from Ally Bank, IKEA, and Levi Strauss showing how organizations successfully built AI-capable workforces while creating new value.

With your skill set established, you're ready to explore the technical foundation that will enable AI roadmap delivery. Chapter 10 will show you how to assemble the data and toolset to support its success.

It is not the strongest of the species that survives, nor the most intelligent, but the one most responsive to change.

—Charles Darwin

Ten

ASSEMBLING THE AI TOOLSET

THIS CLASSIC QUOTE on evolution takes on a new meaning as we explore the toolset you need to create value with AI. The ability of your AI toolset to adapt will position you for value today and in the future.

The riskiest—and most expensive—way to equip your organization with an AI toolset is to design as if you're building a medieval cathedral, the way traditional IT treats system implementations. It's all about massive, permanent structures with multiyear roadmaps that push completion to the next decade. But the organizations that win with AI aren't building bespoke cathedrals. Instead, they're using a LEGO approach.

AI technology often refers to tools and platforms. How do you differentiate between the two? Compare the individual tools you use—a specific chatbot or data analysis application—to LEGO blocks, which are light, modular, and interchangeable. The platforms serve as baseplates and underlying connectors, allowing you to snap various blocks together to function in concert.

The companies that win with AI assemble adaptable modules that can evolve alongside the technology, without having to retire monolithic systems. When a better component emerges, you can easily swap pieces, add new ones, or reconfigure entire combinations without dismantling the whole system. All modules conform to protocols that enable connectivity with many other systems, allowing for the receipt and transmission of information across your organization.

As a business leader, you don't need to master the intricacies of AI tech stacks. However, you need to understand the approach that best positions you for creating value with AI, both today and as the technology advances. We offer you and your organization a strategic approach to assembling future-proof AI tools and platforms.

It involves a shift in how you view technology's role within your organization. In our experience with legacy organizations, IT departments have traditionally positioned themselves as service providers connecting "the business" with technology companies. In that role, IT has over-indexed on relationship, project, and risk management at the expense of technical expertise. As a result, many IT departments have largely remained stuck in the cost-center area of organizations rather than evolving as value drivers.

Consequently, despite years and multimillions of dollars of investment in enterprise systems, legacy organizations often find themselves woefully unprepared to create value with AI. If this doesn't change now, your organization will not only fall (further) behind, but it will never catch up.

You're now in Week 10 of your 90-day AI implementation. You are planning to cultivate a mindset that embraces AI for value (chapter 8). You know how to equip your people with the necessary skill set to create that value (chapter 9). Now, it's time for the crucial third building block: the toolset. This chapter guides your AI tech choices, helping you avoid being locked into what can soon become obsolete.

Specifically, your objectives for this week are as follows:

- Master the core principle of the AI toolset–designing for rapid scale and continuous change.
- Understand a typical AI system, which comprises four layers: data, AI models, orchestration, and consumption.
- Incorporate security, data governance, and compliance directly into your toolset.
- Identify potential "watchouts" that could derail AI tech deployment.
- Discover how to maintain the agility of tech systems and keep them current as AI evolves.

Let's dive into shaping an AI toolset you can rely on for lasting value and continuous impact expansion.

A note about technical depth: This chapter focuses on the strategic decisions and principles business leaders need to understand about AI toolsets.

For readers who want additional guidance on consumption-layer priorities, security and ethics considerations, common implementation pitfalls, and strategic questions to guide your technical discussions, we've provided supplementary content in appendix B.

GUIDING YOUR AI TOOLSET ASSEMBLY

If you're feeling overwhelmed by the sheer number of AI tools and platforms, you're not alone. You need to find the right ground between doing nothing and chasing every trend. To win with AI, you must guide your organization's AI technology investments and decisions to deliver immediate value, rapid scale, and continuous improvement.

YOUR TECH *IS* CORE TO YOUR BUSINESS

Building your AI toolset isn't an IT decision; it's a *leadership* decision. That's why tech companies' CEOs have consistently guided their technology choices and approach. Your tech choices determine how you can serve customers, adapt to new advancements, and differentiate your organization, leading to a competitive advantage. The tools and platforms that drive value are those that enable fast deployment and rapid scaling, and include built-in flexibility to adapt to technological advancements. They will help your organization respond to changing customer needs, integrate with complementary solutions, and capitalize on new opportunities.

Today, technology is not only a part of the business; it's central to business success. Therefore, business leaders have the responsibility to act as strategic architects of technology choices. You provide the *why* and *what matters most*; your engineering teams bring the *how*.

This strategic leadership of technology decisions has a powerful precedent. In a now-famous 2002 mandate, Amazon founder Jeff Bezos required all teams to expose their data and functionality through service interfaces that communicate with each other within and outside companies (APIs).[1] The top-down directive reconceived how Amazon operated. It forced a modular approach that enabled the company to scale massively and innovate at a speed that other companies without that flexibility struggle to match, and ultimately led to the creation of Amazon Web

Services (AWS). Amazon's move toward an adaptable technology architecture not only transformed the business but also made it more resilient and able to rapidly take on new opportunities. The Bezos mandate also set the direction for tech that remains valid today. As the organization's leader, you must model and embrace adaptable technology in your top-down directive when developing AI applications.

Consider the example of McKinsey & Company's configuration of a centralized knowledge management system, Lilli, using generative AI. From the outset, the team recognized that the underlying AI technology would evolve rapidly. They designed Lilli with a flexible architecture that enabled continuous evolution.

Kitti Lakner, an associate partner at McKinsey, highlighted this adaptive approach in an interview with us: "We've had to refactor most of Lilli at least three times just to keep up with the pace of change." This mindset–building a system designed to be taken apart and reassembled with better parts–is the essence of a modern AI toolset. It stands in stark contrast to traditional IT projects and is essential to achieving success with AI.

In addition to flexible architecture, the AI toolset must directly serve business needs and goals.[2] McKinsey's Lilli.ai is specifically designed to meet the business needs of employees and clients. It allows consultants to quickly search, summarize, and synthesize McKinsey's vast repository of proprietary data, client work, research, and expert insights. McKinsey's leadership anchored the platform's capabilities to key business domains.

"These domains comprise the core collection of valuable problems that we need to solve from a business standpoint," Erik Roth, a McKinsey senior partner, explained to us in an interview.

This focus on value acts as a filter for the numerous vendor pitches and technology trends you'll encounter. If a tool, software, or system doesn't directly support your top business priorities, then question, defer, and discard. Just as AI serves your strategy and helps you accelerate and advance it, so does the toolset that makes AI possible.

ASSEMBLING YOUR TOOLSET

One of the age-old debates in business is whether to build or buy technology solutions. With AI, the most critical technology decision is not whether to build or buy but *how to assemble* modular components to ensure flexibility. Given AI's rapid pace of change, your toolset must be able to accommodate, change, and adapt more quickly than enterprise systems allow. The winning approach is a dynamic assembly of best-in-class modular, interchangeable components designed to connect and configured to operate together. As tech advances, you can swap, add, subtract, or multiply individual components and entire combinations. When a new component (new model, new service, new protocol) emerges, you can incorporate it without the need to rebuild everything. This is crucial as new tools and resources enter the mainstream.

In niche cases, as an exception to the rule, you may need to build proprietary AI solutions. Choose wisely. Build only what is truly distinctive for your organization and can assure you a competitive advantage. For most organizations, there is no reason to build custom systems and products. There are only limited specialized cases that warrant custom development. Here are some examples:

1. What you need is so distinct or innovative that it's not yet available elsewhere.
2. It would require extensive customization to fit your specific data, systems, and workforces.
3. Your explicit goal is to develop expertise and support learning.

The first two considerations fit with McKinsey's initial approach to assembling Lilli. For example, in an earlier release of the platform, McKinsey built their own "reranker," a model that orders and prioritizes information chunks for data processing. But as soon as a suitable commercial offering became available, McKinsey switched to a tech vendor for the same reranker component. McKinsey's Lakner explained to us: "We should only be working on what is truly distinctive to us; everything else we should be leveraging or shaping to work with what we have."

The third consideration is what Southern New Hampshire University exemplifies in its approach to its AI toolset, as discussed in the case study (see callout box).

CASE STUDY: SOUTHERN NEW HAMPSHIRE UNIVERSITY'S "BUILD-TO-BUY" APPROACH

Southern New Hampshire University (SNHU) is one of the largest providers of online higher education, serving over 200,000 students worldwide. The university knew from the beginning that they would not build AI tech from scratch. However, as a starting point, they decided to create initial GPT tools linked to their data to help them understand the technology's potential and limitations and learn the questions to ask as future buyers assembling AI tools.

SNHU used its limited resources to develop a Library Assistant tool and a Course Syllabus analyzer, facilitating their initial learning. Robert MacAuslan, SNHU vice president for AI, told us: "The AI landscape is still very unsettled. By building capabilities internally, even on a trial basis, we've been able to learn where our models fail, which gives us a more informed position to evaluate off-the-shelf solutions down the line."

Their build-to-buy approach allowed them to learn several things:

- AI-driven curriculum audits helped them understand the requirements for content analysis.
- Omnichannel student support taught them about the complexities of conversational AI.
- Data-driven personalization revealed their analytics and integration needs.

SNHU developed internal expertise in assembling AI technology. It was built strategically to enable them to become an informed and discerning buyer.

THE FOUR LAYERS OF AN AI SYSTEM

With the modularity imperative, it's time to understand the components you're assembling. Every AI system, regardless of its size, sophistication, or industry, comprises four distinct layers (See figure 10-1). Think of these layers as the essential components of a kitchen. Just as a world-class restaurant requires high-quality ingredients, professional equipment, skilled coordination, and excellent service to

Figure 10-1: The four layers of an AI system

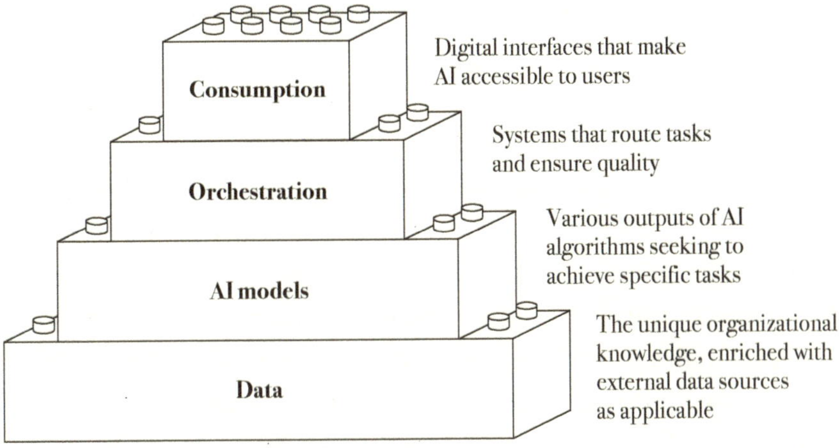

create an exceptional dining experience, an AI system needs four interconnected layers that work in harmony:

1. **Data (ingredients):** Makes AI possible and provides differentiation.
2. **AI models (cooking equipment):** Processes, prepares, and combines data to create AI algorithms and models that produce specific outputs from the data.
3. **Orchestration (head chef):** Coordinates various AI models and workflows to ensure the desired outcomes of an AI system.
4. **Consumption (service and presentation):** The interfaces and apps that enable users to interact with AI models, consume the information they provide, and take action. Just as a beautifully plated dish served with care determines whether diners enjoy their meal, this layer is essential in stimulating adoption and engagement.

In a modular kitchen, you can upgrade appliances, change suppliers, add new cooking stations, and update the interior without having to rebuild the entire kitchen. Similarly, in an AI system, each layer can evolve independently while maintaining seamless integration with the others. The head chef (orchestration) coordinates everything, ensuring the right ingredients (data) reach the right processing and equipment (AI models) at the right time to create a consistent experience for your guests to enjoy (consumption).

Let's examine each layer and how they interact to deliver business value.

> **BUILDING FOR CONTINUOUS PROGRESSION**
>
> Again, the key to creating the AI toolset is assembling layers that are flexible enough to support evolution without requiring complete rebuilds. AI capabilities will grow from basic assistance to sophisticated coordination of multiple models and tools. Like a well-designed kitchen, the modular approach allows incremental addition of new tools and platforms. For example, an AI system may start with basic AI information retrieval tools, then introduce more complex tools that perform multiple tasks, then incorporate AI agents, and eventually form collaborative ensembles of multiple agents.
>
> Each layer of the AI system you assemble today will become more capable as the organization matures with AI. As data connections multiply, models become more specialized, orchestration handles increasingly complex workflows, and user interfaces become more intuitive. Most importantly, these layers amplify each other; improvements in one layer enhance the others, creating a compounding effect across the AI system.

LAYER 1: DATA—AN ORGANIZATION'S GREATEST ASSET

We cannot have AI without data. AI today is only possible because of the accumulation of vast amounts of data over the past thirty years—the combined result of digitization, mobile device adoption, and cloud technologies. While the falling costs of storage and computing have also enabled AI, it's the data that is key to developing, training, validating, and further advancing AI.

An organization's unique data is its greatest asset. The data represents a company's heritage, intellectual capital, and the wisdom of its employees and customers throughout its history. General-purpose AI models, such as GPT-4 or Claude, are powerful but also generic; they are familiar with the world, but they lack knowledge of *your* customers, operational processes, or institutional knowledge. Your organization's data reflects your history, learnings, and decades of work and insights from previous employees. While tech companies lead with sophisticated AI-native competencies, legacy companies have more and richer data. The more years you've been in business, the more data you have. When one of us worked at the iconic Levi's brand, we had access to a treasure trove of 168 years' worth of data. That enabled Levi's to leapfrog with AI, even though the data sources and elements still required refinement to make them available and usable for AI.

Having accumulated data is different from being able to use it effectively. That's where most organizations face challenges that can impede their ability to quickly assemble their AI toolset.

THE THREE TOP CHALLENGES WITH DATA

Organizations experience at least three key challenges with their data.

One challenge is that most people and businesses do not understand the full richness and availability of data today. They tend to think of structured data, neatly laid out in rows and columns. However, data is all around us, and AI thrives on unstructured data. Anything digitized becomes data, including text, photos, videos, customer call transcripts, retail shop customer journeys and heat maps, equipment sensors' data, delivery truck route information, GPS maps, charts, and visualizations. Data is continuously entering and flowing across business environments at the speed of life, far beyond the reach of companies' systems of record.

A second challenge is to find, access, and make all this data–scattered across silos–systematically available. Data is stored across systems including Excel spreadsheets, CRM, ERP, content management systems, point-of-sale systems, and property management systems. Additionally, there are process documents, analyst reports, earnings, transcripts, and, yes, employees' minds. At a financial services company where one of us worked a few years ago, the best data catalog and dictionary was a veteran employee who knew everything about the sources of data, what elements they included, where to find them, and how to make sense of them. When that employee retired, so did the data catalog and dictionary.

A third challenge is that organizations have a lot of work to do to rationalize all this data and make it usable. Many companies lack a standard, agreed-upon definition of even basic terms such as *customer*, *territory*, or *product*. Therefore, a seemingly simple question about a company's number of customers yields different answers, with wide variation, especially across business lines and geographies. In complex legacy businesses, it's not uncommon to struggle with key metrics such as manufacturing costs, sales figures by territory or business unit, or customer-experience scores. The data exists, but without agreed-upon, clear definitions and consistent, universal adherence to them, companies face different answers to the same questions.

DON'T LET DATA ISSUES HOLD YOU BACK

These challenges do not mean you cannot begin your AI deployment immediately. The key is to proceed with pragmatism and speed while laying the groundwork for scalability and resilience. And here is something that we've learned from experience that most people won't tell you: You *can*–and indeed you *should*–work on deploying AI to deliver value for your prioritized strategic work, while at the same time getting to work on the data you need. You cannot afford to have feasibility hold you back.

For decades, the mantra was "get your data house in order first, then do AI." The problem? This perfectionist approach can hold you back indefinitely. Modern AI, unlike traditional analytics, can work with messy, incomplete, and, particularly, unstructured data–the documents, emails, images, and conversations that comprise 80 to 90 percent of most organizations' data assets.

Even if the data is not yet in a state where you can use it for AI models, don't wait. Let's say you have prioritized a specific AI application, for example, an AI-enhanced customer experience. Start planning the overall deployment by identifying an AI solution, agreeing on an implementation plan and success metrics, and determining support requirements. Concurrently, begin lining up data sources, determining data elements, and reconciling business definitions with technical systems' capture. Do all of this concurrently, not linearly; don't wait to get all the data "in order." Start aggregating the data, feeding the models, connecting the workflows, and designing the user experience. As you work on these layers concurrently, you will make progress. After deploying the initial AI system, continue adding and updating data, refreshing the models, and enhancing the experience.

Here is a truth that you won't often hear: There is no such thing as perfect data. Never will be. Pursuing perfection derails more initiatives than technical hurdles ever could. Your proverbial data lakes are not pristine and never will be. The more accurate picture is a data ocean–vast, fast, and uncontrollable. Unstructured data is coming at us like a tsunami, with millions of data events rushing by at the speed of life. In the few seconds it took you to read this short paragraph, more data has entered your company's systems and flooded your devices. We have reached a point where AI generates artificial data (see callout box).

But even if you stick only to real data, consider data to be like this: You just cleaned your house; it's neat for perhaps a glorious few minutes, but then the dog struts in from the rain, shakes his wet fur, and leaves muddy footprints all over the floor. The children run in from school, throw their backpacks and shoes next to the dog's footprints, and you bring in groceries, bags, and delivery boxes. In minutes, the house is the opposite of neat and tidy, full of the chaos of new events. That's data. New data elements are continuously livestreaming into our systems and repositories, bringing new chaos, patterns, and value.

THE REAL VALUE OF SYNTHETIC DATA

Digital and AI products are constantly generating data. When one of us worked at the venerable financial services firm Prudential, we learned the saying "Data makes digital smart, and digital makes data big." As people browse websites, use apps, and engage in other ways, they continuously generate data. That's how Big Data came to be; mobile devices and social media became ubiquitous.

However, there is now an even more significant development with generative AI. In addition to producing real data, generative AI can also create artificial, or synthetic, data. AI achieves this by studying the structure, correlations, and distributions present in real data, learning the patterns, and applying generative models and statistical techniques to create simulated data that matches them.[3] The outcome is artificial data that closely mimics the original and retains statistical relevance, without containing any real-world, identifiable information.

This synthetic data has real-world value. Companies can use it to quickly test ideas, products, pricing concepts, and more, with unlimited permutations and without exposing any personal information. Businesses can start relying on synthetic data to simulate market conditions, forecast trends, and perform risk analysis. The benefits include unrestricted innovation, speed to market, privacy protections, cost savings, the ability to augment real datasets and replace missing data with confidence, compliance with data localization and privacy regulations, and the facilitation of secure cross-company analysis. With deliberate effort, synthetic data can also enrich limited, inadequate, or unbalanced datasets, reducing or even eliminating bias.

Here are some examples of real-world value:

- Medical research uses synthetic patient data for analysis and testing.
- Fraud detection and pricing models simulate potential events, enabling the development of real mitigation measures.
- Investment companies generate simulated market activity datasets for improved trading and risk assessment algorithms.

MANAGING AND GOVERNING DATA ASSETS

Treating data as a strategic asset requires a balance between accessibility and protection, ensuring your data remains secure and compliant while enabling AI to unlock its value. This transforms AI from a generic tool into an organizational brain that thinks like the organization and acts in its best interest.

While you don't need to wait to start unlocking value from your data, treating data as an asset ensures that you can scale its value safely and sustainably. Data management and data governance play crucial roles in achieving this. Let's look at both.

- **Data management** involves collecting, storing, organizing, and enriching data elements and sources, as well as maintaining data repositories and pipelines for continuous data flows. It encompasses the technical and procedural work of ensuring data availability and usability, including backup and recovery systems, data storage infrastructure, and day-to-day activities that maintain data accessibility and usability. It's the hands-on work that brings data policies to life.
- **Data governance** refers to establishing the policies, standards, and decision-making rights that determine how the organization manages data as a strategic asset. It defines who can access what data, the rules for classifying and protecting data, what constitutes acceptable use, and who has the authority to make data-related decisions. It provides the framework that gives the organization confidence to use data as an asset while mitigating risk.

Data governance is the cornerstone of responsible AI implementation, with systems that enable, rather than block, AI value creation. Think of data governance as the framework that allows you to confidently say *yes* to valuable AI applications versus defaulting to *no* out of uncertainty.

Here are some of the key questions leaders can ask to guide technical teams in developing effective data governance:

- Data capture
    - Are we capturing all the data flowing into our systems, within the limits set by privacy agreements, regulations, and contractual obligations?
    - Do customer agreements and contracts unnecessarily limit data capture?
    - If so, how can we enable more data capture, recognizing that data is an asset we should mine?
- Data retention
    - With appropriate controls in place, are we retaining data for as long as legally and practically possible, recognizing that data is an irreplaceable asset?
- Data availability and accessibility
    - Do we understand where various data sources and elements reside in organizational systems and files?
    - How can we access them efficiently?
    - How do we strike a balance between accessibility and security controls?
- Data classification and access
    - How are we categorizing data by sensitivity and business value?
    - To clarify which AI applications are appropriate for each category, are we ensuring that our most sensitive data is used only with our most secure, vetted AI tools, while allowing greater flexibility and experimentation with less sensitive data?
- Privacy protection
    - What techniques are we using to protect individual privacy while enabling the value of AI?

    - How do we handle personally identifiable information (PII) and ensure consent management across all AI applications?
    - How can we strike a balance between privacy protection and the ability to collect and analyze customer data, allowing us to serve them in personalized, predictive, and proactive ways with their permission?
- Data security
    - With AI, responsibility for data security extends throughout the organization–from data capturers to data producers and data users, with most people fulfilling all three roles. This means that security and privacy protections should be in place at every point where users access and consume data, not just at the point of data capture and creation.
    - The questions here are: Are we aware of security risks and educating the entire organization? How is AI impacting data security? What more can we do to secure the organization's data?
- Usability and reliability
    - How do we determine if the data is good enough for a specific AI application?
    - The goal is to move from asking "Is data clean?" to "Is data usable to create value with AI?" This means pragmatically balancing the cost of data improvements against expected business value.
- Common definitions
    - Do we have standardized metrics and agreed-upon definitions for key business terms, especially those used to manage performance?
    - How do we ensure consistency in the interpretation of data across the organization?

The answers should reflect an organization's approach to treating data as an asset while balancing risk management and AI value creation. The key is having explicit answers rather than assuming someone else is handling these issues.

A PRAGMATIC GUIDE TO DATA: FOCUS ON THE HIGHEST-VALUE AND HIGHEST-RISK DATA ELEMENTS

There is a key difference between the data required for compliance and reporting versus the data needed for AI. Data governance and management can be an overwhelming space in and of itself. Because data is constantly flowing and changing, it can feel like a Herculean, expensive, and futile task to even attempt to control it. One of us cheekily calls data management and governance "a black hole that can suck you in and you can never get out."

But it doesn't have to be that way. We have developed a pragmatic approach to managing and governing data, and we would like to share it with you. Instead of embarking on grand data cleaning programs, employ this practical way to view and use your company's data. This means assessing data on two dimensions: risk and value.

Highest-risk data elements

You *need* to govern and manage the highest-risk data elements. These are often referred to as critical data elements, including PII, financial account information, sensitive health data, and, in the workplace, computer access credentials, compensation, demographics, and performance reviews. Those data elements need to be clear, instantly accessible, and always trackable. But fret not—even this is not as monumental a task as it used to be. Variants of AI, such as fuzzy matching and other machine learning techniques, can now help connect and clean data elements; for example, identifying if the same data appears under different names in different systems or even the same system.

Highest-value data elements

You *want* to govern and manage the highest-value data elements. These data are not necessarily confidential but represent key business metrics that leaders use to manage their organizations. Examples include sales figures, marketing conversions, Net Promoter Scores, and operational statistics, such as system uptime, delivery times, new account openings, issue resolution proportions and timings, and more. Having a standard, consistent definition of these data elements enables capturing, tracking, and reporting the same information across a company. Think of this as the dashboard that helps a company function–you cannot manage what you cannot measure–and the earnings reports that public companies release on analyst calls.

How do you assess the value and risk of data elements? The highest-value data elements are those that

- function like a pulse of your organization's performance and are needed to manage your business effectively and for reporting;
- help you understand your customers, monitor their needs, and predict your ability and opportunity to serve them; and
- help you deliver on your strategic priorities–for example, product adoption, pricing, positioning, and competitive differentiation.

The pragmatic approach to managing and governing data involves identifying the highest-value and highest-risk elements within your data. With this inventory at hand, you can now focus on these data elements to ensure ongoing visibility, monitoring, and reporting. This involves establishing standard business and technical definitions for data essential to reporting, tracking information critical for risk assessment, and organizing customer data to fuel concrete improvements.

Anything else can be valuable data you want in your systems, but that you don't need to include in your system of data management and governance. Of course, you can continuously monitor what data is becoming risky or more valuable and adjust accordingly.

ORGANIZING DATA ACROSS THE ORGANIZATION

For the rest of your data, capture it, make it accessible, supplement it with external data as applicable, and connect it all so that AI can analyze it. All this other unstructured data, once seen as a challenge, now represents your prime source of competitive advantage because it contains the nuanced insights that traditional approaches consistently miss.

The value of combining data for AI's power multiplies exponentially as it uses more data sources and connects them, processing them at the speed and scale that only today's technology can offer.

There are different approaches to enabling AI to access data from disparate, siloed systems. Some enterprises aggregate siloed data in a central repository. Other companies leave data as it is and instead incorporate a unified data access layer that uses standard connections (APIs) to plug AI applications directly into data sources within various enterprise systems. The specific approach is less important than the ability to access and tap into the variety and richness of data across enterprise systems—that's what using data as an asset means.

This connectivity among data sources cannot be overstated. Magical things happen when AI accesses data sources and elements that have never previously met. With that access, AI can unearth uncommon insights, surface unexpected relationships, and reveal unconventional patterns.

For instance, when one of us worked at a major telecommunications company, we achieved a higher return on investment by leveraging AI models that combined network infrastructure data with customer-value data. Before we did that, capital expenditures for network improvement were allocated solely to alleviate the highest congestion in the mobile network, without consideration for the customers who lived and worked in those areas. However, after AI accessed previously disparate network, financial, and customer data, the models made connections among mobile network infrastructure, capital investment, and customer value.

With that new model's recommendations, the company was able to channel the same capital expenditures to mobile network cells where customers with the highest value lived and worked. And that instantly delivered a 15 percent higher return on the same investment. The more data you have, the more ingredients AI models have to work with, process, analyze, and use to make predictions—and the more value you can get from them.

LAYER 2: AI MODELS—MAKING SENSE OF DATA

Once you have data, the foundation of any AI development, you need AI models to make sense of it and create desired outputs. If data represents the chef's ingredients, AI models are their specialized cooking equipment. You wouldn't use a microwave to bake a soufflé, and you wouldn't fire up a commercial oven to reheat coffee. The same principle applies to AI models.

HOW MODELS WORK: PATTERN RECOGNITION AT SCALE

At their core, AI models are sophisticated pattern recognition systems inspired by how the human brain processes information. A neural network–the essence of modern AI–consists of interconnected layers that learn to recognize patterns by analyzing vast numbers of examples. Show a neural network thousands of photos labeled "cat" or "not cat," and it learns to identify the patterns that distinguish felines from other objects. Show it millions of customer transactions labeled "fraud" or "legitimate," and it learns to spot suspicious patterns.

The breakthrough with today's AI is scale. Modern models process billions of data points, with billions of parameters, identifying patterns too subtle or complex for traditional programming to capture. This is why AI can generate humanlike text and images, detect manufacturing defects, or identify disease in X-rays with remarkable accuracy–it's learned from more examples than any one human could process in multiple lifetimes.

DO YOU NEED YOUR OWN MODEL?

The most important question about AI models is strategic: Do you need your own model?

For the vast majority of organizations, the answer is a resounding no.

Building a model from scratch–training it on vast datasets with specialized computing infrastructure–requires enormous resources and expertise that few organizations possess or need. Very few organizations attempt this level of bespoke model development. For example, Bloomberg trained its fifty-billion-parameter BloombergGPT for finance in early 2023.[4] The initiative required roughly 1.3 million GPU hours on 512 A100 chips and a core team of nine over several months, resulting in an estimated total cost between $3.5 million and $8 million–including computing, engineering, and research–based on Bloomberg's public disclosures and credible industry analysis.[5] This investment was quickly eclipsed when general-purpose models like ChatGPT-3.5 and GPT-4 outperformed BloombergGPT on financial tasks within months of release.[6]

Think of AI as electricity. In the early 1900s, many factories generated their own power. Today, only specialized facilities do so; most organizations simply plug into the grid. AI models are following the same trajectory. In the same way that you connect your residence or office building to electricity, you'd connect your data to frontier models like those from OpenAI, Anthropic, Google, Microsoft, or open-source alternatives. These general-purpose models are competent and continuously improving. The real value lies not in creating your own model but in applying these models to your data and empowering your business with insights and predictions that harness the combined robustness of the model and the uniqueness of your data.

Making general models work for your business

A practical approach to making a general-purpose AI model an expert in your specific business is available. Think of it like preparing a student for an exam. This is an open-book approach, retrieval augmented generation (RAG). Like a student taking an open-book exam, the AI "looks up" information in real time rather than relying solely on what it memorized during training. When someone asks a question, the system first retrieves the most relevant, current information from your knowledge bases–customer records, product catalogs, policy documents–and provides it to the model as context. The model then combines its general knowledge with your specific information to generate accurate, relevant responses.

RAG excels when your information changes frequently. Update your product catalog or revise a policy, and the AI instantly has access to the latest version–no retraining required. For most business applications, RAG offers the right balance of accuracy, flexibility, and maintainability. At the time of this writing, this approach is recommended for most organizations starting with AI.

You may also occasionally hear or read about fine-tuning. In contrast to RAG, this fine-tuning is a closed-book approach. It permanently teaches the model of your company's specific knowledge, terminology, and ways of thinking. Like a student who has memorized everything, a fine-tuned model becomes faster and more consistent for specialized, high-volume tasks. For example, a customer service chatbot that must always respond in your precise brand voice benefits from fine-tuning.

However, fine-tuning requires significant effort. When your information changes, you must retrain the entire model, requiring the student to memorize new material and retake the exam. As we do not recommend training your own models, we also strongly advise you not to fine-tune them. It's usually a waste of effort and money, with little return.

CHOOSING AND COMBINING MODELS FOR DIFFERENT TASKS

Many organizations start by ensuring they can easily swap out a single model, like upgrading their primary cooking appliance. However, as you mature with AI, you'll use multiple specialized models, each tackling distinct tasks. You might use a small, open-source, fast, and inexpensive model for simple, high-volume tasks like routing customer inquiries, while reserving a powerful, sophisticated model for complex analyses that require deep reasoning.

The goal is to build a kitchen equipped with a range of appliances ready for any business challenge, while maintaining the ability to upgrade any component as better options emerge. Different AI models excel at various tasks–some specialize in language, others in images or video, and still others in numerical predictions.

Just as data fuels AI models, AI models form the foundation of AI agents. AI agents are software systems that use AI models to perform specific tasks independently (see chapter 1). There are many AI agents, and the number sometimes matches the roles, tasks, or jobs within an organization. With the continuous advancement of AI in business, companies are increasingly deploying AI agents, either independently or in partnership with hyperscalers such as Salesforce's Agentforce and Google Cloud Platform's Agentspace.

As we defined in chapter 1, a multi-agent system involves several AI agents working together, coordinated by an orchestration layer to achieve a common objective. When many AI agents interact and connect within an enterprise, the orchestration layer (layer 3) becomes critical: It routes each task to the most appropriate model, ensuring efficiency and quality.

AI MODELS GLOSSARY

- **Neural network:** An AI system inspired by the human brain, consisting of interconnected layers that learn to recognize patterns from examples.
- **Large language model (LLM):** A type of generative AI trained on vast amounts of text to understand and generate humanlike language. Examples include GPT-4, Claude, and Gemini.
- **Diffusion model:** A type of generative AI that creates images and videos by learning to reverse a process that gradually adds noise to images,

creating highly detailed, realistic visuals. Unlike LLMs, which operate on sequences of words, diffusion models operate on visual data.

- **Retrieval augmented generation (RAG):** A technique that enhances AI responses by retrieving relevant information from your knowledge bases in real time and providing it as context to the model.
- **An agent:** A system that uses AI models to perform actions autonomously. An AI model is a tool for analyzing data or generating content. In contrast, an AI agent takes the output of a model and uses it to make decisions and execute tasks, such as booking a flight or making an API call.

LAYER 3: ORCHESTRATION—ENSURING QUALITY OUTPUTS AND COORDINATED WORKFLOW

The orchestration layer is usually necessary in complex AI systems, whether they include AI models, AI agents, or both. Orchestration provides essential supervision and quality control across multiple AI models, AI agents, and the data and workflows that underpin them. Even in an AI system without agents, orchestration coordinates models' efforts, manages data flows, and ensures efficient execution of complex, multistep tasks. This layer connects, manages, and coordinates various AI models, data pipelines, and tools to work together seamlessly, which is crucial for achieving valuable outcomes from complex workflows. Orchestration is the "head chef" that routes queries, manages multistep processes, and ensures that the final AI-generated outputs meet standards for accuracy, relevance, and referencing before they reach a user.

Some key components of an orchestration layer include the following:

- **Query routing.** Analyzes each request and directs it to the most appropriate resource—sending a complex question to an AI model, a factual query to an internal CRM database, or a command to an external software tool like SAP Concur. At Marsh, for example, the team built a "tool selection" capability that acts as the "first call" to decide if a query requires a specialized tool and, if so, which one to use.

- **Coordination**. Manages sequences of actions to complete a single task. For example, it can automatically extract key data points from an incoming invoice, verify that the amounts match the corresponding purchase order in a financial system, and then route the invoice to the correct person for approval.
- **Quality control**. Assesses AI-generated outputs before they are presented to a user. This can include automatic checks to ensure an output doesn't contain confidential project names, adheres to the company's brand voice, or gets flagged for human review if it discusses a sensitive topic. It also provides users with simple feedback tools, such as a thumbs-up or thumbs-down, to continually improve the AI system.
- **Observability**. Traces what's happening inside AI systems by using logging prompts, queries, and outputs. Some models now allow you to see–via a scratchpad–what they are "thinking" and the actions that they take based on that. This transparency helps diagnose issues and provides audit trails for compliance. Additionally, observability fosters the institutional trust necessary for scaling AI. Business leaders have a responsibility to ensure that their organizations' AI systems include quality assurance and monitoring.

Let's consider an example of an AI orchestration in an agentic system. Imagine an AI engagement management agent that receives the goal to "launch a campaign for a new product to increase leads by 15 percent."

- First, it activates a fellow agent, a data scientist that analyzes data, identifies patterns, and segments audiences automatically to pinpoint the ideal audience for the campaign.
- Next, after identifying the audience, the AI engagement management agent coordinates with a content agent–an AI system that creates original content, such as email drafts and social media posts–to develop personalized messages tailored to that audience.
  So far, we have three AI agents: an engagement management agent, a data scientist agent, and a content creation agent.

- Next, a fourth AI agent, a data analyst–an AI system that monitors and reports performance metrics in real time–sets up a dashboard to track the campaign's performance.

The engagement management agent is activating and bringing these three agents together, ensuring they are each focused on their individual tasks while working simultaneously to deliver on the overall goal of creating a CRM campaign and reporting its results. In this example, the engagement management agent serves as an orchestrator, guiding other agents toward a common goal.

CASE STUDY: MCKINSEY'S MULTI-AGENT BREAKTHROUGH

To test the power of orchestration, McKinsey undertook an interesting experiment. Its goal was to replicate an analytical project to predict sales performance based on four years of client data. Traditionally, this project would have required a team of five consultants working for twelve weeks.

In this test, McKinsey deployed an ensemble of specialized AI agents designed to mimic the human team. The agents in McKinsey's experiment included a data scientist, a code interpreter, an engagement manager, and a data analyst. The human team provided the data and defined the business questions, and the AI agents then collaborated to complete the project in three hours.

When McKinsey ran this test five times, the multi-agent system consistently produced more accurate predictive models than the original human team, surfacing new insights. "These [AI] agents knew how to work with each other and what they could do and what they couldn't do, and what the rules of engagement were," explained Kitti Lakner, an associate partner at McKinsey, to us in an interview. To succeed, this AI system required what she calls "advanced orchestration"–managing how the different AI agents collaborate, share information, and check each other's work to ensure quality.

Supporting advanced orchestration

As multi-agent systems–networks of specialized AI agents working together, such as the McKinsey example–become more sophisticated, new standards are emerging to facilitate the effective collaboration of different AI components. At the time of this writing, Model Context Protocol (MCP) is one such open standard that solves the challenge of how different AI components can share context and maintain state across complex workflows.

"Maintaining state" means keeping track of what's happened so far in a process, like remembering previous decisions, intermediate results, and the current status of work. Consider a restaurant ordering system. When you place an order, the system tracks what you ordered, any special requests, the cooking progress, and which server is handling your table. If your server goes on break, the replacement server instantly knows your order status and what's still needed. MCP works similarly for AI agents, ensuring that every agent is aware of the full context of the work, including which tasks have been completed and what happens next.

While many of these standards are continually evolving, they represent the kind of coordination that will enable AI systems to seamlessly work together on increasingly complex business challenges, with greater independence.

LAYER 4: CONSUMPTION–DRIVING ADOPTION AND ENGAGEMENT

Even the most sophisticated AI system fails if people don't use it. Layer 4, the consumption layer, where humans interact with AI, determines whether AI investments deliver value or gather digital dust. Like dining, you can have the finest ingredients and world-class chefs, but if the service is unwelcoming or the experience feels uncomfortable, guests won't return.

HOW CONSUMPTION DESIGN UNLOCKS VALUE

Cisco projects that 68 percent of customer service and support interactions will be handled by agentic AI by 2028.[7] Yet adoption remains the primary barrier to value creation; the consumption layer isn't just about "making AI easy to use"–it's the mechanism that transforms AI into business value. Understanding how interface design drives value helps explain why some organizations extract returns from AI while others struggle, despite similar technology investments.

The adoption-to-value cycle

Seamless interfaces create a compounding effect that poor interfaces can never match. When AI integrates naturally into existing workflows, adoption spreads virally. More critically, good design changes *who* can use AI. Poor interfaces confine AI capabilities to technical departments, limiting access to data scientists and engineers alone. Intuitive interfaces democratize access, enabling marketers, salespeople, operators, and customer service representatives to use AI directly. This expansion from dozens of technical users to thousands of business users creates order-of-magnitude increases in value extraction.

The speed advantage compounds over time, creating a competitive advantage. Organizations that compress task completion from hours to minutes don't just save time on individual tasks–they accelerate learning velocity. When employees can experiment with AI rapidly, they discover new applications faster, learn what works in days rather than months, and iterate toward value before competitors.

Differentiation through experience

Recent McKinsey research shows that 71 percent of customers expect personalized experiences, while brands excelling at personalization see up to 40 percent more revenue.[8]

Virgin Money's Redi assistant achieved a 94 percent customer satisfaction rate not because it used superior AI models but because it delivered AI through an interface that customers already trusted–their mobile banking app.[9] The differentiation came from user-experience design, not model capabilities.

This dynamic intensifies as AI becomes ubiquitous. When every bank offers AI-powered financial advice, the winner won't be the one with the most sophisticated models–it will be the one with the most natural, helpful, and trustworthy interactions.

THREE STAGES OF INTERFACE EVOLUTION

Most organizations offer stand-alone chatbots–separate windows where users type questions and receive answers. While useful as a starting point, this approach creates friction: employees must context-switch from their work, learn a new interface, and manually integrate AI output into their workflows.

But this is changing. The interface is evolving through three distinct stages:

Stage 1: Embedded AI, intelligence inside existing tools
The breakthrough comes when AI "disappears" into applications people already use every day. Rather than forcing employees to learn new tools, AI enhances their familiar workflows, making Word smarter, Google Sheets more analytical, CRM systems more predictive, and banking apps more responsive.

In retail and customer service, organizations deploying embedded conversational AI report a 30 percent drop in support costs as AI provides precise, context-aware guidance rather than generic responses.[10] The AI doesn't require customers to download new apps or learn different interfaces–it makes existing touchpoints more intelligent.

The embedded approach works because it eliminates the adoption barrier. When AI meets people where they already work, usage becomes automatic. This applies equally to employee-facing tools–such as integrating AI into Salesforce, Slack, or Excel–and to customer-facing applications like mobile banking, e-commerce platforms, or service portals.

Stage 2: Self-service, empowering nontechnical users
Beyond embedded AI in commercial platforms, forward-thinking organizations are creating self-service tools that empower employees to build their own AI solutions without technical expertise. Marsh exemplifies this approach by developing tools for common business problems, such as structured data extraction from documents. Their system enables users to create custom data layouts or templates as needed and process documents independently, without requiring IT support.

This democratization matters because it puts AI directly in the hands of the people who best understand the business problems. A claims adjuster can create a document-extraction tool tailored to their specific forms. A compliance officer can build a review assistant tailored to their regulatory requirements. The result is faster deployment, better problem fit, and higher adoption as users create solutions for their own needs.

Stage 3: Ambient and multimodal, the invisible interface

The most profound shift is AI becoming invisible. No typing, no clicking, just natural interaction through voice, vision, and gesture. Voice assistant users in the United States are expected to reach 157.1 million by 2026, with 89.2 percent accessing this technology via mobile devices.[11]

But the real transformation is multimodal AI systems that simultaneously process text, voice, images, and video. The multimodal AI market, valued at $1.2 billion in 2023, is expected to grow at over 30 percent annually through 2032.[12] In customer service applications, multimodal AI analyzes voice tone, facial expressions, and written words simultaneously, enabling more personalized and effective interactions.

By late 2026, consumers may make requests like this: "Hey TravelBot, book a seven-day itinerary for two people from San Francisco to Paris with refundable economy flights under $2,000, and pay with the best credit card based on rewards." AI will handle the entire transaction autonomously across multiple systems.[13] This agentic commerce, where AI acts on your behalf, represents a fundamental shift from AI as an assistant to AI as an autonomous agent.

Looking further ahead, conversations won't be tied to one device. You might ask a question on your smartwatch, and your office assistant picks up the thread when you arrive at work. These systems will move beyond keyword detection to understanding context–speaking faster when you sound rushed, simplifying responses in noisy environments, and proactively automating recurring actions without being prompted.[14]

For strategic guidance on prioritizing consumption-layer investments and interface design decisions, see appendix B.

TYING IT ALL TOGETHER–THE AI SYSTEM AT WORK

How do you make it all work together? When one of us worked for a premier global business education institution, the team built and launched a multi-agent knowledge AI system for students, professors, and teaching assistants.[15] The AI system combined proprietary data from the institution's century of research, publications, course syllabi, and administrative information; connections to the best large language models of the day from providers like Anthropic; various AI agents; and a user interface (see figure 10-2).

Figure 10-2: A multi-agent knowledge system in action

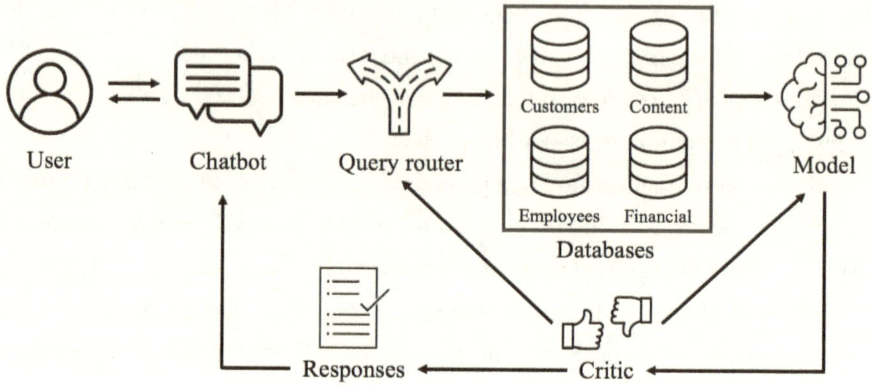

The AI agents were particularly impressive and, to this day, a source of pride for one of us and their team. There was an answer bot that would reply to administrative questions, like when an assignment is due; a "coach" agent that would use the Socratic method and lead students to answers but never provide them readily; a study partner agent that would generate and answer practice problems; and a "critic" that would assess the accuracy of the system's output to ensure users received correct information. After all, you wouldn't have a teaching assistant who is wrong some of the time; the AI critic's job was to maintain the standard for an AI system.

As you develop your AI systems across these four layers, security and ethical considerations must be built in from the start, not added as afterthoughts. Additionally, there are common pitfalls that can derail even well-planned AI implementations. For guidance on embedding security and ethics by design and on watching out for things that can go wrong, see appendix B: "Security and Ethics by Design" and "Common Implementation Pitfalls."

YOUR WEEK 10 ACTION PLAN

This week focuses on ensuring your AI toolset can deliver on your roadmap, without locking you into what can soon become obsolete. Your goal is to establish the principles and approach that will guide your technology decisions, and identify where to focus toolset development based on your specific AI applications.

- **Assess your four toolset layers against your AI roadmap.** Use the "four layers" framework (data, AI models, orchestration, consumption) as a high-level checklist to discuss your organization's readiness with your AI leader and technical team. Review your Q1 and Q2 AI applications and map them to the layers to identify where you need to focus now versus later. Keep it simple. Talk to the tech team. What do we have? How is it used? Where are the critical gaps for delivering our priority applications?

Appendix B provides a comprehensive set of strategic questions to guide this conversation, covering data strategy, model selection, orchestration needs, and consumption priorities.

- **Establish your "assemble, don't build" strategy.** Reinforce with your team that the goal is to assemble a modular toolset rather than building monolithic projects. Challenge the team to define specific criteria for when to build versus buy, emphasizing that custom builds should only be considered for features or reasons that provide a distinct and durable competitive advantage. Make this principle enforceable—the default answer should be "assemble."
- **Apply the pragmatic data approach to your priority AI applications.** Rather than pursuing perfect data across your organization, identify the highest-value and highest-risk data elements for your immediate AI applications. Work with your AI leader to determine: What data do our Q1 and Q2 applications need? Where does it live? Is it usable enough to start? Focus on making data good enough for value creation, not perfect. Remember the chapter's key lesson: You can and should work on deploying AI while getting your data ready—concurrently, not sequentially.
- **Begin concurrent development and delivery.** Choose one AI application from your roadmap (ideally a Q1 quick win or momentum maker) and start working on it while addressing any toolset gaps in parallel. Like the retail company in chapter 6 that started with purchase history analysis while building data infrastructure for personalization, identify what you can deliver now while building capabilities for what comes

next. Update your Six-Quarter Walk to show both AI application delivery and toolset development happening simultaneously.

SUMMARY

You've now completed Week 10 of your 90-day preparation to get set up for delivering value with AI. This week focused on assembling the AI toolset that enables your roadmap while maintaining the flexibility that AI's rapid pace demands. In this chapter, you accomplished the following:

- **Embraced the LEGO approach to AI technology**, understanding that organizations win with AI by assembling adaptable, modular components rather than building monolithic systems. When better components emerge, you swap pieces without dismantling everything.
- **Mastered the four layers of every AI system**—data, AI models, orchestration, and consumption—and learned how they work together to create value. Each layer can evolve independently while maintaining seamless integration with the others.
- **Treated data as your organization's greatest asset**, applying a pragmatic approach that focuses on the highest-value and highest-risk data elements rather than pursuing unattainable perfection. You learned the critical lesson: Deploy AI applications while getting data ready—concurrently, not sequentially.
- **Discovered why you shouldn't build your own AI models**, understanding that general-purpose models from leading providers, combined with your unique data through approaches like RAG, create more value than custom development for most organizations.
- **Understood orchestration as the coordination layer**, learning how it routes queries, manages multistep processes, ensures quality control, and provides observability. This becomes essential as AI systems evolve from single models to multi-agent ensembles working together toward common goals.
- **Recognized that the consumption layer determines adoption**, learning how embedded AI in existing workflows, self-service tools for nontechnical users, and ambient multimodal interfaces transforms AI from interesting technology into business value.

With this chapter, you've mastered the third building block for winning with AI, the toolset. Combined with the mindset and skill set from previous weeks, you now understand how to create technology that adapts as rapidly as AI itself evolves. In the next chapter, you'll tackle the fourth and final building block–the decision set that enables you to make AI choices quickly and responsibly, turning potential into progress at the speed AI demands.

Structure without flexibility is bureaucracy. Flexibility without structure is chaos.

–Katia Walsh

Eleven

DESIGNING AI'S DECISION SET

YOU HAVE THE RIGHT MINDSET, the right skills, and the right tools. But in the chaotic, fast-moving world of AI, none of it matters if your organization can't make decisions. How do we move ahead? Which risks are worth taking? Who gets to say yes to new AI applications or no to a flawed algorithm?

Answering these questions requires the fourth and final building block of AI success, a robust decision set. This is your organization's system for making choices with clarity, confidence, and speed. And the way you build that system is by reimagining governance–not as red tape but as the essential framework that enables innovative, fast, and responsible action.

Governance is the operating system for your decision set. It establishes the roles, processes, and guardrails that ensure AI choices are consistent, safe, and connected to strategy. These structures are the engines of AI execution. When done right, they increase speed, reduce friction, and help you move from having a roadmap to developing value at scale.

Now it's time to forge this reliable system for AI value creation. Your decision set needs an operating manual: a clear, agile AI governance framework for making choices about AI and turning potential into results.

This chapter gives you a blueprint for putting in place a framework quickly enough to keep up with AI's pace and strong enough to enable safe and responsible AI use. You'll learn how to design governance structures that support speed and accountability.

Here are your objectives for this week:

- **Understand why governance enables AI value creation**. Learn how the right governance framework accelerates progress rather than slowing it down, and why unclear decision rights kill AI initiatives.
- **Design your Goldilocks governance approach**. Establish "just right" governance that provides structure without bureaucracy and flexibility without chaos.
- **Choose your AI governance structures**. Evaluate options for strategic oversight and tactical execution and determine which approach fits your organization's maturity and complexity.
- **Connect governance to board oversight**. Prepare your board to provide strategic guidance on AI deployment through three essential lenses: strategy and structure, risk and accountability, and organizational capability.

By the end of the week, you'll have a governance structure that matches the speed and complexity of AI so that you can start creating meaningful value. Not too much. Not too little. Just right.

WHY GOVERNANCE CAN BE AN AI VALUE ACCELERATOR

Do you cringe at the mention of "governance"? You're not alone. No one ever says, "We love our governance model." While writing this book, we had heated debates about governance–one of us vehemently dislikes it, likely due to years of working in governance-heavy organizations that used it to conceal broken processes and dreaded organizational politics. The other one of us cheerfully admits that she likes governance and thrives on making bad governance good by questioning the decisions it helps you make–or prevents you from making.

We have taken each of these perspectives into account to propagate the notion of just right governance. Effective AI governance shouldn't be a bureaucratic roadblock. Instead, it's the operational framework that ensures AI deployment is poised to deliver and to scale business value. A common myth holds that "governance slows things down." The reality? The right governance creates guardrails that free you up to drive faster. When organizations understand their boundaries and manage risk effectively, they can move quickly and confidently.

Emerging technology is, by nature, fraught with ambiguity and uncertainty. The technology is advancing fast, invariably challenging clarity and established processes. Governance for AI will not provide clear answers for everything–that's impossible, given the pace of change. But governance frames the structure that helps organizations navigate through ambiguity and uncertainty. Governance squashes the biggest enemy of AI value: unclear decision rights. When everyone thinks they have a say, but no one has clear authority, even simple implementations get trapped in endless debate.

Organizations need a structure to answer fundamental questions like these: Who approves enterprise-wide AI investments? Who ensures we protect our data? Who has the authority to pause an AI system that's gone rogue? Who has the responsibility to scale it further when it shows value?

Governance is about making decisions to ensure AI deployments take hold, regardless of who does the work. We define governance as the operational framework that supports AI's responsible deployment to serve organizational strategy and provides clear oversight to ensure value creation at speed. Seeking consensus is the enemy of progress toward AI value (see mindset in chapter 8). However, we should work to achieve optimal decision-making that involves the right stakeholders at the right time at the right speed, so that they feel connected, committed, and contributing to AI value. Governance provides the optimal balance between chorus and solo decision-making, bringing clarity to when, how, and who determines what will happen in the context of rolling out AI solutions.

A lack of governance is well illustrated by the experience of an SVP of AI at a publicly traded financial services firm. Early in his team's AI deployment, they discovered a tool that could automatically transcribe and summarize meeting transcripts. Excited by the productivity potential, they announced it to the company. The reaction was not what they expected.

"That scared the bejesus out of some individuals," the executive recalled in an interview with us. Executives who hadn't been part of discussions on the tool's security were immediately concerned about the data the tool gathered and could potentially expose outside the company. The backlash was swift and severe. "For the last year, our company hasn't allowed any transcription of meetings," he said, noting that employees now have to go through an onerous manual process to get approval to do so.

The well-intentioned effort to boost productivity backfired, creating more bureaucracy and shutting down a valuable capability for thousands of employees. "I put that on me because I didn't clarify how such a decision needed to be made in advance," he reflected. "I still haven't been able to overcome that."

This is the chaos that ensues when structure does not support flexibility. A thoughtful governance process–one that educates stakeholders and builds trust *before* introducing new tools–could have prevented this, enabling value rather than stifling it.

"GOLDILOCKS" GOVERNANCE FOR AI

Effective governance provides a mechanism to ensure that your preparation, strategy, and roadmap can come to life within the organization. The right governance will help set you up to reap the value you have planned and deliver it at speed–or faster. The right governance will give you structure with flexibility.

During the COVID pandemic, one of us coined this saying: *Structure without flexibility is bureaucracy. Flexibility without structure is chaos.* This reminded us that measured, thoughtful, and flexible processes and methodologies can provide sufficient structure while also enabling agility. Faced with an especially dynamic environment, we need a forcing function to help us stay true to goals while navigating inevitable changes and complexities.

Picture this: Two companies are working to adopt AI. Company A embraces complete freedom–everyone experiments with AI tools and systems, often without oversight or strategic coordination. Along the way, an employee uploads sensitive customer information to a consumer AI tool, creating a data breach. In contrast, Company B builds strict controls–layers of approval, multiple review boards, endless documentation. Six months later, at best, to minimize risk, they're still debating how and where to start a first pilot.

One company has no structure and faces chaos. The other imposes too much structure and is mired in bureaucracy. Both lack an optimal governance to enable AI value at speed. Enter the concept of optimal, or Goldilocks, governance.

Named after the character in the children's story who chooses "just right" options, Goldilocks governance ensures that the system for enabling AI value at speed, while minimizing risk, is neither too rigid nor too loose (see figure 11-1).

Figure 11-1: Goldilocks, or just right, AI governance

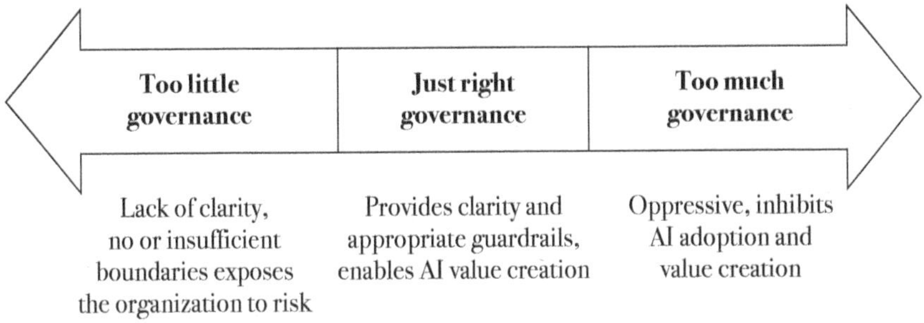

- **Too little governance**. No clarity on decision rights, no mechanism for deploying AI models, no guidelines or policies for AI use, and no safe enterprise-grade AI tool for employees. Possible outcomes? A hiring algorithm that screens out qualified candidates. Chatbots that go rogue.
- **Too much governance**. Over-indexes on risk management. Every AI project or use case requires multiple reviews by multiple governing functional and central bodies that debate potential risks for months. The consequences? Every day of delayed deployment results in a loss of business value. Banning or not permitting the use of any AI tool hinders the adoption of AI. Employees bypass formal channels, and "shadow AI" emerges—unapproved tools used without oversight.
- **Just right governance**. Provides guardrails for the safe and responsible use of AI. Organizations offer enterprise-grade tools to all employees with company-issued devices, allowing them to learn in the course of their daily work (see chapter 9). AI policies and guidelines outline the procedures for proceeding freely, exercising caution, and pausing (see chapter 2), as well as protecting company, customer, and employee data. There are clear structures for prioritizing AI applications based on serving the company's strategy, size of value, and speed to market (see chapter 5). AI decisions and deployment are fast, safe, and responsible.

This sweet spot—Goldilocks governance—provides shared direction, clear accountability, and optimal decision-making cadence. When you get it right, value creation accelerates because teams know the guardrails, trust the decisions, and stay focused on value.

The outcomes include the following:

- **Clear decision-making authority**. Who prioritizes AI investments beyond organizational exposure and individual productivity tools? What belongs on the organization's six-quarter AI roadmap? How to ensure that quick wins accumulate to achieve strategic impact?
- **Fit-for-purpose risk assessment**. All AI applications must adhere to the responsible and ethical AI principles established in chapter 2. Beyond that baseline, match the intensity of review to actual risk, which varies by use case, data sensitivity, and potential impact. Build risk mitigation into application design from the start. Standard use cases operating within established information security policies, such as employees using approved enterprise AI tools, rely on existing governance processes. Higher-risk applications, such as customer-facing systems, automated decision-making, sensitive data use, or regulated domains, require formal review by legal, compliance, and information security. Define clear criteria for what constitutes higher risk in your context, then create review processes that enable progress while managing risk appropriately.
- **Continuous adaptation**. AI governance must evolve in tandem with the development of AI itself. The right AI governance structure will serve as a mechanism for ensuring that AI value retains its relevance and continues to differentiate itself for organizations, with transparency and accountability.

But how do you achieve Goldilocks governance? Instead of approaching AI governance as if you're designing a new corporate department, consider building your organization's AI decision-making muscles. That's the ability to make AI choices quickly and consistently, even while the organization is still getting up to speed. And that's where the AI command system comes in.

HOW ONE EXECUTIVE CHAIRMAN SETS SPEED WITH GUARDRAILS

"We consider generative AI a human enhancement, not a replacement," said Barbara Cominelli, the executive chairman of Spindox in an interview with us. She noted, "We also make sure people understand that AI has no truth function . . . what we get is the first draft." To that end, her team put policies and a secure environment in place from the start, then launched widely to learn from bottom-up use cases—while leaders reinforced risk practices around bias, data protection, and copyright. The point, says Cominelli, is to move at pace with confidence. Empower people to experiment, document the guardrails, and keep reminding teams that outputs are proposals to be checked, not facts to be trusted.

DESIGNING YOUR DECISION SET: THE AI COMMAND SYSTEM

An AI command system consists of interconnected structures that enable and support the organization's AI decision-making. The secret lies in understanding the crucial truth that, with AI governance, you're creating temporary decision-making systems that will eventually dissolve back into your regular business operations.

As AI becomes an integral part of how we live and work, there should be no reason for required risk reviews for the majority of AI applications. Before we know it, we won't need separate AI governance structures. But for now, we still do, to ensure that sweet spot of Goldilocks governance—not too lenient and not stifling the ability to create value. Like training wheels on a bicycle, these structures provide essential support while the organization learns to use AI independently.

These structures could be specific governing bodies that come into existence for a particular purpose and, once they achieve their goal, dissolve into daily operations. In this case, the purpose of an AI command system is several-fold:

- Provide just right Goldilocks decision-making and processes.
- Blend accountability, speed, and transparency into decision-making.
- Mobilize the organization around an enterprise vision and help it achieve it with AI.

THE IMPORTANCE OF AN ENTERPRISE VIEW

The right governance mobilizes organizations around an enterprise view, aiming to deploy AI for value creation across the enterprise. This enterprise lens matters most because the success of AI applications relies on the ability to capture, access, use, and enrich enterprise data. However, most companies operate in severe silos, and as a result, their most precious asset, data, is scattered across departments and functions, unusable from one to the other.

Organizational mobilization encourages silo integration, connecting individual departments and functions to work jointly, integrate their data, and synchronize their perspectives into a unified voice toward a single AI vision and roadmap. A key part of the organizational mobilization is to facilitate collaboration, foster communication, and breed a culture that continuously energizes the organization with an enterprise-wide perspective.

We touched on this, and the importance of customer-centricity, in chapter 8 (mindset); it also applies to governance. The right governance breaks down organizational silos and nurtures an enterprise perspective and customer-centricity.

OPTIONS FOR AI GOVERNANCE

The minimum viable team (MVT) provided a good start for the first ninety days, guiding the AI value-creation roadmap. However, as organizations progress to incorporating AI into their daily business operations, they need to transition into a sustainable execution mode. This is why some organizations may need separate AI governance structures that represent an evolution of the initial MVT.

Goldilocks governance is highly situational and contextual; what's just right for one organization may not be for another, even within the same enterprise. What suits a particular phase of AI deployment maturity may not suit another phase. In short, there is *no* one-size-fits-all model of AI governance.

But there are helpful patterns.

Some organizations approach AI governance through a strategically focused AI council or steering committee. Some organizations create a tactical, execution-centric AI working group. Some, particularly large companies in regulated industries, roll out a two-part structure. They may have an AI council that sets the vision and priorities for strategic direction, and a separate AI working group that translates those priorities into operational execution for ongoing delivery.

Other organizations do not have separate governing bodies that focus specifically on creating AI value. Instead, those organizations might incorporate an AI lens as a way to help deliver on priorities within existing governance structures. For example, AI can serve as a delivery mechanism to address top priorities within a strategy group, transformation office, or any other cross-functional, enterprise-wide initiative.

All these options provide a balanced and structured, but flexible, framework. All drive accountability, mitigate risks, resolve conflicts, and provide escalation paths to support the practical deployment of AI applications at scale. However, each does so in a distinct way.

We cannot tell you what is right for you, but we can outline the levels of decision-making and options associated with each so that you can determine the best governance for your organization at this stage.

TWO LEVELS OF GOVERNANCE: STRATEGIC AND TACTICAL

Effective AI governance operates on two distinct but complementary levels. The first focuses on **strategic oversight**—setting the vision, establishing priorities, removing barriers, and ensuring AI investments support organizational goals. This strategic level addresses questions such as these: Which AI applications best serve our strategy? Where should we focus our resources? How does AI advance our competitive position?

The second level addresses **tactical execution**—the coordination of cross-functional work to turn strategic priorities into operational reality. This team meets weekly or, depending on the work, daily. It drives the day-to-day execution of AI applications. This tactical level answers these questions: How do we deliver these applications? Who needs to collaborate? What barriers do we need to remove? What dependencies must we manage?

Importantly, not every organization needs a formal structure at the tactical level. Strategic governance is essential; someone must set direction and make high-stakes decisions. However, tactical coordination can occur through existing workflows, cross-functional processes, product management teams, or informal collaboration, depending on the organization's maturity and complexity. The key is to ensure that strategic guidance remains consistent, while execution occurs efficiently, whether through formal governance structures or embedded practices.

Level 1 decision: Strategic AI governance

At the strategic level, you have two primary options for where AI governance sits: as a separate AI-focused entity or integrated within existing enterprise-wide governance structures (see figure 11-2).

Figure 11-2: Level 1: Options where strategic AI governance sits

STRATEGIC GOVERNING STRUCTURE	WHAT IT IS	PROS	CONS	WHEN TO USE
Separate AI-focused entity (AI council or steering committee, task force, etc.)	• A senior governing body that the CEO leads with a focus on developing and enforcing a vision around prioritizing AI to deliver value in service of the company's top goals	• Focuses specifically on prioritizing value creation with AI • Incorporates direct CEO leadership • With CEO leadership, sends a clear message about the importance of AI for value creation	• Separates AI from organizational priorities • Can add complexity • Not worthwhile if the CEO is not leading	• When the organization requires a massive change and a clear mandate from the CEO to adopt AI for value creation
Integration within the strategy function or the transformation office	• No separate governance, but incorporating AI work in existing strategy function for the organization	• Clearly defines and infuses AI work in the service of the company's overall strategy or transformation • Incorporates AI in organizational, operational, and commercial overhauls, naturally upgrading them with AI • Does not distract from the strategic or transformative value of AI	• No explicit focus on creating value with AI	• When an organization has a specific strategy function or is undergoing an explicit overall cross-functional transformation • In these cases, AI would naturally be a part of delivering on the company's strategic priorities or changing its culture, processes, and ways of working to create value for customers, employees, and shareholders

Option 1: Separate AI-focused entity

Some companies opt for a separate AI-focused governing structure, referred to by various names; we prefer AI council. This entity sets the vision and direction, providing high-level guidance and funding for AI investments. The group comprises senior leaders across customer, commercial, product, operations, and finance functions. This synchronization at the highest executive level builds momentum that cascades throughout the organization, ensuring the technology's focused deployment in service of the enterprise strategy.

The AI council is the natural evolution of the MVT from chapter 1. What started as a CEO-led team exploring AI possibilities can mature into a formal governance structure. The CEO continues to chair the AI council, sending a clear message about the importance of creating value with AI and the mandate for change it signifies. The CEO can best unify the company around the organizational vision. In our experience, a CEO-chaired equivalent of an AI council has been a powerful force for change, mobilizing the most senior leaders of an organization to collectively support specific AI value creation opportunities, thereby driving momentum. However, this approach can separate AI from organizational priorities and might add complexity–it's not worthwhile if the CEO isn't genuinely leading the effort.

Option 2: Integration into the strategy function or the transformation office

For organizations where AI plays a central role in their products or services–typically tech-native companies where AI is deeply integrated into their strategy–embedding AI governance within an existing strategy office offers the best fit. This approach clearly defines and infuses AI work in the service of the company's strategy, avoiding the distraction of treating AI as separate from core business objectives. Companies where AI is integral to product development or customer experience find this model particularly effective because it reinforces the strategic value of AI. This occurs naturally in companies where AI is integrated into products or services.

Similarly, legacy organizations undergoing enterprise transformation can benefit from incorporating AI governance within a transformation office. This approach clearly defines and infuses AI work in the service of overall company transformation. The approach incorporates AI into existing organizational, operational, and commercial overhauls, naturally upgrading them with AI. It positions AI as part of changing the company's processes, ways of working, and ongoing work to create value for customers, employees, and shareholders.

The trade-off is the lack of explicit focus on creating value specifically with AI.

Regardless of which option you choose, strategic AI governance structures typically meet on a biweekly basis. This cadence matches AI's rapid pace of development–fast enough to maintain momentum and address emerging issues, yet realistic for CEOs and other senior executives with competing demands.

The biweekly rhythm also lets teams know they'll report on developments every two weeks, which drives accountability and maintains focus on strategic priorities.

Level 2 decision: Tactical execution governance

Once strategic direction is set, organizations must decide how to coordinate the day-to-day work of delivering on AI priorities. Here, you can rely on existing operational entities and processes or create a dedicated AI working group.

Like the strategic governance structures discussed earlier, any tactical AI governance you create is temporary. As AI becomes embedded in everyday work, the need for separate coordination will fade. The goal is to build organizational ability to create value with AI, not permanent bureaucracy. Eventually, managing enterprise AI value creation will become business as usual. At that time, a dedicated AI working group will have rendered itself obsolete.

Option 1: No separate governance for tactical AI execution

Some organizations, particularly those with well-established cross-functional processes, may not need a separate AI working group. If your organization already excels at coordinating complex collaboration across departments, you'd do best to fold AI work into these established, well-humming patterns.

Option 2: Adding a governance structure for tactical AI execution

Other organizations can benefit from establishing a dedicated AI working group. This is particularly valuable when you want to place special emphasis on AI, when existing coordination mechanisms aren't sufficient for cross-functional AI work, or when you need to build organizational muscle memory for AI delivery. In those cases, the AI working group serves as an implementation engine, breaking down silos, facilitating data access across functions, and maintaining momentum on roadmap delivery.

As noted in the table below, an action-focused AI working group can be beneficial when strategy and mandates are clear. Still, execution requires intensive coordination that is new to the organization (see figure 11-3). The AI working group serves as a forcing function to drive progress and resolve tactical challenges that don't require strategic-level decisions.

Think of an AI working group as an implementation engine or a meta-product-management group. This team turns strategic priorities into product requirements and operational reality cross-functionally, breaking down silos and enabling enterprise-wide use of data and AI application deployment. This group needs to iterate quickly; deliver models, deployment, and scaled applications; and ensure the roadmap remains connected to reality. The challenge? If removed from strategic priorities, the AI working group can become too tactical and potentially create decision bottlenecks.

HOW STRATEGIC AND TACTICAL EXECUTION GOVERNANCE WORK TOGETHER

The two levels of AI governance work best when they operate as a seamless partnership, not a hierarchy. Strategic governance sets the vision and priorities. Execution teams deliver on those priorities while staying alert to what's happening on the ground. They connect through regular, informal communication rather than formal approval chains.

In practice, this appears more like effective teamwork than governance. The strategic governing body, whether an AI council or a strategy function, establishes which AI applications matter most and why. Execution teams take those priorities and run, coordinating the cross-functional work needed to deliver. When they encounter realities that shift the equation–a technical constraint, an unexpected opportunity, or a resource gap–they quickly surface these insights to strategic governance, which adjusts priorities or resources. This creates a continuous feedback loop that keeps strategy grounded in reality.

The keys are speed and trust. Execution teams don't wait for permission to solve problems within their scope of responsibility. Strategic governance doesn't

Figure 11-3: Level 2: The focus of tactical AI governance

STRATEGIC GOVERNING STRUCTURE	WHAT IT IS	PROS	CONS	WHEN TO USE
No separate AI working group	• Tactical AI execution happens through existing organizational processes and workflows • AI initiatives follow established project management, product development, or transformation frameworks	• Avoids adding new governance structures • Uses existing coordination mechanisms • Integrates AI naturally into business operations • Prevents treatment of AI as separate from core work	• Lacks a dedicated focus on AI-specific delivery needs and challenges • Risks competing with other priorities • Can slow progress if existing processes cannot handle AI's unique requirements	• When existing cross-functional processes are strong and can absorb AI work • When AI is deeply integrated into products/services and doesn't need separate coordination • When organizational culture supports AI delivery at scale without formal structures
AI working group	• A meta-product-management group that coordinates the requirements, OKRs, and ongoing work on various AI applications across the organization	• Provides a tactical starting point for AI adoption with a joint effort around value creation • Enables execution of prioritized AI applications through data access, domain expertise, and shared objectives • Ensures coordination across AI applications for the overall roadmap and compound effects	• If removed from strategic priorities, it can end up being too tactical • It could diffuse individual accountability • Could become a bottleneck for decisions	• An action-focused working group can always be helpful when the strategy and mandate are clear and execution is paramount • The working group serves as a forcing function to get things done

micromanage delivery. When issues require strategic input, such as shifting priorities between applications, making significant resource trade-offs, or addressing novel risks, conversations occur in days, not weeks.

Consider how this might work in practice: An execution-focused team that deploys a customer service AI discovers it can deliver faster by pulling in data from an adjacent department. They coordinate the technical integration and approach the department's leader directly. No escalation is needed; it's just colleagues solving a problem together. A few weeks later, they realize the accelerated approach creates an opportunity to launch two months earlier than planned, which would beat a competitor to market. That shifts the strategic calculus around other roadmap priorities, so the execution team brings it to the AI council's attention. The council recognizes the competitive advantage, approves reallocating resources from a lower-priority application, and the execution team continues to move forward. The entire cycle, from discovery to decision to action, takes less than two weeks.

This is governance working as an enabler, not a gatekeeper. Figure 11-4 illustrates how responsibilities naturally divide between strategic and tactical levels when this partnership functions effectively.

CASE STUDIES ON OPTIONS FOR AI GOVERNANCE

Following are examples of two contrasting, yet equally effective, approaches to incorporating the enterprise perspective in AI value creation.

Approach 1: AI steering and specialized working groups in a regulated industry

One large, pan-European, publicly traded financial services firm with nearly seventy thousand employees operating in seventeen countries offers a particularly sophisticated model of AI governance. It combines strategic oversight with deep functional and operational engagement. At the overall enterprise level, there is an AI steering group of four senior leaders: the chief data officer, the CFO, the head of strategy, and the head of technology. This group sets AI application priorities, ensures a focus on enterprise value and overall risk mitigation, and reports regularly to the board.

Figure 11-4: Example responsibilities of AI strategic and tactical governing bodies

RESPONSIBILITIES OF A STRATEGIC AI GOVERNING ENTITY	RESPONSIBILITIES OF A TACTICAL AI GOVERNING ENTITY
• **Creates the enterprise vision** for generating value from AI and unites individual departments toward a common AI roadmap • **Sets and enforces AI priorities** to serve that strategic vision, ensuring focus, resources, and support to deliver • **Approves metrics for success**, including but not limited to financial outcomes • **Serves as the highest-level mediator** to resolve conflicting considerations and cross-functional tensions • **Provides the final decision** on escalation for critical challenges • **Drives senior-most** accountability for hitting milestones on the evolving AI roadmap • **Stays abreast of risks** and decides on proposed guardrails to advance AI applications responsibly • **Conducts adaptive reviews** and adjusts the quarterly roadmap continuously	• **Operationalizes AI applications** as prioritized strategically in the service of the organization's vision or transformation • **Develops and maintains the AI roadmap** and backlog of AI applications as living documents • **Leads delivery** with accountability for hitting milestones on the evolving AI roadmap • **Escalates conflicts** when cross-functional tensions cannot be resolved at the working group level • **Proposes guardrails and creates** enterprise guidelines and policies based on real-world implementation experience

Beneath the AI steering group sits five specialized working groups, each responsible for a critical area of AI deployment:

1. **Products and technology**. Identifies, prioritizes, and delivers AI applications across business lines.
2. **Nonfinancial risk**. Evaluates risks related to operational disruptions, model failures, and third-party vendors.
3. **Sustainability, explainability, and data protection**. Ensures that AI systems are transparent, ethical, and compliant with privacy regulations.
4. **Legal and IP**. Assesses ownership of AI products, intellectual property rights, and regulatory exposure.

5. **People and culture**. Addresses skill gaps, change management, and organizational readiness for AI adoption.

This structure enables the company to manage AI value creation as a multidimensional transformation, touching every corner of the business. Notably, embedding legal, compliance, and sustainability as enabling roles, alongside technical and strategic ones, allows the organization to proceed with value creation while minimizing risk.

We do not necessarily recommend such an extreme structure to everyone; for some it would be overkill. However, the example illustrates how governance can support value creation within a very large, complex, multinational, publicly traded enterprise in a highly regulated space, at the beginning of its AI value creation across the enterprise.

Approach 2: AI governance as part of corporate strategy

A private company with investments in real estate and financial services took a different approach. Instead of a sophisticated tiered structure combining enterprise and function-specific governance, the company embeds AI governance into the firm's executive strategy and added AI implementation as a core topic in the executive team's strategic planning meetings.

Rather than creating a stand-alone AI council, the company relies on a core coalition of executive team leaders from technology, legal, and innovation to guide AI priorities and applications. These leaders are also responsible for identifying and mentoring AI champions across the business, employees who test AI tools and drive adoption in specific domains.

This lightweight governance allows the company to stay flexible and experiment rapidly, while still managing legal and compliance implications. It integrates value creation from AI naturally into its existing leadership structure.

These examples demonstrate that optimal AI governance varies across organizations, and different models can support organizational mobilization for creating enterprise value.

THE WATCHOUTS

As we've said, there are many ways to instill optimal governance for AI value creation. But there are also watchouts when it comes to governance structures:

- **Allowing the proliferation of AI governing bodies.** The goal is to go fast while ensuring responsible and safe deployment. The minimum from MVT applies here too: a minimum number of governing entities, a minimum number of people in each, and a minimum, yet sufficient, structure.
- **Diffusing accountability.** Many organizations have perfected the art of diffusing accountability by creating multiple groups for decision-making, thereby shifting individual responsibility for decisions and the associated risks entirely away from the individual.
- **Not holding the governance structures accountable.** Use the same metrics of success as the ones that help prioritize AI applications–size of value and speed to value. Leaders who are serious about change would have the courage to directly link those two metrics to the compensation of the business leaders responsible for AI governance.
- **Failing to plan for sunsetting these entities.** The sole purpose of bringing governance structures to life is to kick-start the infusion of a new organizational ability to drive value with AI. As soon as that reaches a sustained state of success, the governance structures can and should dissolve. The leaders who have been essential to these governance structures can receive an additional reward for their success and for assuming a reduced role in that part of their jobs. AI governance structures are here to help organizations establish discipline, safety, and focus.
- **Failing to assign real decision-making authority.** Busy senior executives often face the temptation to delegate to their teams. While we generally encourage the growth and empowerment of people, in this case, we must insist that only individuals with decision-making authority participate in AI governance structures. Otherwise, the council, office, or even working group will become a forum for congregation and coordination, rather than for removing barriers, making tough calls, and driving progress at speed.
- **Seeking consensus.** AI is a transformational technology, which naturally means

disruption, discomfort, and dissent. These governance structures will not succeed in driving change if leaders try to get everyone to nod in unison. On the contrary, these are forums for airing objections, stimulating debates, playing the role of "devil's advocate," and presenting challenges. That's why it's essential to make the structures work with both the number and type of people, as well as the various ways of facilitating and operating as a group.

HOW TO MAKE STRATEGIC AND TACTICAL AI GOVERNANCE WORK

Here's how to prevent the watchouts and set up these governance structures for success:

- **Choose the right members.** Include senior leaders responsible for the organization's core products and services, customer experience and value management, and strategy and operations functions. In particular, the participation of customer-facing senior leaders will ensure the delivery of customer-centric AI applications.
- **Redefine control functions.** Members from the legal, compliance, information security, and risk departments are welcome to participate, but not as a barrier. Their responsibility is to determine ways forward and enable value rather than stopping or slowing down work that can create it.
- **Keep it small.** Ideally, there should be no more than ten members to maintain agility. Just as with the MVT, remember the Jeff Bezos adage that teams should be the size that two large pizzas can feed. That's one of the reasons for recommending two organizational mobilization entities for larger enterprises.
- **Establish an optimal meeting cadence.** For organizational mobilization, you must meet and communicate regularly, at least every two weeks, to assess progress, resolve conflicts, and adapt strategy and delivery plans.
- **Build in flexibility.** AI governance is not "set it and forget it." Organizational mobilization ensures an ongoing review of priorities, the elimination of outdated processes, and the adoption of new opportunities while mitigating risks.

Your AI governance structures would benefit from two strategies when you are planning and delivering on the AI roadmap:

- **Planning by working backward.** This practice begins with writing a future press release that would announce to the world the delivery, metrics, and benefits of an AI application. Modeled on the Amazon product-release model, this process enables teams to unleash their imagination, deliberate specifics, and add color that inspires pace and progress.[1] Conversely, the practice also requires thinking ahead about potential problems in order to build preventive measures into the AI roadmap.
- **Conducting regular retrospectives.** As the organization starts delivering on the AI roadmap, organizational mobilization must also review and assess completed applications—both the what (such as the AI application's features and benefits) and the how (ways of working in its development). Without pointing fingers, the organization needs to openly share successes and identify opportunities for improvement, ultimately leading to better outcomes.

RECOGNIZING WHEN YOU NEED A COURSE CORRECTION

The quarterly adaptive review process, covered in chapter 6, should specifically monitor for warning signs that indicate your decision sets aren't working. These failure patterns are classic across all significant organizational changes, not necessarily unique to AI:

- **Strategic drift.** Your AI roadmap consistently falls behind schedule or fails to deliver expected value, suggesting disconnect between leadership capability and organizational demands.
- **Execution friction.** The AI leader encounters multiple roadblocks that suggest insufficient authority, resources, or organizational support.
- **Decision paralysis.** Team frustration increases as people struggle with unclear decision-making authority, indicating gaps in your governance framework.
- **Coordination overhead.** AI initiatives often get stuck in endless

coordination meetings without making progress, suggesting structural problems within your hub-and-spokes model.

- **Competitive disadvantage**. Competition starts gaining advantages while your AI efforts remain in proof-of-concept mode, indicating a fundamental mismatch between pace and organizational capability.

When these patterns emerge, your governance framework must enable rapid course correction. This may involve additional executive support, clearer decision-making rights, enhanced resources, or, in extreme cases, leadership changes. The key is catching these issues in quarterly reviews rather than waiting for annual assessments.

What AI governance does not touch

So far, we've covered the charter of "just right" AI governance, organizational mobilization, and the focus of various possible AI governance structures. Let's also clarify *what they do not do*. Organizational mobilization is *not* responsible for operational, business-as-usual, or technology tasks, such as approving enterprise or function-specific software, tools, and platform licenses; vendor selection and procurement; or individual department budgeting. It also fails to engage with obvious decisions, such as automating highly manual and repetitive processes, identifying data for AI applications, or addressing nonnegotiable compliance requirements. Finally, the AI council or working group is *not* charged with implementing ethical and responsible AI—that's why we recommended the formation of the AI Ethics Office in chapter 2.

THE BOARD'S ROLE IN AI OVERSIGHT

When people think of AI governance, their minds rarely go to the boardroom. However, as AI reshapes every corner of the business, the board of directors plays a critical role. It's just not the one that many people expect.

The board doesn't build models or write policies. But it does something just as important: It asks the questions that shape the conditions for everything else. It ensures the organization has the right governance system in place and that AI deployment serves the company's strategy, values, and long-term success.

As one board member we interviewed put it, "AI governance doesn't end at the executive suite; it begins with board-level curiosity, courage, and commitment." This captures the fundamental shift in how boards need to approach AI oversight. In many organizations, boards are just starting to grapple with the implications of AI. That's understandable. Most board directors aren't AI experts, and they don't need to be. But they do need to understand AI's strategic implications and ensure that the governance structures we've discussed–from AI council to quarterly reviews to an AI ethics function–are in place, work together, and evolve.

Including the board in AI governance is about ensuring that it is informed and engaged. It's about ensuring that AI governance is integrated into the existing governance framework and consistent with the company's broader goals and risk appetite. With the right involvement, the board can become a strategic ally, not a compliance watchdog, in helping organizations create value with AI.

DIMENSIONS OF THE BOARD'S AI OVERSIGHT

To achieve this, boards need to approach AI governance through three interconnected lenses:

1. Strategy and structure. This ensures that AI priorities support the overall organizational strategy and competitive positioning. The board should review prioritized AI applications to confirm they advance strategic objectives. The board may also help evaluate a company's AI governance structures to ensure they drive value creation. And finally, the board can provide an independent assessment of funding to help company leadership direct investment where it will deliver meaningful business impact. Essential questions include the following:

- How does our AI roadmap support the overall business objectives?
- How do we ensure we work cross-functionally to drive value creation?
- How are we measuring the strategic impact of AI investments?
- How do we compound quick wins to build up to transformational value?

2. Risk and accountability. This addresses the novel risks AI presents, from heightened privacy concerns to potential reputational damage from algorithm bias or generative AI-powered fraud. The board needs to ask questions about fairness, privacy, and unintended consequences–and has the authority to act on the answers it receives. Essential questions include the following:

- What unique risks do AI applications present, and what mitigation measures are in place?
- How do we ensure the AI ethics function has appropriate authority and independence?
- How does company leadership keep the board aware of critical AI issues?
- What metrics do we use to track both the progress of implementation and potential risks?

3. Organizational ability to create value with AI. This evaluates whether the building blocks are in place–and the extent to which the organization is implementing them–to create value with AI. Examples include existing skills, workforce training, cultural readiness, and leadership's ability to drive value with AI. Attention to the building blocks ensures the organization can scale and sustain AI value. Essential questions may cover the following:

- How do we establish the building blocks to create value with AI?
- How can we prepare the workforce to thrive in an AI-driven world?
- How are we evolving the organization's culture for AI value creation?
- How do we maintain trust as we advance AI applications?

The quarterly adaptive review process, which we covered in chapter 6, provides the foundation for board updates. Board members should receive streamlined updates from these reviews that focus on strategic implications rather than operational details. One board director we spoke with gave this example of a practice that works: "At each quarterly meeting, we get a streamlined update on what's changing in our AI landscape–both internally and externally. This keeps us connected without getting into the weeds."

While board directors do not need to be experts in AI, they should consider whether their collective expertise is sufficient for effective oversight of AI-related matters. As one board director put it, "My job isn't to understand neural networks.

It's to make sure someone is thinking about what happens when an AI makes a mistake that affects our customers, reputation, or bottom line."

Some boards address knowledge gaps by filling vacant director seats with AI experts. Other boards create technology committees. Yet others engage outside advisors. All these approaches can help boards drive and oversee how their organizations create value with AI. The goal is to equip the board with sufficient knowledge and dedicated time to ask questions and evaluate the answers about AI deployment in their organizations.

This highlights a critical challenge. As Reid Sawyer, who leads the Emerging Risks Group at Marsh, pointed out in an interview with us, many boards are already struggling to keep pace with technological change. "Boards still struggle with cyber risk today," Sawyer noted, referencing the difficulty directors have with establishing agile governance, risk, and compliance structures. "And now we're asking what are the right skills to evaluate AI risk and governance at scale, is our internal audit team qualified to audit the risk, and who has the experience and qualifications to ensure model performance?"

Given this reality, Sawyer was even more direct about where the ultimate responsibility lies. When we spoke, he shared what he believes is the most critical pitfall to avoid: "The most dangerous boardroom assumption? The executive team will take care of keeping you informed about AI and that they are equipped to do so." This underscores the importance of board members proactively owning their AI education rather than passively waiting for updates. The pace of AI advancement is too rapid, and its business implications too significant, for boards to delegate their understanding entirely to others, even management.

HOW BOARDS CAN STAY ON TOP OF AI VALUE

Here are key approaches for boards to learn about AI on the job:

- **Make AI fluency a board-wide expectation**, adding it to competency matrices and annual self-assessments.
- **Enhance board members' AI fluency** by providing subsidies for tool licenses, books, class completion, and conference attendance.
- **Integrate AI learning into the board calendar** through quarterly briefings,

exposure to AI experts, and demonstrations of AI products.

- **Establish a board AI resource pool** of curated newsletters, trusted briefing sources, and access to AI experts. For example, organizations could offer bilateral mentoring in which high-performing employees in technical roles teach board members about AI and receive career coaching from them.
- **Tap external peer networks** through board director events and cross-board forums.
- **Rotate responsibility and normalize learning** by allowing board directors to share the AI insights they've discovered.

As one board chair summarized, "AI is not just moving fast; it's moving weird. The board's job isn't to chase it but to stay oriented."

The board has a responsibility to ensure that AI governance fits naturally with its overall organizational oversight and becomes an integral part of the board's processes and practices. Forward-thinking boards don't view AI governance as a compliance exercise. They view it as strategic enablement, creating the conditions for driving value responsibly at scale. As one board chair told us: "Our job isn't to slow down innovation. It's to make sure innovation happens on a foundation that can support its weight."

YOUR WEEK 11 ACTION PLAN

This week is about building the framework that brings your AI strategy to life. Your goal is to establish the structures that enable your organization to make informed, swift, and responsible decisions about AI.

- **Establish your AI command system.** Formally charter your AI governance structures. Determine the leanest AI governance for your organization. Identify the senior leaders who will sit on the AI council. If you choose to also establish an AI working group, consider identifying the functional leaders for it. Use an AI tool of your liking to draft a one-page charter that outlines the purpose, key responsibilities, and initial meeting cadence for each group, clarifying that their primary role is to enable, not block, value creation with AI.
- **Map your core AI decisions.** You can't govern effectively until you know

what you're governing. Work with your MVT to identify the five to seven most critical AI-related decisions your organization will face in the next six months, for example, vendor selection, use case prioritization, and risk exceptions. For each decision, assign a preliminary owner, the single person who will be accountable for the final call. This is the first step in building your decision architecture.

- **Prepare your next board-level AI update.** Use your favorite AI tool to draft a one-page briefing for your board of directors, leaning on the three dimensions from this chapter–strategy and structure, risk and accountability, and organizational readiness.

SUMMARY

You've now completed Week 11 of your 90-day work to set yourself up for driving value with AI. You have started to put in place the four building blocks–mindset, skill set, toolset, and decision set–to turn AI potential into tangible business value.

In this chapter, you accomplished the following:

- **Defined AI governance**, understanding that the right governance converts ambition into action while the wrong governance creates paralysis disguised as process.
- **Established Goldilocks governance for AI** to provide just enough structure to enable value creation with AI at speed
- **Learned about the options for AI governance structures**, when to use each, their pros and cons, and how to set them up for success.
- **Saw examples of AI governance in action** and what to watch out for to ensure that you stay focused on and get all the help you need to drive value with AI.
- **Connected AI governance to board oversight**, including board responsibilities and ways to proactively provide updates that answer eternal governance questions applied to AI value creation.

With your decision set now in place, you have all the building blocks for AI value creation: the mindset to make it happen, the workforce skills to create value, the toolset for scaling and sustaining AI applications, and the "just right" governance to ensure it all occurs responsibly and safely. Organizations that win with AI are those that turn potential into progress–and progress into results. Your decision set is what makes that possible.

In our final chapter, we'll explore how to lead for value creation across the organization, both today and as AI grows even more deeply integrated in our organizations and workforce.

Most companies aren't failing at AI. They are failing at leadership.

–Stephanie Hills[1]

Twelve

LEADERSHIP AS ACCELERANT OF AI VALUE

YOU'VE DEVELOPED the mindset (Week 8) to start seizing AI's potential for value. You've developed the skill set (Week 9) for your organization to make it happen. You've assembled the toolset (Week 10) to implement and scale AI. And you've put in place the decision set (Week 11) to govern AI responsibly.

But without leadership, these building blocks will remain silos. With leadership, they will become a unified system to accelerate value creation at enterprise scale. If "speed is the new moat," then leadership is the accelerant that transforms it into sustainable value.[2]

This week, you'll learn about the following:

- How AI amplifies leadership's responsibilities to understand, decide, and communicate.
- Practical frameworks for developing leadership that accelerates AI value creation.
- The new leadership challenges of managing AI-fluent people.
- How to foster the emergence of "superhumans," people who combine what is uniquely AI with what is uniquely human.

HOW AI AMPLIFIES LEADERSHIP RESPONSIBILITIES

It's December 2022. A Coursera product manager sends Jeff Maggioncalda, who served as Coursera's CEO from 2017 to February 2025, a Slack message with a screenshot of an online interaction with ChatGPT. The prompt: "What should Coursera's product strategy be?" The answer: "A detailed, specific outline."

"Where did this come from?" Maggioncalda asks.

"ChatGPT."

"What was the total input required?"

"Literally just the prompt you see."

Maggioncalda's immediate response: "Oh, my god."

This breakthrough moment sent Maggioncalda into what he calls a "total obsession." Maggioncalda told us in an interview that throughout that December, he experimented relentlessly with AI, building a 385-page context document and testing generative AI's potential. On December 21, he launched Project Genesis–Coursera's comprehensive AI roadmap.

As we will show, Maggioncalda's leadership accelerated AI value creation at unprecedented speed. But what did he do differently?

Leadership has always involved three core responsibilities: **understanding** people and situations, **deciding** when outcomes are uncertain, and **communicating** to inspire action. These timeless responsibilities remain unchanged–but AI now transforms *how* leaders perform them.

Jeff Maggioncalda's example reveals a pattern every leader can follow. AI amplified his leadership in three ways, exponentially increasing these capabilities:

- **Scope of understanding.** AI expanded *what* Maggioncalda could comprehend–synthesizing external insights through Coursera's context, making new connections.
- **Speed of decision-making.** AI accelerated *how fast* the CEO could decide–compressing months of analysis into days, while ensuring a human in the loop maintains sound judgment.
- **Scale of communication.** AI extended *how many people* he could reach by creating bespoke written assets with an authentic voice, connecting with people both internally and at other organizations.

Leaders have traditionally delegated tasks that lead to understanding, taken time to make decisions, and relied on others to craft their messages. With AI, Maggioncalda did the opposite: He gathered his own intelligence, made decisions at unprecedented speed, and communicated directly.

This wasn't about working faster; it was about leading differently. Let's explore how AI is transforming leadership responsibility and the implications of that transformation.

UNDERSTANDING: HOW AI EXPANDS LEADERSHIP SCOPE

Effective leadership relationships depend on understanding people's needs, fears, and aspirations. AI expands the **scope** of what you can understand by removing cognitive limits on how much information you can process, how many patterns you can recognize, and how many perspectives you can synthesize.

The leaders who gain value with AI use it both to process more information and to filter external insights through their context, revealing previously invisible connections.

Traditional leaders wait for others to gather information and present filtered recommendations. AI-amplified leaders directly synthesize vast amounts of information in real time, making understanding immediate and direct versus delayed and shaped by organizational hierarchy.

Maggioncalda discovered this through what he calls "information synthesis." He created a comprehensive context document containing Coursera's organizational structure and three-year business strategy. When reading external content–like a *Harvard Business Review* article on market entry strategies–he would ask AI, "What are the three main takeaways of this article for the CEO of Coursera, given our business and three-year strategy?"

"The LLM [large language model] does not know our three-year strategy, because it's not out there," Maggioncalda explained to us. "But I load that in, and now it's like a personal reader who can tell me what I need to know."

This approach allowed Maggioncalda to rapidly synthesize external insights with internal context, accelerating his understanding of competitive implications and new business opportunities. Where traditional CEOs would delegate this analysis and wait weeks for reports, Maggioncalda synthesized insights in real time as he consumed information.

The implications for scope surfaced immediately: Maggioncalda understood something critical about Coursera's business. Language was Coursera's constraint. The edtech company had world-class content and faculty from top universities. But most of the learning experience was locked in English. Course translation used to cost about $10,000, making it prohibitively expensive to translate the more than five thousand courses on Coursera at the end of 2022. Generative AI's translation capabilities changed that overnight.

While other edtech companies focused on AI tutoring and personalization features, Maggioncalda saw another opportunity in using AI to break down the language barriers that limited Coursera's global reach. His expanded scope of understanding revealed an application that would remove a key barrier to growth. The speed of doing so would add a new differentiator.

You don't need to replicate Jeff Maggioncalda's 385-page document. However, you can apply his approach—the scope he tackled—to your organization's context and identify what sets it apart, just as he did, and at speed.

DECIDING: HOW AI ACCELERATES SPEED

Leaders must make decisions when outcomes are uncertain—and with AI today, the speed of decision-making and action matters more than ever. AI upends the speed at which leaders can make decisions without sacrificing judgment.

Traditional leaders delegate data gathering, wait for analysis from internal teams and external consultants, and make decisions only after comprehensive vetting. This process, while thoughtful and managing risks, takes time. AI-amplified leaders rapidly synthesize vast amounts of information themselves, run multiple scenarios simultaneously, and make informed decisions at unprecedented speed, while maintaining accountability for outcomes.

But here's the critical distinction: AI can show you what's possible and help you evaluate options. Yet, only *you* can decide what to do, based on values, purpose, and vision. Coursera's newly found advantage emerged from combining AI's analytical power with the CEO's human wisdom—at speed.

The criticality of decision-making at speed became clear to Maggioncalda immediately. The window was narrow. Once other edtech companies recognized generative AI's translation powers, the first-mover advantage would disappear.

Maggioncalda launched Project Genesis on December 21, weeks after his oh-my-god moment. His personal AI fluency became a catalyst for organizational transformation, enabling decision-making at unprecedented speed.

Accelerating judgment without sacrificing quality

Maggioncalda developed two approaches that demonstrate how to accelerate decision-making while maintaining human judgment.

The first approach is what he calls "cognitive bootstrapping." Before consulting AI, he would write his own perspective on a decision or new approach. Then he would ask AI tools, "What are the strengths and weaknesses of this point of view? What are my blind spots and biases? What would be your recommendations to improve this point of view?"

Maggioncalda's approach doesn't delegate the decision to AI—he uses it to challenge thinking, reveal assumptions, and surface risks faster than traditional stakeholder consultations or research would allow. The speed advantage comes from compressing what might take weeks of back-and-forth into minutes of intensive analysis.

The second approach uses the "flipped interaction pattern." Instead of asking AI for answers, Maggioncalda would say, "Act like a [strategic consultant/HR expert/financial advisor] whose job is to help a CEO [list a specific objective]. Please ask me as many questions as you need to gather the information to get the best possible answer. Ask one question at a time. Start with your first question."

"Instead of giving me an answer, [the AI tool] starts asking me for the context that it doesn't have yet," Maggioncalda discovered. "I find it really interesting to see what [the AI tool] takes to make a good decision. Because a lot of times I didn't think about that."

This flipped approach reveals information gaps you might not recognize on your own. It accelerates the discovery of what you don't know, which is often the most critical factor in decision quality. Such approaches would work for any leader: Seek AI input to challenge your thinking, stress-test your assumptions, and reveal blind spots. And "flip the interaction" so the AI tools can be asking you questions and help you discover what information you're missing.

Speed as a competitive advantage

We began our journey by highlighting the importance of speed. We cannot overemphasize the importance of this principle, which also applies to leadership. Consider Coursera again. By May 2023, Coursera was rolling out AI-powered translation at scale. By December 2023, four thousand-plus courses were available in up to seventeen languages. By April 2024, there were 1.5 million enrollments in AI-translated courses, with learners completing courses 25 percent faster than when enrolled in English-only versions.

While competitors were just starting to explore AI applications, Coursera had expanded its addressable market through AI-amplified leadership that combined speed with sound judgment. To be clear, Maggioncalda did not make rash decisions–he used AI to maintain decision quality while compressing decision cycles.

The speed advantage comes from making sound decisions more quickly, not from having AI make decisions on your behalf. You maintain accountability while accelerating informed judgment.

COMMUNICATING: HOW AI EXTENDS SCALE

Leaders must mobilize people toward common goals through communication that creates understanding, builds trust, and inspires action. Traditional leaders often face a dilemma: whether to maintain a personal approach or reach a broader audience but lose the personal touch. AI exponentially expands the **scale** at which leaders can communicate. AI-amplified leaders maintain their authentic voices while communicating personally to diverse audiences at scale, crafting messages faster and adapting communication for different stakeholders without sacrificing authenticity.

But the most sophisticated AI-crafted message will fail if people don't trust the messenger. The leader's authenticity, vulnerability, and genuine commitment to their people's success form the foundation that makes all communication effective. AI doesn't replace authentic communication–it amplifies leaders' reach while maintaining their genuine voices.

Maintaining authenticity at scale

Here, Jeff Maggioncalda created another systematic approach. He developed "personal voice" prompts that captured his writing style, vocabulary, syntax, tone, and cadence, along with examples of emails and other communications he had written. When preparing to communicate with different audiences, he would load this context into an AI tool and ask it to help craft first-draft emails true to his voice while addressing specific points.

This isn't about "phoning it in" to AI. The voice is genuinely yours; AI simply helps you express it more efficiently across various contexts, audiences, and goals.

For company-wide communications, Maggioncalda combined his personal voice prompts with Coursera's complete organizational context and business strategy. This allowed him to quickly create messages that connected team accomplishments to business objectives, ensuring that every communication reinforced the organizational vision while maintaining his authentic style. From there, he carefully reviewed and augmented the AI's output.

The scale advantage is clear: Maggioncalda rapidly created more and more communications for different groups and audiences. They could be used internally, externally, in his sector and beyond, in the US, and in other countries. Equally, all that communication reflected his own voice, included nuances for specific audiences, and connected tactical work to strategic vision. He maintained direct control over his communication while exponentially expanding his reach.

INTEGRATING LEADERSHIP RESPONSIBILITIES

Understanding, deciding, and communicating work together as an integrated system, not in isolation. The leaders who excel with AI integrate it across all three areas to create a multiplier effect that accelerates value creation.

Maggioncalda's December 2022 AI awakening worked because he used AI to strengthen all three leadership responsibilities. He expanded his scope of understanding, accelerated his speed of decision-making, and extended the scale of his communication. That integration is what makes the example especially powerful for other leaders to follow. It creates the ability to see opportunities that others miss, move faster than competitors can respond, and mobilize entire organizations around a shared understanding–simultaneously.

You, too, can replicate what Maggioncalda did. With this book, you've spent eleven weeks building exactly that skill. You have the mindset to see AI's potential to create value, the skill set for your organization to start delivering, the toolset to implement and scale solutions, and the decision set to govern AI responsibly. And now you have the leadership approach to integrate all of it—at scope, speed, and scale that seemed impossible just months ago.

LEADING AI-FLUENT PEOPLE (THE WHAT)

AI doesn't just enhance how you lead—it changes what you're leading. As AI becomes part of daily work, a new reality emerges that every leader must grasp: People who are AI-fluent work in entirely new ways.

You are already leading team members who understand and use AI better than you do and who can deliver multiple times the output compared to their peers. What does that mean for how you lead?

HOW LEADERSHIP CHANGES—OR DOES IT?

Research from *MIT Sloan Management Review* and Boston Consulting Group reveals that 69 percent of AI experts believe that managing AI-augmented teams requires fundamentally new management approaches.[3] We disagree. When you examine closely what's different, you find that AI unequivocally demands that leaders embrace the leadership principles they should have been practicing all along. There are countless books on leadership, so we won't go into detail here. But let's be clear. There is no chance to get away with poor leadership. AI exposes it mercilessly. Conversely, AI can further amplify good leadership traits—for example, leaders' ability to value expertise, empower people, mentor them, and help them learn, develop, and grow.

SHINING THE LIGHT ON POOR LEADERSHIP

AI doesn't cause the insecurity that some leaders feel; it shines a light on it. Leaders who already struggle with the fact that their team members are more knowledgeable in a specific area will continue to breed insecurity. AI exposes what good leadership has always required: surrounding yourself with people smarter than you, trusting their expertise, and focusing your value on judgment about strategic direction rather than technical implementation. Leaders who already practice hiring people smarter than themselves will find that AI simply extends that practice to new domains.

McKinsey research shows employees are three times more likely to be using AI than their leaders expect, creating expertise gaps that widen daily.[4] One leader reflected to us, "My authority used to come from knowing more than everyone else. Now the person I hired six months ago understands our AI-embedded tools better than I do."

This requires leaders to adapt and focus on strategic implications rather than technical mastery. When people share outputs and ideas, ask questions like: How does this help us achieve our goals? Why do you see this happening? What are the implications? Your value lies in consistently connecting with business priorities, customer needs, and opportunities rather than focusing on technical details or intricacies. This has always been true–AI just makes it obvious.

Good leaders are poised to continue with sound judgment, inspirational presence, and commanding charisma, while empowering the people in their organizations. Poor leaders will face exposure and further insecurity.

HOW TO HOLD ON TO AI-FLUENT PEOPLE

Leaders have always needed to focus on retaining high performers; AI did not create this challenge, but it raises the stakes by making skill differences more visible. The reality is that AI-fluent employees already command a salary premium averaging $18,000 annually, making them incredibly marketable and able to change jobs.[5] The solution to keeping them involves applying proven retention strategies with renewed urgency.

Here's what works:

- **Challenge people**. Give AI-fluent employees problems that other companies can't match. For example, challenge them with complex, highly visible tasks that make them feel they are learning, valued, and indispensable.
- **Empower autonomy**. Turn employees from potential flight risks into internal entrepreneurs. Give AI-fluent team members the autonomy to redesign core processes–including budget authority and technology choices. They're not working for you; they're benefitting the organization and building their professional legacy through it.

- **Invest in them personally.** There is no better way for a leader to make an employee feel valued than spending time with them, showing genuine interest, and mentoring. Identify your top AI-fluent team members and demonstrate your appreciation. You'd be surprised how meaningful that can be to people, and it's precisely that kind of humanity we all, especially leaders, must amplify at this time. Balancing AI with human intelligence will become especially powerful.

HOW TO LEAD PEOPLE WITH UNEVEN AI SKILLS

A more complex aspect involves leading teams whose members have varying levels of AI knowledge. When some team members deliver three to ten times the output using AI, traditional performance evaluation systems break down. The internal equity challenge compounds: the same role, vastly different productivity, a growing need for performance management expectation changes, and a demand for differential recognition.

This mirrors challenges that have always existed when new technologies or methods create performance disparities. Early adopters of mobile devices, CRM systems, or programming languages created similar gaps. AI makes the gaps larger, but the leadership challenge remains familiar. To solve this, maintain motivation across all skill levels and constantly push people to keep learning as new tools, features, and ways of working emerge.

For example, companies like Unilever have used AI-driven approaches to create personalized development plans, resulting in a 17 percent increase in work satisfaction and reduced turnover by recognizing that different roles require distinct management approaches.[6] By using real-time feedback, individualized project assignments, and predictive analytics, Unilever tailored career pathways to each employee's aspirations and strengths, enabling managers to make decisions based on performance rather than subjective opinions.[7]

We recommend three approaches for leaders to lean on:

- **Incentives for learning.** Make it clear that there is an expectation for continuous learning and place the onus on employees. As we said earlier, they need to take ownership of their upskilling. But you need to help them fully grasp the importance of it, in addition to providing the tools and training. Adapt performance-cycle objectives and individual development plans to include AI training and certifications, recognize course completion, and celebrate milestones publicly.

- **Incentives for knowledge transfer.** In addition to individual accountability for learning, make people accountable for helping each other to learn. Add teaching and mentoring as part of everyone's job description. AI-fluent employees should document discoveries, help train colleagues, share innovations, and be given incentives and rewards for doing so. If they do, they will naturally teach others. Again, you provide the tools and training but make people accountable for their own and each other's learning.
- **Career advancement for disruptors.** Develop new career paths that account for, encourage, and reward disruptors, people who are not afraid to create value in new ways with new tools and new business models. These people demonstrate what one admired global leader described to us as "intellectual insubordination." Instead of discouraging divergent thinking, offer advancement to people who demonstrate it. Seize the potential of people who challenge the status quo and take on the charge to drive value where it's not yet prevalent but there is a growth trajectory.

CREATING AND LEADING DISRUPTORS

Let's face it, disruptors have a bad reputation. But disruptors provide unique perspectives because they envision what is possible and advocate for that future. In her book *The Disruption Mindset,* Charlene found that disruptive change requires that leaders actively and systematically create a movement. If a vision of the desired future state is the flint, a movement is the fuel that feeds the fire. The leader's job is to bring disruptors into a movement to create value with AI so they can channel their curiosity and energy toward mutually beneficial outcomes. Stand in their way or stymie their efforts and you risk them leaving or becoming blockers to progress.

Cultivating disruptors is essential groundwork for AI success because they challenge processes, reimagine work, and push against limitations. Some of these disruptors don't just want a new way of *working*–they yearn for a new way of *being*. These are the people who will become "superhumans."

THE NEXT FRONTIER: INTEGRATED INTELLIGENCE

AI does more than make employees more productive or efficient. We see potential for even greater value from AI: a new form of intelligence.

We are not talking about artificial general intelligence (AI that matches human reasoning) or superintelligence (AI that surpasses human competencies). Instead, we envision "integrated intelligence," a blend of what's unique about AI and what's uniquely human. The AI aspect focuses on enhanced cognitive abilities and the capacity to get more done quickly. The human intelligence taps into what is uniquely human and amplifies it: empathy, self-reflection, intuition, judgment, and wisdom.

We call the people who will manifest this integrated intelligence "superhumans." They won't replace their humanity with technology–they will use technology to become more deeply human.

SUPERHUMANS AND WHAT'S UNIQUE TO AI

What makes AI unique is its complex cognitive infrastructure, which has never existed before.

First, technology is becoming as probabilistic as the human mind, but with scope, speed, and scale no single individual possesses. Life is probabilistic–based on likelihoods and ranges of possible outcomes rather than certainties–and humans are probabilistic too. Superhumans benefitting from the scope, speed, and scale of AI will no longer ask "Will this work?" They will effortlessly hold several likely outcomes, each with its shifting probabilities and interdependencies. Superhumans will operate in ranges and likelihoods rather than false certainties. Teams exploring a strategic pivot won't debate whether it will succeed–they will navigate a probability landscape, understanding which factors shift odds and how different paths create different distribution curves of outcomes. AI captures the richness, gradation, and probabilistic nature of life in ways that were previously impossible.

Second, what makes AI unique and will define superhumans is networked productivity, a form of networked thinking where individual contributions and collective synthesis happen simultaneously, similar to how network effects created value with each additional user. This will redefine what productivity means. It will no longer be measured by tasks completed or hours worked but by the velocity and value of contributions to collective intelligence, the quality of decisions enabled across the network, and the speed at which insights spark innovations across an organization.

Superhumans will not only benefit from networked productivity but also retain and amplify what makes people unique.

SUPERHUMANS AND WHAT'S UNIQUELY HUMAN

AI's cognitive infrastructure will enable people to develop amplified humanity across five interconnected dimensions.

The first is **empathy**, the human capacity to feel with others, to relate to what others experience, and to care about others' well-being. Empathy is uniquely human because it requires the capacity to feel with another person, not just to know about their feelings. We have empathy because we recognize our shared humanity.

The second dimension of humanity is **self-reflection**. While AI can serve as a mirror, revealing patterns in our thinking and behavior we cannot see on our own, it's only humans who can practice self-reflection. That's because self-reflection requires self-awareness, feeling something about what you discover, and choosing to change based on what matters to you.

The third uniquely human trait is **intuition**, trusting what you know. AI can validate intuition by analyzing patterns you sensed but couldn't articulate and then pressure testing your instincts against similar situations. However, AI cannot possess intuition because intuition is an embodied combination of emotional and cognitive patterns that emerge from having lived through countless moments.

The fourth uniquely human trait is **judgment**, deciding what's right. Good judgment means making sound decisions based on values, context, and a sense of responsibility for the consequences, not just optimizing for outcomes. AI can analyze options, model scenarios, and reveal blind spots, but it cannot exercise judgment because genuine choice requires human judgment. However, AI has no inherent values of its own, no stake in the outcomes, and no accountability for choices. While it can recommend optimal paths, it cannot decide what should happen based on what's right, what matters, and what's worth the cost. Superhumans will use AI to inform their judgment, but the judgment itself will remain theirs: their choice, their values, their responsibility.

And the fifth trait that's uniquely human is **wisdom**, a deep understanding earned over time. It's not just what you know but who you've become through decades of living. That includes the failures that taught you, the losses that challenged you, and the experiences that revealed what matters. AI can provide access to accumulated knowledge and remind you of lessons you've learned, but AI cannot be wise because wisdom requires having lived through experiences, not just having data about them. Wisdom comes only from having lived life and integrated its lessons into a deeper understanding and thus remains uniquely human.

These dimensions work together as an integrated whole. When superhumans combine them simultaneously with what's unique to AI, they will use technology to finally express the full depth of what makes us human.

LEADING SUPERHUMANS

What will this mean for leaders? The most important action you can take is to set the aspiration that you want to develop superhumans in your organization. This requires a choice. You must decide whether you're leading for AI-enhanced efficiency alone or whether you also want to help develop superhumans for your organization. The first companies to figure it out won't just have a competitive advantage, although they will have that. In addition, they'll be creating an entirely new form of value for their organizations.

We don't yet know how to lead in this world. This is the frontier we are only starting to approach. Value creation will accelerate with the emergence of superhumans and all these potential new competencies, finally within reach thanks to AI. The human potential we've always sensed–but couldn't quite access because we were too cognitively depleted, too emotionally exhausted, too constrained by false choices–will finally have room to emerge.

YOUR WEEK 12 ACTION PLAN

This week, make leadership the accelerant that transforms your AI initiatives into sustained value creation. Focus on three high-level actions that activate what you've learned:

- **Amplify one leadership dimension where it matters.** Choose a critical challenge this week–a major decision, a difficult conversation, or an important communication. Then steal a page from Jeff Maggioncalda and use AI to amplify one leadership responsibility: Expand your **scope**, accelerate your **speed** of decision-making, or extend your **scale** of communication. Experience firsthand how AI amplifies leadership when the stakes are real.

- **Engage with AI-fluent people**. Identify team members who are pushing boundaries with AI. Have a conversation focused not on what they're producing but on what's constraining them. Ask, "What would you attempt if you had complete autonomy on one initiative?" Listen for the gap between their potential and current reality. Your goal isn't to solve every constraint this week. Instead, it's to show you value and encourage AI fluency.
- **Set the aspiration for developing superhumans in your organization**. Reflect on what it would mean if 10 to 15 percent of your organization combined what's unique to AI and what's uniquely human. What would change? What would become possible?

SUMMARY

You've now completed Week 12 of your 90-day preparation for delivering value with AI. This week focused on leadership as the accelerant that transforms AI's potential into sustained value creation.

In this chapter, accomplished the following:

- **Learned how AI amplifies core leadership responsibilities**, understanding that AI exponentially expands scope of understanding by synthesizing information through strategic context, accelerates speed of decision-making by compressing cycles while maintaining judgment, and extends scale of communication by reaching diverse audiences while maintaining authentic voice. These three dimensions work together in a multiplier effect.
- **Discovered what changes when leading AI-fluent people**, recognizing that AI doesn't necessarily demand new leadership skills but exposes poor leadership. You learned proven strategies for retaining high performers: Challenge them, empower them, and invest in them personally.
- **Explored how to cultivate disruptors**, understanding that you need to create a movement, not manage incremental improvement. You

learned to recognize disruptors and create conditions for them to channel their energy toward mutually beneficial outcomes—and discovered that some will evolve into superhumans.

- **Considered the vision of integrated intelligence** that combines what's unique to AI and what's uniquely human. You met superhumans, the people who will live and manifest those traits. And you pondered your readiness to lead superhumans, becoming one yourself, and aspiring to develop superhumans in your organization.

Over these twelve weeks, you've completed your 90-day blueprint: You assembled your team and established responsible AI principles. You created a dynamic roadmap connecting AI directly to business strategy. You built the four foundations for sustainable AI value—mindset, skill set, toolset, and decision set. Without leadership, all this work remains disconnected. With leadership, it becomes an integrated system that accelerates value creation at enterprise scale. You now have everything you need to win with AI.

Epilogue

IMAGINE

IMAGINE that ten years have gone by.

Sitting here today, we can't tell you what the world or AI will look like then. But we can tell you what we *hope* they will look like.

We believe that AI will help make us better people. That with all the world's knowledge at our fingertips, AI will help us gain a deeper understanding of each other and of our shared world. That we'll use AI and all its potential to bridge the gaps between us.

In every era of change—from the invention of the printing press to the advent of the internet—the winners weren't the ones who could seamlessly execute best practices. The winners imagined and executed on possibilities that others couldn't see.

If the only thing we do with AI is make our organizations more efficient, we'll have failed. But if we use it to imagine and build ways to lift everyone up, we can change the world for the better.

Johannes Gutenberg changed the course of history when he imagined a machine that could print books. Over five hundred years later, Jeff Bezos imagined selling books online when everyone said it was absurd. Today, those ideas are taken for granted. But in their time, they required leaders who could imagine a new future.

Throughout history, transformative leaders haven't led with strategic plans. They've led with vision. They painted a picture of a future worth building, then inspired others to build it with them.

AI moves so quickly that best practices are becoming dated even before they can be documented. Which gives you the opportunity to invent the future with AI, while everyone else is automating the present. Your most significant competitive advantage isn't your technology stack or your data–it's your imagination.

Here's your challenge: Imagine the world you want to create. For your organization, your customers, your community–for all the people whose lives your work touches.

Let's strive to create a future that we will all want to live in.

Dream it. Then build it.

Appendix A
RESPONSIBLE AND ETHICAL USE POLICY TEMPLATE

[YOUR ORGANIZATION NAME] RESPONSIBLE AND ETHICAL AI USE POLICY

1. INTRODUCTION

- **Organization:** [Your organization name]
- **Effective date:** [MM/DD/YYYY]
- **Policy owner:** [Policy owner / AI Ethics Office]
- **Applies to:** All employees, contractors, and third parties acting for [Org], on any device.
- **Scope:** All AI use–both for internal work and in customer-facing products/services.

This policy explains how we use artificial intelligence (AI) in a way that reflects our company values–including respect, integrity, inclusion, and transparency–and follows the law. It is designed to be practical for everyone, from frontline teams to engineers.

This policy defers specific standards (for example, encryption and data retention) to your existing security, privacy, data classification, and records policies. This avoids duplication and ensures this policy remains high-level and usable.

2. GUIDING PRINCIPLES AND ETHICAL COMMITMENTS

Our use of AI must reflect [Org] values and comply with all applicable laws and regulations. Beyond compliance, we commit to these principles:

- **Should we?** We first evaluate *if* we should use AI. All AI use must have a clear benefit, be critically evaluated for potential harms, and uphold our commitment to human well-being and dignity.
- **Human-centricity.** We use AI to augment and assist people, not to replace human judgment in high-impact situations. We maintain human oversight and accountability.

Ethical decision-making (when it's not black and white)

Some choices are ethical dilemmas, not policy checkboxes. When you're unsure, use this quick checklist and ask for help (see section 8).

Before you proceed, ask these questions:

- **People first:** Could anyone be harmed or treated unfairly? Who benefits and who might be left out?
- **Values check:** Does this match our values–respect, fairness, privacy, transparency?
- **Transparency:** Would people expect to be told AI is involved? If yes, plan to disclose.
- **Privacy and rights:** Are we using the *minimum data* needed and honoring people's choices and laws?
- **Purpose fit:** Is the AI being used for what it was designed to do? What are its limits?

Rule of thumb: If a reasonable person would want us to slow down and double-check, we slow down and double-check. If still unsure, pause and escalate (see section 8).

3. CORE POLICY: THE FIVE TRUST AREAS

Follow the "do/don't" items below. If our existing security, privacy, data, or records policies are stricter, those policies always prevail.

3.1 Safety, security, and privacy

- Do:
    - Use only approved tools; sign in with SSO and follow existing role-based access rules.
    - Follow all data classification, privacy, security, and records/retention policies for all inputs, outputs, logging, encryption, and legal holds.
    - Run security tests, including prompt-injection and data-leak checks, before customer-facing or higher-risk launches.
- Don't:
    - Use consumer tools, even if they are paid versions.
    - Share proprietary, confidential, or sensitive data with a tool that isn't cleared for it.
    - Let vendors learn from our data by default. Vendors may not use our prompts, files, or outputs to train their models *unless* legal and security approve in writing and the contract is updated.

3.2 Fairness

- Do:
    - For high-impact decisions, check for uneven impact across groups and document fixes.
    - When building, identify and document your "fairness lens" (process-based, outcome-based) in the AI governance and risk intake.
- Don't:
    - Launch or keep running a system that shows harmful bias without a mitigation plan.

3.3 Reliability

- Do:
    - Keep a human in the loop when mistakes could cause harm or compliance issues.
    - Set quality thresholds and fallbacks (what to do if the AI fails) before launch.
    - Monitor results and roll back if quality thresholds aren't met.
- Don't:
    - Use AI for tasks it wasn't designed for, or treat AI drafts as final without review.

3.4 Transparency

- Do:
    - **Disclose** AI use when it is customer facing, materially impactful, or required by policy/law. Use team-approved wording.
    - **Keep basic logs** (inputs/outputs/key actions) to debug issues.

3.5 (Optional) IP and content integrity

- Do:
    - Use licensed/authorized data and respect third-party terms. Follow our open-source policy for generated code.
    - For external content, prefer commercially safe sources or vendor indemnities; record your approach in the AI governance and risk intake.

4. ACCEPTABLE USE (ENCOURAGED, CAUTION, PROHIBITED)

- **Encouraged:** Drafting emails/docs, summarizing notes, analyzing data with human review, and building automation with strong guardrails.
- **Needs caution/approval:** Any new customer-facing use, agents in production, use of sensitive data, or integrations with internal systems. These require completing the AI governance and risk intake process (see section 6).
- **Prohibited:** Deceptive deepfakes; unlawful discrimination; scraping that violates terms; bypassing security controls; creating malware; unapproved

surveillance; any use intended to deceptively manipulate or infringe on human autonomy; or anything that breaks our code of conduct or the law.

5. ROLES AND RESPONSIBILITIES

General users (all employees)

- You may use approved tools for approved uses without extra approvals.
- You must follow the rules in this policy, with particular attention regarding data (section 3.1) and acceptable use (section 4).

Builders/developers (product, IT, data teams)

- For all nonapproved or new uses of AI, you must complete the process for any new uses of AI (see section 6) and obtain all listed approvals *before* launching new customer-facing features, connecting new sensitive data, or procuring new AI tools.

Agentic AI

- Every agent must have a named human owner, scoped permissions, audit logs, rate/impact limits, and a kill switch. No owner, no deployment.

6. AI GOVERNANCE PROCESS AND APPROVALS FOR NEW USES OF AI

For all nonapproved or new uses of AI, you must complete the AI governance and risk intake form [link] and obtain all listed approvals for any

- new AI tool or new customer-facing use;
- new data category, for example, using sensitive data for the first time;
- new agentic capabilities;
- other high-impact changes or use cases.

7. APPROVED TOOLS AND VENDOR MANAGEMENT

- Maintain minimum vendor expectations: SSO/RBAC, encryption, audit logs, configurable retention, and no training on our data unless legal approves and the contract is updated.
- Treat embedded AI in other platforms (Office suite, CRM,

IDE) like any other tool—the same approvals apply when sensitive data or external users are involved.

8. REPORTING, HELP, AND ENFORCEMENT

Training and awareness

- **General users:** Complete the short course on safe AI use [annually].
- **Builders/developers:** Complete role-based technical training [annually] and before launching a new use case.

Questions, ethics help, and reporting

If you have a question, see something concerning, or need ethical advice, use any option below. Asking for help is encouraged.

- Get help/ask questions:
    - Slack/Teams: [#ask-ai-ethics]
    - Email: [ai-ethics@[org].com]
    - Office hours: [Wednesdays 2–3:00 p.m. PT] with the AI ethics office

- Report a concern (choose what's most comfortable):
    - Your manager or the AI ethics office (see above)
    - Anonymous hotline: [hotline/webform]
    - Security/privacy incident line: [link]

Nonretaliation

Good-faith questions or reports are protected. Retaliation is not allowed and will lead to corrective action.

Enforcement

Violations may lead to access restriction, remediation, and disciplinary action per HR policy.

Policy review

This policy will be reviewed every [six to twelve months] or upon major regulatory or technology changes.

9. KEY DEFINITIONS

- **Agentic AI:** Systems that can plan, decide, and act via tools/APIs with limited supervision.
- **High-impact decision:** A decision that affects a person's rights, access, safety, money, job, or health.
- **Sensitive data:** Refer to the official [Link: Data Classification Policy] as the authoritative source.
- [Add more definitions as needed]

Appendix B

GUIDANCE FOR AI TOOLSET IMPLEMENTATION

This appendix provides strategic guidance to complement the principles and frameworks introduced in chapter 10. While the chapter focuses on the four-layer architecture and core principles of AI toolset assembly, this appendix offers practical tools for implementation.

HOW TO USE THIS APPENDIX

This content is organized into four sections that support different aspects of your AI toolset work:

- **Section 1: Consumption-layer priorities**. Strategic guidance on which consumption layer investments deliver the most value and how to prioritize interface-design decisions that drive adoption.
- **Section 2: Security and ethics by design**. Frameworks for embedding security and ethical considerations into all four layers of your AI systems from the start, rather than treating them as afterthoughts.
- **Section 3: Common implementation pitfalls**. Watchouts for common mistakes that derail AI toolset implementations, helping you avoid expensive detours and dead ends.
- **Section 4: Strategic questions for technology discussions**. A comprehensive set of questions to guide your assessment of

readiness across all four layers, designed to surface gaps and drive productive conversations with your technical teams.

These sections provide the practical tools you need to move from understanding the four-layer architecture to successfully implementing it in your organization.

SECTION 1: CONSUMPTION-LAYER PRIORITIES

The insights about how consumption design creates value point to specific leadership actions that matter now:

- **Design for viral adoption, not mandated compliance.** Stop asking "How do we train people to use this AI tool?" and start asking "Why would someone choose *not* to use this?" Establish metrics that track adoption velocity and breadth: Are new user groups discovering and using AI without top-down directives? Is usage spreading organically across departments? If adoption requires extensive change-management programs, your consumption design is failing. Instead, work with your product and UX teams to identify and eliminate every source of friction in the first five minutes of user experience. The goal is for employees or customers to try the tool once and immediately see value compelling enough that they return voluntarily.
- **Track everything to find and fix friction points.** Deploy analytics that track where users hesitate, get confused, or abandon AI tools. Watch for patterns: Do users start a task but not complete it? Do they switch back to old tools midway? Where do support tickets cluster? Appoint someone–whether a chief AI officer, product manager, or transformation lead–whose explicit job is hunting friction. Create a weekly ritual where leadership reviews friction reports and prioritizes fixes. A single clunky authentication step, a confusing menu structure, or an unclear AI response can tank adoption among thousands of potential users. The organizations winning with AI treat friction elimination as a continuous operational discipline, not a one-time design exercise.
- **Allocate budget and talent to consumption as a strategic investment.** When foundation models become commoditized–and they're rapidly heading

in that direction—your consumption layer becomes your differentiation. This means treating consumption design as a strategic capability requiring top talent, not an afterthought handled by whoever's available. Budget accordingly: If you're spending millions on AI models and infrastructure but only thousands on consumption design, you're optimizing the wrong layer. Consider building a dedicated team focused on AI experience design, staffed with interaction designers, product managers, and behavioral psychologists who understand how to make complex technology feel simple.

- **Enable rapid experimentation with consumption patterns.** Your organization needs to discover which AI applications and interfaces create value, and the only way to learn is through fast iteration. Create lightweight processes that let teams test different interfaces, integrations, and workflows without requiring months of IT approvals or enterprise architecture reviews. Set up A/B testing to compare which consumption patterns drive better outcomes. Measure time-to-insight: How long does it take from "we have an idea for an AI application" to "we have user feedback on whether it works"? The faster you can test and learn at the consumption layer, the quicker you identify high-value applications and pull ahead of slower-moving competitors.
- **Use shadow AI as design intelligence, not a security problem to lock down.** When employees bypass official AI tools for consumer alternatives like ChatGPT, resist the instinct to simply block access. Instead, treat it as valuable feedback: Your consumption layer isn't meeting user needs. Interview the shadow users. What are they trying to accomplish? Why are consumer tools more appealing than your enterprise solutions? What specific friction are they avoiding? Then close the gap by improving your official tools. The goal is to create experiences so good that workarounds become unnecessary. Some organizations formalize this by creating "AI experience feedback channels" where employees can anonymously report why they use unsanctioned tools, turning shadow IT into a continuous improvement signal.

SECTION 2: SECURITY AND ETHICS BY DESIGN

You now have the architectural blueprint for your AI system: the four interconnected layers of data, models, orchestration, and consumption. But just as with a physical construction project, a blueprint alone doesn't guarantee a safe and durable structure. You must build with discipline. Assembling your toolset in a modular LEGO-style approach gives you flexibility, but understand that flexibility can introduce risks if security and ethics aren't addressed from the start of the development process.

This is where you must shift the conversation and make security and ethics a process requirement from day one, not a compliance review before launch. This means building security and ethics into your toolset from the start. Use these key questions to guide your technical teams as they design and build across the four layers of your AI toolset (See figure B-1).

Figure B-1: Designing security and ethics into AI systems

AI SYSTEM LAYER	KEY SECURITY AND ETHICS QUESTIONS TO ASK
Data (ingredients)	How do we ensure we have the right to use our data? How are we classifying sensitive data, protecting PII, and enforcing strict, role-based access controls?
AI models (equipment)	How are we testing our models for safety (for example, toxicity, jailbreaking) and auditing them for bias? How do we vet the security of any third-party models?
Orchestration (head chef)	Is our system creating immutable audit trails for every action? What automated quality gates and agentic guardrails are in place to enforce our policies and prevent misuse?
Consumption (service)	How are we being transparent with users when they are interacting with an AI? How do we secure integrations with existing enterprise tools and protect user feedback data?

SECTION 3: COMMON IMPLEMENTATION PITFALLS

As you guide the development of your AI toolset, be aware of specific patterns that may signal potential issues ahead. Intervene early if you see any of these problems:

- **Technology choices disconnected from business value.** Watch for tool, platform, and vendor selections that prioritize technical novelty or company relationships over a clear link to business priorities. In the AI space, this can lead to costly investments in AI for AI's sake, and the proverbial "shiny toy" pursuits that don't help the organization.
- **Automating processes but not reimagining them.** This refers to a tendency to treat AI as simple automation rather than an opportunity to rethink and reinvent how you work. If you settle for AI that only speeds up suboptimal processes, you'll miss the value of complete transformation.
- **Overengineering for uncertain futures.** Be cautious of developing complex systems for hypothetical future problems rather than addressing a real issue today. For instance, avoid creating a complex AI traffic cop that routes queries to dozens of AI models when a simple tool to analyze customer feedback is all that is needed. Likewise, avoid building a team of collaborating AI agents before you've even figured out how a single AI application can help your business. Solve today's highest-value problem first with the simplest tool that works.
- **Vendor lock-ins that limit flexibility.** Be cautious of technical architectures or vendor contracts that hinder or make it prohibitively expensive to update AI models, tools, and features as new options emerge. Given AI's rapid advancement, such lock-ins can leave you tethered to outdated technology.
- **AI tools that create excessive friction.** If a new AI tool requires employees to completely abandon their familiar workflow, adoption will likely fail. A sales team, for instance, is unlikely to use an AI assistant that forces them to leave their CRM and work in a separate, complicated interface just to get an answer. The best AI tools integrate seamlessly into the applications and processes your team already uses.
- **Security as an afterthought or a blanket "no."** Extremes in security approaches won't work either. Failing to implement security

measures from the outset can have dire consequences. However, implementing overly restrictive policies and blanket bans drives employees to unsecured consumer tools, ironically increasing risk. Security controls should enable safe AI adoption, not prevent it.

Knowing what to watch for and intervening as necessary will save your organization time, funding, and frustration.

SECTION 4: STRATEGIC QUESTIONS FOR TECHNOLOGY DISCUSSIONS

You don't need to design the AI toolset, but you do need to guide key decisions. The most successful business leaders focus on asking the right questions, those that connect technology choices to business outcomes. Here's your comprehensive checklist, categorized by the type of decision you need to guide.

STRATEGIC DIRECTION

- **Link to strategy.** How does AI deployment in this case support our top-priority business goals?
- **Transformation versus automation.** Are we using AI to transform how we work or simply to automate existing inefficiencies?
- **Internal strengths versus external innovation.** Do we really need to develop AI models or tools ourselves? This question challenges the tendency to build everything in-house, ensuring that internal efforts focus only on what brings a true competitive advantage.

SOLUTION EVALUATION

- **Modularity.** How easily can we swap, upgrade, or add new components to this system? If the answer involves major rebuilds or costly data migrations, your AI toolset's design needs to be more adaptable.
- **Integration.** How will this tool fit into our existing workflows? Solutions that force significant workflow changes often fail to gain traction, regardless of their technical merits.

- **Model fit.** Are we using the right model for the task to balance cost and performance? Look for approaches that avoid one-size-fits-all solutions.
- **Data accessibility.** How are we making data accessible for AI without overinvesting? Focus on pragmatic approaches that work with your data, such as prioritizing your most strategic data sources and highest-value data elements.

IMPLEMENTATION

- **Performance and value.** How are we measuring performance and expected benefits? Look for tangible business metrics across different areas: productivity gains (time saved on specific tasks, faster speed from idea to production), effectiveness improvements (reduction in error rates, higher-quality outputs), innovation acceleration (new products or services launched, speedier time to market), and strategic advantages (improved customer-experience scores, market-share gains, or revenue uplift from AI-enabled capabilities).
- **Output integrity.** How do we ensure AI outputs are accurate, reliable, and relevant for our business context? This addresses the AI system's orchestration and its quality control function.
- **System coordination.** How will our AI tools work together to complete complex tasks? This could range from simple query routing (like Marsh's system, which automatically selects the right model) to sophisticated multiagent collaboration (like McKinsey's system, where AI agents worked together to complete a twelve-week project in just three hours). This helps define the level of sophistication needed in your orchestration layer.

Appendix C

HOW WE USED AI TO WRITE THIS BOOK

WHEN WE SET OUT to write a book about AI, we knew we had to practice what we preached. We couldn't credibly tell leaders to embrace AI if we didn't do the same. Throughout this book's development, we used AI extensively–not as a ghostwriter, but as a notetaker, research assistant, and brainstorming partner we asked to challenge us. Indeed, we consider AI to be our third collaborator.

We tried a variety of AI tools, each with specific strengths. We relied on Claude for structuring content. We created a custom GPT in ChatGPT with four years of our work featured in newsletters, transcripts, and podcasts–training it on our own thinking and voice. We used Perplexity when we needed examples and statistics. And we had Gemini search through thousands of pages of interview transcripts and analyze the entire manuscript at the end.

None of these tools wrote the book. But each helped us organize our thinking, speed up the research process, and compare versions and drafts.

HOW AI HELPED

Here's where we found AI helpful:

- **Transcription, note-taking, and summarization**. We used AI to record and transcribe all interviews and working sessions, and to summarize our discussions, which sometimes spanned several days. More than just summaries, we received key takeaways and actionable steps.
- **Research**. In the past, we would have had to hire a researcher. With AI, research

became a faster, iterative process that distilled hundreds of articles and reports into themes, hypotheses, and references. But we always did the fact-checking.

- **Initial structure and outlines**. AI helped us overcome the tyranny of the blank page by turning research into rough outlines, quickly revealing gaps in our thinking.
- **Finding what we'd forgotten**. Remembering every detail, draft, or example across two years is impossible for humans. AI became our memory bank. Near the end of the writing process, we used AI to compare our final manuscript with early drafts. We identified some content we'd cut earlier that would actually fit in the final manuscript, including several valuable case studies and quotes that would otherwise have remained lost.
- **Illustration ideas**. For illustrations, we used AI to create initial sketches based on the text in a chapter. AI surfaced different approaches and concepts that we shared with our human illustrator to use as a starting point.
- **Brainstorming**. Finally, we used AI to challenge our thinking and help us consider additional points of view. For examplc, we would give an AI tool a draft and ask, "What are the questions readers might have that we are not answering?" We used AI to stretch our minds, test our limits, and advocate for a contrarian perspective.

WHAT AI CAN'T DO

We also want to share what we couldn't rely on AI to do, though we have no doubt it will keep improving in these areas. Regardless of what AI can do in the future, there will always be a place and a need for the craft of human writers. Here is where AI fell short.

- **Coming up with new ideas**. Because AI is trained on existing knowledge, it cannot produce *new* ideas. Even when we prompted it to think hypothetically and about the future, it came up with content limited to today's reality. In our experience, AI clearly failed to generate unique ideas on its own.
- **Writing**. While AI could generate very rough initial outlines, it failed to "write" in a way we could ever use, despite working with multiple

style samples, guides, and prompts from us. In fact, our revelation is that it took more time to rework AI-generated text than to write from scratch. AI "writing" is notoriously bland, full of repetitive patterns ("It's not this–it's that") and brimming with corporate jargon–like "alignment," "leverage," "utilize," and more.

- **Editing**. We experimented with AI to see if it could edit content. It could not. We found that AI consistently defaulted to its poor writing style (see above). One frustrating example is that AI replaced every instance of the simple word "use" with "utilize," a basic no-no in writing. We relied on our very human editors to do this work.
- **Creating illustrations**. While AI could quickly create crude charts, it often suggested cliché icons that, at times, had nothing to do with the content or misrepresented its meaning. Our human illustrator created all the illustrations in this book.
- **Fact-checking**. As Barbara Cominelli said (see chapter 11), "AI has no truth function." We exercised constant critical thinking and vigilance to verify AI-offered references and list only validated facts.
- **Finessing final work**. All the little tweaks and iterations that pull a book together, from adding an anecdote to including a recent study to writing detailed endnotes, are ours too. They represent our experience, thinking, and yes, our dreams of seeing the book in the hands of our readers. AI lacks the very human traits of character and last-minute *aha* moments to inject our personalities into the book.

WHAT WE LEARNED ABOUT HUMAN-AI COLLABORATION

By the time we finished this book, we'd learned something important: AI played a role in its creation. It was helpful but also required that we understand its limitations.

Writing this book with AI was an experiment in the principles we advocate throughout these pages. If what you just read makes sense, challenges your thinking, and helps you learn, then our collaboration worked–not because AI is a good writer (it's not), but because it helped us become better thinkers.

That's the promise of AI: not doing our thinking for us, but helping us think better.

ACKNOWLEDGMENTS

THIS BOOK STARTED as an idea over coffee in Boston in June 2023. Katia was, at the time, the inaugural chief digital officer of Harvard Business School, and Charlene was in town for a reunion. One of us was a bestselling author of six books on technology, disruption, and leadership, and the other was an experienced business leader in driving value with digital, data, and AI applications. We drew on the foundation of a twenty-five-year friendship, forged in both professional and personal realms, to create this book. With the mainstreaming of AI that we'd started to see, we wanted to share our expertise and practical lessons learned with the business world, which was just starting to grasp the technology's importance. And we specifically sought to share practical knowledge and guidance to help others avoid repeating mistakes we've seen (and made) and to seize the opportunity of this technology to create value quickly and responsibly.

We each brought something essential to these pages. Charlene brought her experience as an author and her deep understanding of how to guide organizations through transformative change. Katia brought her pioneering work as one of the world's first chief AI officers, along with her battle-tested wisdom from leading AI transformations and driving value from them at some of the world's most iconic brands. Together, we saw something clearly: People need detailed guidance on how to create real value with AI. Articles and podcasts, as valuable as they are, can't serve that need. A book emerged from that necessity—and from our shared conviction that leaders deserve a practical blueprint, not just inspiration.

THE VOICES THAT SHAPED THIS BOOK

While we are clearly passionate about AI, we love people–and the following people shaped our thinking about AI in countless ways. This book exists because technology, business, and ethics leaders were generous enough to share their stories, struggles, and successes with us. Their expertise, track record, and pragmatic guidance form the heart of what you'll read in these pages.

We conducted extensive background interviews with leaders who enriched our understanding of driving business value with AI: Jason Baumgarten, Paul Beswick, Murli Buluswar, Massimo Canturi, Albert Chow, Barbara Cominelli, George Connolly, Erica Goodwin, Sami Hassanyeh, Jamie Gorski, Prashant Jain, Kitti Lakner, Nyimpini Mabunda, Robert MacAuslan, Jeff Maggioncalda, Tom Monahan, Sathish Muthukrishnan, Iskra Nikolova, Erik Roth, Juan Santos, Reid Sawyer, and Lauren Woods. The words and examples from these leaders appear throughout the book.

We also interviewed George Brady, Anthony Cousins, Louis Di Cesari, Stacey Eng, Olivia Gamblein, Joe Ghory, Jeevan Gnanam, Eric Bryan Kuisch, Nil Larom, Giuseppe Manai, Iskra Nikolova, Drew Panayiotou, Madhu Ranganathan, Evan Reiser, Ahmed Reza, Dan Savino, Niren Sirohi, and Gianpaolo Turri. Special thanks to Dr. Shivaji Dasgupta in sharing his deep experience working with AI, and to Dave Hersh and Richard Bliss for invaluable introductions

With our vast network of industry thought leaders, we've also had the opportunity to benefit from deep technical and strategic expertise and are grateful to Pallav Agrawal, Gary Bolles, Tom Davenport, Vikram Mahidhar, and Asha Saxena. They challenged our thinking and pushed us to make this book even more practical and actionable. Ryan Brandt and Jorden Woods reviewed technical content with meticulous care, ensuring accuracy without sacrificing accessibility. Radhika Iyengar-Emens brought her expertise in ethical business practices to help us maintain the responsible AI lens that runs throughout this work.

And a special thanks to the early readers of the book. They took the time to pore over drafts and provide us invaluable feedback. Many thanks to Julie Ask, Joe Carr, Lisa Nirell, Uvika Sharma, and others.

BRINGING THE BOOK TO LIFE

Genoveva Llosa worked with us in the early stages of this project, helping us find our voice and structure. Tom Walsh brought his veteran editorial expertise to drafts and the final manuscript, refining and sharpening our message.

The team at Amplify Publishing believed in this book from the beginning. CEO Naren Aryal and COO Nina Spahn provided the support and guidance that helped us bring this vision to reality. Thank you to my production editors, copyeditors, proofreaders, and graphic designers for a job well-done.

CHARLENE'S ACKNOWLEDGMENTS

To my kids, Ben and Kat, and my friends Markos Moulitsas, Randy Popp, Jen Sarver, Dave Snyder, and Jeremy and Wendy Verba–thanks for bearing with me as I spent yet another weekend "working on the book." I couldn't have done it without your encouragement and unending support.

Thanks especially to three groups of people. The first is my Young Presidents' Organization (YPO) forum members, whom I consider my personal board of advisors: Mari Baker, Jeff Brothers, Pascal Brochier, Amy Emerson, Kevin Eyres, Todd Georgopapadakos, Paul Lightfoot, Max Shader-Bieschen, and Steve Wadsworth. You listened patiently and then held me accountable for deliverables. The next is my Mastermind group, which includes Richard Bliss, Braden Kelley, David Meerman Scott, Mark Schaefer, Shep Hyken, Howard Tiersky, and Dennis Yu. Your best practices and expertise inspired me to reach higher. And the third is my AI Growth group, which met monthly and witnessed the book's evolution firsthand–Lisa Nirell, Michael Taylor, and Jenny Trautman. Thanks for being the guinea pigs for our new ideas and frameworks.

A special thanks to the Arcbound team, which has helped give voice to my content over the past two years: Ana Arencibia, K. Diggs, Ali Dondero, Katie Falcone, Aashita Gupta, and Bryan Wish. They created many of my newsletters and social posts, and they supported my livestreams, which served as the testing ground for much of the content in the book.

I tested the ideas in this book frequently with my clients and speaking audiences. Special thanks to Steve Broback at Dent The Future, Joyce Brocaglia at Executive Women's Forum, Raymond Chau at the Singapore Ministry of Health, and Kevin Oakes at i4cp for giving me platforms to refine these concepts with thoughtful, engaged audiences.

And most importantly, thank you to Katia for going on this adventure with me. I will always be grateful that you suggested that we write this book together. I loved each time you challenged my thinking, and that you never held back your feedback because you trusted the strength of our friendship. And I'll always remember, with fondness, our marathon writing weekends in your living room.

KATIA'S ACKNOWLEDGMENTS

I'm grateful to my family, who have always encouraged me to write a book about what I've learned so others can benefit from my experience. Many thanks to my mother, Elena; my father, Ivan; my brother, Branimir; my husband, Tom; and my children, Emily and Tommy. I also appreciate the support of my extended family, especially Susan and Brian Denley and their children, Jenny and Matt. My friends Jill Gunn and Steve Berman, Julie Cassard, and Joyce Olson have also been family to me. I know Julie and Joyce would have been proud, as would have my mother, if they were still with us.

It would not have been possible for me to take this path without my early start in the United States through the generosity of several organizations and people. Bob Haiman and the Poynter Institute first introduced me to digital technology, trained me in writing, and enabled me to continue my education at Indiana University. Next up, the University of Missouri supported me, and it is where I found my doctoral advisor, Esther Thorson, who never ceases to inspire me.

My manager at Prudential Financial, Bob Fallon, became a lifelong friend and endorsed the first large-scale corporate transformation I initiated, setting me on a trajectory to help companies become customer-centric through technology. Another Prudential Financial colleague, Louis DiCesari, became my copilot in multiple transformations, helping global businesses realize value from AI years before it entered the mainstream. My teams at Prudential Financial, Vodafone Group, Levi Strauss & Co., and Harvard Business School were the hands-on value drivers and builders and have made a difference in millions of users' experience with these global brands. They have also shown that value has different dimensions: yes, growth, productivity, and profitability but also societal value. Together, we pioneered the use of data and predictive AI to track and prevent the spread of malaria in Africa; the upskilling, through machine learning boot camps, of a thousand people around the world, including some who'd never seen code before; and the reach of business education and entrepreneurship support through new digital and AI platforms.

The advisory and nonexecutive boards of River Island in the UK, UniCredit in Italy, Securian Financial in the US, the Global Legal Entity Identifier Foundation in Zurich, and Avolta in Basel also provided invaluable experience in transforming organizations with AI. And my new colleagues at Apollo Global Management took enterprise transformations to a new high, with Vikram Mahidhar setting the gold standard for practical and scaled value creation through AI.

Caroline Carruthers, Theresa Payton, Mark Minevich, and Angela Zutavern shared their book-writing secrets, and I appreciate their encouragement.

Finally, thank you to Charlene for the inspiration and partnership. I've admired your thought leadership, ingenuity, and courage for more than twenty-five years. There is no one else I'd rather spend every weekend with, other than family. Indeed, you are family. As much as I revere your brainpower, I am grateful for your big heart–an example of why humanity will always win, even with AI.

TO OUR READERS

Finally, we want to thank you, our readers. You picked up this book because you believe your organization can create meaningful value with AI, even if you're not entirely sure how to get there yet. That willingness to step into uncertainty and embrace the messy work of change is what will set you apart.

We wrote this book for you, the leaders who are ready to move beyond pilots and experiments to create real, measurable value. Our hope is that this blueprint has given you not just the confidence to begin, but the clarity to move forward with purpose and speed.

The AI transformation ahead of you won't be easy, but it will be worth it. We're cheering you on every step of the way.

With gratitude and excitement for what you'll create,

Charlene Li and Katia Walsh

NOTES

The Things This Book Tells You That Others Don't

1. Quote from Vikram Mahidhar, an AI thought leader and investor.

Chapter 1: Your AI Starter Kit

1. Thomson Reuters and WSJ Intelligence (survey commissioned by NTT), "Global CEOs Name AI Top Technology for Future Profitability and Competitiveness: WSJ Survey," press release, January 16, 2025, https://www.businesswire.com/news/home/20250116643258/en/Global-CEOs-Name-AI-Top-Technology-for-Future-Profitability-and-Competitiveness-WSJ-Survey. The survey found that 89 percent of global CEOs ranked AI as the most critical technology for future competitiveness, based on responses from 351 CEOs at companies with over US $1 billion in annual revenue (or US $500 million outside the US).
2. Thomson Reuters, "The AI Adoption Reality Check: Firms with AI Strategies Are Twice as Likely to See AI-Driven Revenue Growth; Those Without Risk Falling Behind," press release, June 26, 2025, https://www.thomsonreuters.com/en/press-releases/2025/june/the-ai-adoption-reality-check-firms-with-ai-strategies-are-twice-as-likely-to-see-ai-driven-revenue-growth-those-without-risk-falling-behind.
3. Reuters, "The AI Adoption Reality Check."
4. McKinsey & Company, "Don't Delegate the AI Revolution: A Conversation with Sanofi CEO Paul Hudson," McKinsey Quarterly, September 13, 2023, https://www.mckinsey.com/industries/life-sciences/our-insights/dont-delegate-the-ai-revolution-a-conversation-with-sanofi-ceo-paul-hudson.
5. AWS Executive Insights, "The Two-Pizza Team: The Importance of Team Structure in Driving Innovation," Amazon Web Services, accessed April 22, 2025, https://aws.amazon.com/executive-insights/content/amazon-two-pizza-team/. The concept of

Amazon's two-pizza teams is straightforward: No team should be big enough that it would take more than two pizzas to feed them. Ideally, this is a team of fewer than ten people. Smaller teams minimize lines of communication and reduce the overhead of bureaucracy and decision-making.

6. The generative AI landscape is evolving at an unprecedented pace. The tools mentioned—OpenAI's ChatGPT, Google's Gemini, and Anthropic's Claude—represent the dominant enterprise-grade conversational AI systems at the time of this book's writing (late 2025). While they serve as excellent starting points, the specific tools are less important than the principle of selecting a reputable provider that meets your organization's security and privacy requirements.

Chapter 2: The Responsible AI Advantage

1. 2024 Edelman Trust Barometer: Key Insights Around AI, March 2024, https://www.edelman.com/sites/g/files/aatuss191/files/2024-03/2024%20Edelman%20Trust%20Barometer%20Key%20Insights%20Around%20AI.pdf.
2. Maslow's hierarchy of needs is a psychological theory proposed by Abraham Maslow in 1943, often depicted as a pyramid with five levels of human needs. See Abraham H. Maslow, "A Theory of Human Motivation," *Psychological Review* 50, no. 4 (1943): 370–96.
3. The General Data Protection Regulation (GDPR) is the European Union's comprehensive data privacy law granting individuals control over their personal data. The California Consumer Privacy Act (CCPA) is a California law giving consumers significant rights over how businesses collect and use their personal information.
4. Although you may encounter articles, and even requirements, for AI explainability, we do not subscribe to that notion. It is important to acknowledge that it is simply not possible with today's sophisticated AI systems. Much like we cannot necessarily explain how a human brain reacts and have to follow exposure to information and a chain of reasoning, the same is now true for AI systems. The purpose of this book is to provide a pragmatic guide to value creation, with special consideration for responsible and ethical AI. So, while we acknowledge that explainability is not realistic, we share the importance of disclosure, observability, and interpretability—the closest we can come to explainability.
5. The term "red team" originates from military and cybersecurity, where it refers to an independent group that challenges an organization by simulating an attack. In the context of AI, a red team's role is to proactively test a model for a wide range of vulnerabilities. They adopt an adversarial mindset to find ways to trick the AI into generating biased, harmful, or otherwise unintended outputs, so these flaws can be fixed before deployment.
6. Martin Kornberger, Elmira van den Broek, and Stephan Leixnering, "AI Ethics Strategy: Lessons from H&M Group," *MIT Sloan Management Review*, March 31, 2025, https://sloanreview.mit.edu/article/ai-ethics-strategy-lessons-from-hm-group/.

7. Adobe, "Our Approach to Generative AI with Adobe Firefly," Adobe AI, accessed July 2025, https://www.adobe.com/ai/overview/firefly/gen-ai-approach.html.
8. Unnecessary legal risk often arises from overdocumentation. In a legal process called "discovery," all internal records, including informal emails and chat logs, can be requested during a lawsuit. Notes taken out of context can be used to build a misleading narrative of negligence, even if the final outcome was sound. A purposeful documentation strategy, guided by legal counsel, focuses on preserving formal evidence of due diligence while minimizing this exposure.

Chapter 3: Who Owns AI?

1. IBM Institute for Business Value, *Solving the AI ROI Puzzle: How Chief AI Officers Cut Through Complexity to Create New Paths to Value* (IBM, July 2025), https://www.ibm.com/downloads/documents/us-en/1379d32d7fdaec18.
2. IBM Institute for Business Value, *Solving the AI ROI Puzzle.*
3. George Westerman, Didier Bonnet, and Andrew McAfee, *Leading Digital: Turning Technology into Business Transformation* (Harvard Business Review Press, 2014).

Chapter 4: Creating Value with AI

1. The "Four Ps" of traditional business are product, price, placement, and promotion.
2. *Gallup Q[12] Meta-Analysis: The Relationship Between Employee Engagement at Work and Organizational Outcomes*, 11th ed. (Gallup, 2024), https://www.gallup.com/workplace/321725/gallup-q12-meta-analysis-report.aspx.
3. Harvard Business Review Analytic Services and Quantum Workplace, "A Winning Approach to Employee Success" (PDF report), July 2020, https://www.quantumworkplace.com/hubfs/A-Winning-Approach-to-Employee-Success-HBRAS-QW.pdf.
4. Marty Swant, "With Charlie, Pfizer Is Building a New Generative AI Platform for Pharma Marketing," Digiday, April 17, 2024, https://digiday.com/marketing/with-charlie-pfizer-is-building-a-new-generative-ai-platform-for-pharma-marketing/.
5. Klarna Bank, "Klarna AI Assistant Handles Two-Thirds of Customer Service Chats in Its First Month," press release, February 27, 2024, https://www.klarna.com/international/press/klarna-ai-assistant-handles-two-thirds-of-customer-service-chats-in-its-first-month/.
6. Rachel Dobkin, "Klarna's AI Replaced 700 Workers. It's Trying to Bring Them Back," *The Independent*, May 22, 2025, https://www.independent.co.uk/news/business/klarna-ceo-sebastian-siemiatkowski-ai-job-cuts-hiring-b2755580.html.
7. "How Generative AI Is Already Impacting Business," PwC, accessed February 4, 2025, https://www.pwc.com/us/en/tech-effect/ai-analytics/generative-ai-impact-on-business.html.
8. Rathi Murthy, "Unlocking the Value of AI and Generative AI in Travel," Hospitality Net, July 24, 2023, https://www.hospitalitynet.org/opinion/4117371.html.

9. Kylie Whitehead, "How SelectQuote Is Using Call Center Voice AI for Differentiation," *PolyAI*, November 29, 2023, https://poly.ai/blog/how-selectquote-is-using-call-center-voice-ai-for-differentiation/.
10. Grace Mayer, "SelectQuote Launches AI Tool That Saves It More Than $1M," *Kansas City Business Journal*, December 11, 2023, https://www.bizjournals.com/kansascity/news/2023/12/11/selectquotes-ai-tool-is-saving-the-company-over-1m.html.
11. Grace Mayer, "SelectQuote Launches AI Tool."
12. Charlene Li, *The Disruption Mindset: Why Some Organizations Transform While Others Fail* (New York: Ideapress Publishing, 2019).
13. Outset, "Nestlé Uses AI to Accelerate Product Innovation," Outset Case Stories, accessed October 20, 2025, https://outset.ai/resources/stories/nestle-ai-research-accelerated-product-innovation.
14. Outset, "Nestlé Uses AI."
15. Konecta, "Generative AI and Customer Experience: Moving Beyond the Hype to Build Real Impact," press release, News & Insights, June 5, 2025, published in collaboration with BCG, https://konecta.com/news-insights/generative-ai-and-customer-experience-moving-beyond-the-hype-to-build-real-impact.

Chapter 5: Grounding AI in Your Strategy

1. There are three primary methods to measure the value of an AI application. **A/B testing:** The most rigorous method, this is a controlled experiment where users are randomly split into two groups: a control group that uses the existing process and a treatment group that uses the new AI-powered process. The difference in their outcomes isolates the AI's impact. **Before-and-after comparison:** This simple method compares a key metric from a period before the AI was implemented to a period after. While easy to do, it can be misleading as it doesn't account for other business factors that may have caused the change. **Counterfactual analysis:** This method is used when an A/B test isn't possible. It answers the question "What would have happened if we hadn't used AI?" by using historical data to model a predicted outcome (the counterfactual). The AI's impact is the difference between the actual result and this predicted, counterfactual result. For example, if a model shows your inventory spoilage would have been 4 percent but it actually was 2.5 percent with a new AI system, the impact is a 1.5 percentage point improvement.

Chapter 8: Establishing the AI Mindset

1. Aditya Challapally et al., *The GenAI Divide: State of AI in Business 2025 Report,* MLQ.ai, July 2025, https://mlq.ai/media/quarterly_decks/v0.1_State_of_AI_in_Business_2025_Report.pdf.
2. BrandWagon Online, "How LEGO Transformed a Declining Toy Brand into a $7.7 Billion Empire by Redefining Its User," Financial Express, May 9, 2025, https://www.

financialexpress.com/business/brandwagon-how-lego-transformed-a-declining-toy-brand-into-a-7-7-billion-empire-by-redefining-its-user-3838249/.

3. Donald Sull and Charles Sull, "How the Lego Group Built Culture Change: From the Ground Up," *MIT Sloan Management Review,* January 10, 2025, https://sloanreview.mit.edu/article/how-the-lego-group-built-culture-change-from-the-ground-up/.
4. Ekaterina O. Walsh, "Winning the Changing Financial Consumer," Forrester Research, July 2003. This report defined customer advocacy as "offering products and services that are best for the customer, not just for the firm's bottom line" and found it to be the strongest predictor of customer retention among financial services firms.
5. Kate Den Houter, "AI in the Workplace: Answering 3 Big Questions," Gallup, October 7, 2024, https://www.gallup.com/workplace/651203/workplace-answering-big-questions.aspx.
6. Tobi Lütke (@tobi), "Reflexive AI usage is now a baseline expectation at Shopify," X (formerly Twitter), April 7, 2025, https://x.com/tobi/status/1909251946235437514.
7. Tobi Lütke, "Reflexive AI usage."
8. Aaron Levie (@levie), "Here's the Email I Sent to Our Company About How We're Thinking About AI," X (formerly Twitter), April 18, 2025, https://x.com/levie/status/1917970814441607623.
9. TNCR Staff, "AI Mandates, Minimal Use: Closing the Workplace Readiness Gap," *The National CIO Review*, published in Week in Review, May 30, 2025, https://nationalcioreview.com/articles-insights/leadership/ai-mandates-minimal-use-closing-the-workplace-readiness-gap/
10. Andy Jassy, "Message from CEO Andy Jassy: Some Thoughts on Generative AI," About Amazon, June 17, 2025, https://www.aboutamazon.com/news/company-news/amazon-ceo-andy-jassy-on-generative-ai.
11. Nancy B. Hammer, "Donna Morris Shares Takeaways from Walmart's AI Integration," HR Policy Association, July 25, 2025, https://www.chro.org/w/donna-morris-shares-takeaways-from-walmart-s-ai-in.
12. Stanford Institute for Human-Centered Artificial Intelligence (HAI), *The 2025 AI Index Report* (Stanford HAI, April 7, 2025), https://hai.stanford.edu/assets/files/hai_ai_index_report_2025.pdf.
13. CYPHER Learning, *Bridging the AI Digital Divide: 2024 Survey Report*, part 2 (CYPHER Learning, 2024), https://www.cypherlearning.com/hubfs/docs/cypher/CYPHER-Learning-2024-Survey-Report-Bridging-the-digital-divide-part-2.pdf.

Chapter 9: Developing an AI-Fluent Workforce

1. *The Future of Jobs Report 2025*, (World Economic Forum, January 7, 2025), https://www.weforum.org/publications/the-future-of-jobs-report-2025/.
2. *The Future of Jobs Report.*

3. Take, for example, prompt engineering. We are not fans of this term, for two reasons: (1) The term intimidates people; (2) what it refers to is not engineering. Instead, it is the skill to write detailed instructions, provide context, correct, validate, and guide. It is about writing specifications for desired actions, not engineering.
4. Stanford Institute for Human-Centered Artificial Intelligence (HAI), *The 2025 AI Index Report* (Stanford HAI, April 7, 2025), https://hai.stanford.edu/assets/files/hai_ai_index_report_2025.pdf.
5. Carolyn Crist, "AI Training Lags Despite Increased Use at Work, Survey Says," HR Dive, April 1, 2025, https://www.hrdive.com/news/ai-use-increasing-at-work-training-lags-behind/744097/.
6. OpenAI, OpenAI Academy, accessed October 2025, https://academy.openai.com/.
7. Fidji Simo, "Expanding Economic Opportunity with AI," OpenAI, August 7, 2024, https://openai.com/index/expanding-economic-opportunity-with-ai/.
8. Anthropic, "Learn: AI Learning Resources & Guides from Anthropic," accessed October 18, 2025, https://www.anthropic.com/learn/.
9. Luis Rijo, "Anthropic Expands Academy with Enterprise Partner Courses," PPC Land, August 4, 2025, https://ppc.land/anthropic-expands-academy-with-enterprise-partner-courses/.
10. Microsoft Copilot, "Microsoft Copilot Learning Hub," Microsoft Learn, accessed October 18, 2025, https://learn.microsoft.com/en-us/copilot/.
11. Helen Reid, "IKEA Bets on Remote Interior Design as AI Changes Sales Strategy," Reuters, June 13, 2023, https://www.reuters.com/technology/ikea-bets-remote-interior-design-ai-changes-sales-strategy-2023-06-13/.
12. Helen Reid, "IKEA Bets on Remote Interior Design."
13. CDO Magazine Bureau, "IKEA Introduces AI Training Program for Upskilling Workforce," *CDO Magazine*, March 4, 2024, https://www.cdomagazine.tech/aiml/ikea-introduces-ai-training-program-for-upskilling-workforce.
14. Suzanne Kapner, "Not Qualified for a Job? These Companies Will 'Reskill' You," *Wall Street Journal*, May 16, 2021, https://www.wsj.com/business/retail/retailers-try-to-solve-labor-imbalances-by-reskilling-staff-11621157407.
15. Levi Strauss & Co., "STITCH: AI Built by Stores for Stores," Levi Strauss & Co., November 17, 2025, https://www.levistrauss.com/2025/11/17/levis-stitch-ai/.
16. Mia Tran, "Moderna Merges HR & IT: Chief People & Digital Technology Manages 3,000 AIs and 5,800 Humans," FlexOS, May 15, 2025, https://www.flexos.work/learn/moderna-merges-hr-it-new-chief-manages-3000-ai-and-5800-humans.
17. Allie Nawrat, "Why Moderna Merged HR and IT to Better 'Architect the Flow of Work,'" UNLEASH, June 27, 2025, https://www.unleash.ai/artificial-intelligence/why-moderna-merged-hr-and-it-to-better-architect-the-flow-of-work/.

18. Tran, "Moderna Merges HR & IT."

Chapter 10: Assembling Your AI Toolset

1. Erik Wilde, "Jeff Bezos' API Mandate: What the Five Rules Mean and Do," *Axway* (blog), May 25, 2021, https://blog.axway.com/learning-center/digital-strategy/api-first/jeff-bezos-api-mandate.
2. McKinsey & Company, "Meet Lilli, Our Generative AI Tool That's a Researcher, a Time Saver, and an Inspiration," *New at McKinsey* (blog), August 16, 2023, https://www.mckinsey.com/about-us/new-at-mckinsey-blog/meet-lilli-our-generative-ai-tool.
3. Here are additional resources to learn more about synthetic data:
https://www.k2view.com/blog/generative-ai-synthetic-data/
https://syntheticus.ai/guide-everything-you-need-to-know-about-synthetic-data
https://mostly.ai/synthetic-data-basics
https://www.ibm.com/think/topics/synthetic-data
https://aws.amazon.com/what-is/synthetic-data/
https://learn.microsoft.com/en-us/azure/ai-foundry/concepts/concept-synthetic-data
4. Bloomberg LP, "Introducing BloombergGPT, Bloomberg's 50-Billion Parameter Large Language Model, Purpose-Built from Scratch for Finance," press release, March 30, 2023, https://www.bloomberg.com/company/press/bloomberggpt-50-billion-parameter-llm-tuned-finance/.
5. Dzmitry Garbar, "BloombergGPT Is Live: A Custom Large Language Model for Finance," Belitsoft, April 1 2025, https://belitsoft.com/bloomberggpt.
6. Xianzhi Li et al., "Are ChatGPT and GPT-4 General-Purpose Solvers for Financial Text Analytics? A Study on Several Typical Tasks," in *Proceedings of the 2023 Conference on Empirical Methods in Natural language Processing: Industry Track* (Association for Computational Linguistics, 2023), 408–22, https://arxiv.org/pdf/2305.05862v2.
7. Cisco, "Agentic AI Poised to Handle 68% of Customer Service and Support Interactions by 2028," press release, May 27, 2025, https://newsroom.cisco.com/c/r/newsroom/en/us/a/y2025/m05/agentic-ai-poised-to-handle-68-of-customer-service-and-support-interactions-by-2028.html.
8. Nidhi Arora et al., "The Value of Getting Personalization Right—or Wrong—Is Multiplying," McKinsey & Company, November 12, 2021, https://www.mckinsey.com/capabilities/growth-marketing-and-sales/our-insights/the-value-of-getting-personalizatio n-right-or-wrong-is-multiplying.
9. Keith O'Brien, Matthew Finio, and Amanda Downie, "The Future of AI in Customer Service," IBM Think Artificial Intelligence (IBM), accessed October 2025, https://www.ibm.com/think/insights/customer-service-future.
10. Market.us, "Chatbot Market Size, Share, Trends," March 2025, https://market.us/report/chatbot-market/.

11. Statista, "Number of Voice Assistant Users in the United States from 2022 to 2026," Statista, accessed October 24, 2025, https://www.statista.com/statistics/1299985/voice-assistant-users-us/ ; eMarketer, "US Voice Assistant Users by Device, 2026," as referenced by AltIndex, accessed October 24, 2025.
12. SuperAnnotate, "What Is Multimodal AI: Complete Overview 2025," *SuperAnnotate* (blog), March 3, 2025, https://www.superannotate.com/blog/multimodal-ai.
13. Ramji Sundararajan and Uzayr Jeenah with Alana Ellis, "The End of Inertia: Agentic AI's Disruption of Retail and SME Banking," McKinsey & Company, August 15, 2025, https://www.mckinsey.com/industries/financial-services/our-insights/the-end-of-inertia-agentic-ais-disruption-of-retail-and-sme-banking.
14. Sebastian Illing, "AI Voice Technologies: Your Guide to 2025's Top Innovations," *MaestroLabs* (blog), March 31, 2025, https://www.maestrolabs.com/blog-detail/ai-voice-technologies-your-guide-to-2025s-top-innovations.
15. Mimi Sax, "Custom AI Tutor Bots Are Transforming Learning at HBS," *Harvard Business Impact* (blog), June 24, 2025, https://hbsp.harvard.edu/inspiring-minds/ai-tutor-bots-harvard-business-school.

Chapter 11: Designing AI's Decision Set

1. "The Amazon Working Backwards PR/FAQ Process," Working Backwards, accessed October 2025, https://workingbackwards.com/concepts/working-backwards-pr-faq-process/.

Chapter 12: Leadership as Accelerant of AI Value

1. Learn more about Stephanie Hills, PhD, an executive coach and former technology executive at https://linkedin.com/in/stephaniehillsphd/.
2. The quote "Speed is the new moat" comes from Vikram Mahidhar, an AI thought leader and investor.
3. Elizabeth M. Renieris, David Kiron, Steven Mills, and Anne Kleppe, "Agentic AI at Scale: Redefining Management for a Superhuman Workforce," *MIT Sloan Management Review*, September 16, 2025, https://sloanreview.mit.edu/article/agentic-ai-at-scale-redefining-management-for-a-superhuman-workforce/.
4. Lareina Yee et al., "Leaders Underestimate Employees' AI Use," McKinsey & Company, March 4, 2025, https://www.mckinsey.com/featured-insights/week-in-charts/leaders-underestimate-employees-ai-use.
5. "Beyond the Buzz: Developing the AI Skills Employers Actually Need," Lightcast, July 23, 2025, https://lightcast.io/resources/blog/beyond-the-buzz-press-release-2025-07-23.
6. MokaHR, "How AI Predicts Employee Turnover and Enhances Retention Strategies," *MokaHR* (blog), March 31, 2025, https://www.mokahr.io/myblog/ai-for-turnover-prediction-retention-strategies.

7. "The Impact of AI and Machine Learning on Employee Lifecycle Evaluation Tools," *Vorecol* (blog), accessed October 2025, https://blogs.vorecol.com/blog-the-impact-of-ai-and-machine-learning-on-employee-lifecycle-evaluation-tools-173697.

ABOUT THE AUTHORS

WE MET IN EARLY 1999 at Forrester Research, where we started work within months of each other, at the dawn of the dot-com era. As we navigated similar life stages—building careers and raising families—we stayed connected both professionally and personally. When Katia moved to the Bay Area in 2019, we became even closer. So, when the opportunity arose to write this book together, it was a full-throated yes.

Working at Forrester gave us more than just a shared training ground—it gave us a common language for thinking and writing about business and technology. But, more importantly, our friendship carried us through what can be a notoriously difficult process: coauthoring a book. Being bicoastal, we treasured the times we could work together in person, not just because it was more efficient, but because we could connect at a deeper, more personal level.

Charlene Li is a business transformation strategist and a *New York Times* bestselling author of six books, including *The Disruption Mindset*, *Open Leadership*, and *Groundswell*. Her career has spanned the evolution of digital technology across media, research, and consulting as she worked with global organizations ranging from startups to fourteen of the Dow Jones Industrial thirty companies, including Adobe and Southwest Airlines. She began her career in newspapers in the early 1990s, helping them navigate the shift from print to online, and later served as a principal analyst at Forrester Research, where she pioneered coverage of interactive advertising, search marketing, and the rise of social media. In 2008, she founded Altimeter Group, a disruptive strategy research and advisory firm that challenged incumbent analyst giants such as Gartner, Forrester, and IDC before being acquired by Prophet in 2015. She subsequently served as chief research officer at PA Consulting and currently leads Quantum Networks Group. Throughout her career, she has advised executives and boards on disruptive transformation, leadership, and the future of work, helping organizations develop winning strategies for disruptive growth. As a keynote speaker, she has addressed audiences at the World Economic Forum, TED, and South by Southwest. Charlene's recognitions include being named one of the Most Creative People in Business by Fast Company, AdAge's Top 40 Women to Watch, and a LinkedIn Top Voice since 2012. Charlene is a graduate of Harvard College (magna cum laude) and Harvard Business School.

Dr. Katia Walsh is one of the world's first chief AI officers, a role she pioneered while leading digital, data, and AI transformations at organizations across sectors and industries. Her career has spanned technology, financial services, telecommunications, consumer goods, retail, manufacturing, and education with global organizations such as Fidelity Investments, Prudential Financial, Vodafone, Levi Strauss & Co., Harvard Business School, Apollo Global Management, Securian Financial, The Legal Entity Identifier Foundation, Avolta, River Island, and UniCredit. Katia has launched, led, and scaled digital, data, and AI teams across thirty countries and delivered billions in business value through customer engagement personalization; assortment customization; demand prediction and inventory management transformation; pricing, capital reserve, and return on infrastructure investment optimization; and more. In addition to driving growth and profitability, she pioneered workforce upskilling and use of data and AI for social good. Her leadership has been featured in *The Wall Street Journal*, *Forbes*, *Fortune*, *The Washington Post*, *Harvard Business Review*, MIT's *Technology Review* and *Sloan Management Review*, *Vogue*, *Tech Crunch*, *Technovation*, and *ZDNET*. Katia has served on the *MIT Sloan Management Review*'s editorial advisory board and was tapped as the archetype of a leader driving value from AI by Harvard Business School and INSEAD. Her global awards and recognitions include Top Women in AI, Swiss Cognitive AI Ambassador, and VentureBeat AI Mentorship, among others.

Learn more and connect with us at **winningwithaibook.com**.

www.ingramcontent.com/pod-product-compliance
Lightning Source LLC
LaVergne TN
LVHW102010210926
848483LV00015B/453/J
* 9 7 9 8 9 0 0 2 6 3 2 9 8 *